THE
EVERYTHING
PERUVIAN COOKBOOK

Dear Reader,

I was only seventeen years old when I discovered Peruvian food. I was recently married and my husband introduced me to the many wonderful dishes of his childhood; each one accompanied by an interesting anecdote or story. I was in awe of all the new and exotic flavors I had in front of me, but trembled at the idea of preparing any of those incredible dishes by myself. First of all, I knew nothing about cooking, and those beautiful dishes seemed like something only the masterful Peruvian cooks could do with grace.

At the time, I marveled at the freshness of *cebiche* and the sweetness of the many colorful fruits in the Peruvian markets, all of them so different in size and flavor from the tropical ones I was used to. Every season brought new vegetables and produce, cereals and grains, amazing fish and seafood. Every visit to the market was exciting and educational. And my love and curiosity for these striking ingredients, and for the wonderful way Peruvian people prepare them, has never tired.

If you have picked up this book, chances are you have already tried or heard of the fascinating food Peru has to offer. If you haven't, don't worry! The popularity of Peruvian food has been a long time coming, and is finally starting to become a reality.

This has been a fascinating journey, and I hope you enjoy this introduction to Peruvian cooking as much as we enjoyed putting it together.

Buen Provecho!

Morena Cuadra

Welcome to the EVERYTHING® Series!

These handy, accessible books give you all you need to tackle a difficult project, gain a new hobby, comprehend a fascinating topic, prepare for an exam, or even brush up on something you learned back in school but have since forgotten.

You can choose to read an Everything® book from cover to cover or just pick out the information you want from our four useful boxes: e-questions, e-facts, e-alerts, and e-ssentials.

We give you everything you need to know on the subject, but throw in a lot of fun stuff along the way, too.

We now have more than 400 Everything® books in print, spanning such wide-ranging categories as weddings, pregnancy, cooking, music instruction, foreign language, crafts, pets, New Age, and so much more. When you're done reading them all, you can finally say you know Everything®!

QUESTION

Answers to
common questions

FACT

Important snippets
of information

ALERT

Urgent
warnings

ESSENTIAL

Quick
handy tips

PUBLISHER Karen Cooper

MANAGING EDITOR, EVERYTHING® SERIES Lisa Laing

COPY CHIEF Casey Ebert

ASSOCIATE PRODUCTION EDITOR Mary Beth Dolan

ACQUISITIONS EDITOR Lisa Laing

DEVELOPMENT EDITOR Eileen Mullan

EVERYTHING® SERIES COVER DESIGNER Erin Alexander

Visit the entire Everything® series at *www.everything.com*

THE EVERYTHING®
PERUVIAN COOKBOOK

Morena Cuadra and Morena Escardó

Founders of PeruDelights.com

Adamsmedia

Avon, Massachusetts

To Enrique Escardó V-G, for teaching us to
love Peru and its food.

———————

An Everything® Series Book.
Everything® and everything.com® are registered trademarks of F+W Media, Inc.

Published by Adams Media, a division of F+W Media, Inc.
57 Littlefield Street, Avon, MA 02322. U.S.A.
www.adamsmedia.com

ISBN 10: 1-4405-5677-6
ISBN 13: 978-1-4405-5677-7
eISBN 10: 1-4405-5678-4
eISBN 13: 978-1-4405-5678-4

Printed in the United States of America.

10 9 8 7 6 5 4 3 2

Always follow safety and common-sense cooking protocol while using kitchen utensils, operating ovens and stoves, and handling uncooked food. If children are assisting in the preparation of any recipe, they should always be supervised by an adult.

Photographs by Morena Cuadra.

This book is available at quantity discounts for bulk purchases.
For information, please call 1-800-289-0963.

Contents

Acknowledgments

To Eduardo, my son, my inspiration, and my best friend, with unconditional love and gratitude. Your infinite faith in me, and your permanent encouragement no matter what, mean the world to me. Thanks to my parents for being the best role models. Much love to my brothers Eduardo and Roberto, friends and partners in so many adventures. To the best sisters a girl could have: Belinda, Roxana, and Veronica. Thanks to Antonella, for sharing her family recipes for this book. I enjoyed our several hours working together. To my dear cousin Carolina Alvarez, for sharing so many funny conversations over breakfast. Special thanks and love to my personal angel, Sharon Peyus, and her husband, Al, for making me feel like family.

Heartfelt thanks to Peru, and my Peruvian family and friends, for welcoming me and teaching me all I know about this wonderful country. And last but not least, my eternal love and gratitude to my daughter, the other half of this team, and the soul of *www.perudelights.com.* You've kept me going with love and care since day one. I couldn't dream of a better partner. You are the best! Love you always.

—Morena C.

First of all I would like to thank my mom, my grandmother, and Amelia, the three women I grew up with in the kitchen. They prepared the most delicious and comforting food while sharing beautiful stories that taught me not only about food, but also about life. The recipes and thoughts you so lovingly shared with me will stay in my heart forever.

A big thank you to Alex Smith, Rachel Bowen, Hector and Eduardo Escardó (my brothers), Andrea Franco (my sister!), and Ana Flores, for being the steam behind this machine, sharing your time with us so generously, and helping us from the start, when we still had no clue what we were doing. Your knowledge, advice, and inspiration have been invaluable. On that note, thanks to Alexandra Collas (another sister!) for being our very own cheerleader. Your super enthusiastic support never gets old.

Roberto Cuadra, Ximena Llosa, Antonella Delfino, Valentina Cordero, Jorge Tali: Without your rockstar contributions, Peru Delights wouldn't be the same. We hope you will keep sharing your delicious food and great knowledge with us and with the rest of the world for a very long time to come. And Roberto, thank you also for boldly sharing the food of Peru in Central America, and for feeding us your exquisite food every time we come to visit. You are an amazing chef.

Thank you Rob, for proofreading my English writing even when you're tired or have much more important things to do. And thanks, especially, for being the guinea pig for my cooking experiments, and eating them with a smile.

And to Lisa Laing and the team behind this book at Adams Media: You've made *The Everything® Peruvian Cookbook* a reality, bringing the wonderful culinary tradition of our country to many homes, and for that, we are extremely grateful.

—Morena E.

Introduction

WITH SO MANY REGIONS, climates, ingredients, traditions, and cooking techniques that vary extensively across Peru, is it possible to really talk about Peruvian food as a united cuisine? A quick look at the difference in looks, clothes, religion, even in language, and the people that inhabit this eclectic land would make anyone question the relation of one culinary heritage to the next.

For example, people on the coast of Peru shy away from eating alpaca meat or the Amazonian worm known as *suri*. Andeans wouldn't dream of eating all the sweets and desserts that are lusted for in the capital. With so many differences between them, it is clear that it would be better to talk about the many Peruvian cuisines that, put together, make up these endless array of dishes.

There is, however, common ground between them; and it is not just the geographical ground they all share. Probably the biggest, strongest bond that glues Peruvian food together is the way Peruvians feel about it as a whole, whether it is a native from the dry desert along the Pacific Coast, from the river valleys up in the cold Andes, or from the colorful, joyous towns in the deep Amazon jungle. Just as sports or historical triumphs make the people of some countries chant the same song with one loud voice, in Peru, food, and the people's love and respect for it, is the factor that joins Peruvians together as one, despite their differences. This is far from being a new thing, although the culinary "boom" of the last few years has ignited an even stronger flame in Peruvian cuisine. Looking back through history, though, food has always been at the center of the life and culture of the people who inhabit this fertile, magical, and mysterious land.

Columbus discovering America in 1492, and Francisco Pizarro finally arriving in the land of the Incas many years later, was, with no doubt, a military and economical success for Spain. But above all, what happened in what is now Peru was a cultural domination, which completely changed the technology, religion, language, and social order of an entire civilization. Food was no exception. And despite the Europeans' determination to turn their "new" world into a faithful copy of the "old," "better" world, not all European influences produced positive outcomes (such as the introduction of famines). But what was found in America influenced the entire world.

For example, it may have taken over 200 years for it to happen, but when famine threatened the European continent in the seventeenth century, settlers had luckily discovered potatoes, a breakthrough that saved much of Europe from starvation. Potatoes are now a culinary staple in many countries and continents; certainly in France and the United States, with the omnipresent French fries and *pommes frites*. And it may have taken almost 300 years, but eventually, Western men accepted tomatoes on their tables, which are now an irreplaceable ingredient in Italian cuisine, amongst others. Can you imagine the world without ketchup or tomato sauce?

CHAPTER 1

Everything You Need to Know about Peruvian Food

The many cultures that influenced the way Peruvians eat today created a thriving gastronomy that is anything but monotonous. Incredibly colorful and unique native ingredients have mixed with staple foreign ingredients. Techniques that are as old and connected with nature as the people found in pre-Incan tombs have fused with ancient ways from other continents, and with technology, producing infinite possibilities in the kitchen. The history of the country is long, full of glorious and painful moments. But all of it comes together and makes sense when one sits in front of a plate of fresh, exquisite food that is full of traditions, stories, and passion.

A Love Affair with Nature

Once dismissed as "primitive" by white settlers, it has been argued that the Incans were the only past civilization able to completely avoid any problems with food. Over a hundred years before the Spanish Conquistadors arrived in the region now known as Peru, the area had gone through a great agricultural revolution thanks to the sophisticated engineering and irrigation techniques inherited from pre-Incan times. When the Incans paired these methods with their use of astrology and astronomy, their skill at selecting and improving native species, and the wide use of manure as a powerful earth fertilizer, they turned the already rich area that forms Peru today into a Garden of Eden other civilizations could only dream of.

In the Incan civilization, famines were unheard of. The government, by law, made sure every person had enough food to eat at all times. Of course, Peru was hit by natural disasters and dying crops, just like any part of the world. By sun- and freeze-drying excess crops (which they had at all times), they always had a stockpile of food ready to help them recover quickly in times of hardship.

The Incan Diet

In the glory days of the Incan Empire, people ate three meals a day. The morning and evening meals were eaten at home, but the main meal, consumed in the middle of the day, was given by the government and eaten communally in the town plazas. This ensured that, no matter what, everyone ate good food and everyone ate equally. Not only did Incans share their culture of food with one another; they also shared it with other animals and with *Pachamama* (Mother Earth), who they believed gave them all their sustenance.

In the Incan culture, eating eggs or milk was completely taboo, except when someone became ill, in which case the shaman (healer) occasionally prescribed these foods as medicine. Incans refused to eat a life in process (the egg), or an infant's sustenance (the milk). In this way, they were similar to the ancestral Chinese and Japanese cultures. Their diet was also mostly vegan, except for the occasional meat that they ate in times of celebration or during religious rituals.

The native diet of the Incan people was simple, without strong sauces and flavors. This does not mean that they ate tasteless dishes, though, as they used chili peppers and some herbs to enhance each preparation. Their food was made to nourish and enjoy, but also to heal and bring people back to an equilibrium and a state of general well-being.

The most important products used on a daily basis were carbohydrates with high amounts of quality proteins, such as the native potato, corn, quinoa, and *kiwicha* (amaranth). Fish and seafood were also very welcomed by the Incans, and even raw fish was sometimes eaten (sometimes raw llama, too), a culinary custom which later became the inspiration for *cebiche*.

The main dish of the Incan diet was a soup made of Andean tubers, which was called *rocro* (now called *locro*) in its more solid versions, *lawas* in its more watery versions, and *chupis* in its regular version (now called *chupe*).

FACT

> The Incas used a system of irrigation called Andenes, which allowed them to grow produce in all the different altitude levels of the country. This way they really made good use of all the land, even in the highest, driest of climates. Andenes look like giant stairs in the mountains, and they are still used today.

The Spanish Influence

Francisco Pizarro arrived in Peru in 1532, several decades after America had first been discovered. The Spanish who settled in this area quickly became rich, thanks to the gold and silver they discovered and sold back in Europe, and the luxurious lives they lived allowed them to import all the food they wanted.

They made sure they got constant supplies of rice, wheat, sugar cane, bananas, figs, dates, grapes, cilantro, olive oil, garbanzo beans, garlic, onion, cows, goats, lambs, pigs, and hens. They also saw to it that local farmers started growing these products so they would have them on hand (and at cheaper prices) at any time.

One of the first obvious signs of the culinary fusion of Spanish and Incan cuisines was the use of eggs, cheese, and milk in many previously vegan Andean stews and soups. *Chupes*, *locros*, and *picantes*, all the ancestral dishes that were previously made without dairy, then became even more delectable once these ingredients were added during preparation. Another big step was the use of *aderezo*, which is now found in virtually every Peruvian savory dish. *Aderezo* is nothing more than the use of onions and garlic sautéed in oil—with the addition of some kind of *ají*—to flavor the food.

Around this time, dried alpaca and llama meat were replaced with beef, lamb, and chicken. Staples from Spanish kitchens became popular among colonial people, served with Peruvian additions such as chili sauces, *huacatay*, corn, and sweet potato. Also *cebiche*, as we know it today, was born.

ESSENTIAL

The Spanish Conquistadors not only increased the cultivation of foreign produce like wheat and sugar, they also made sure native ingredients were still grown, because they needed them to feed the indigenous workers, soldiers, and servants.

The Fame of *Cebiche*

There are many versions of *cebiche* found around the world, and they all have different methods of preparation, but any food connoisseur will agree that Peruvian *cebiche* is one of the best. This raw fish appetizer is very simple. All that is needed to make it is the freshest fish possible, some good acidic limes, a few slices of red onion, chili peppers, and salt. Simple, right? Raw fish with chili had been enjoyed by Peruvians and other cultures for many centuries, but it wasn't until the Spanish brought onions and limes to Peru that the famous *cebiche* everyone loves was born. *Cebiche* is a Spanish-Peruvian success story.

FACT

Cebiche is usually accompanied by a cold glass of beer, but this took a long time to happen. Cebiche was, at first, considered a cheap dish, eaten by the poor locals, and beer was considered almost too international and aristocratic.

The Arab Factor

The local cuisine was rapidly changing in Peru due to the introduction of these new products to the markets, and that's how the first big transformation of native Peruvian food came about. Even though a big part of the Spanish influence was originally from Spain, some of it really came from Arab countries, since Spain had just freed itself from many centuries of Arab domination and had thus been strongly influenced by it.

The Spanish Conquistadors traveled to the "new world" accompanied by Arab wives and servants, who kept their cooking traditions alive in their new destination. *Empanadas* are a great example of this influence. In fact, the Peruvian tradition of stuffing all kinds of vegetables, cereals, and doughs comes from these Arab women, who were extraordinary cooks. The immense amounts of mouthwatering sweets and desserts Peruvians still love also have an Arab origin (*alfajores*, rice pudding, *suspiro*, *mazamorra*, and candied limes, to name a few).

FACT

Very little sugar was consumed in Peru until the mid-nineteenth century, when it started to be produced in the country and exported to Europe and other countries. Since there was such an abundance of sugar and the price was so low, many Peruvian women (with Arab recipes as inspiration) began creating an incredible number of new sweets and desserts to serve.

African Spice

Unfortunately, like many countries, Peru was not immune to African slavery. The killing of natives by the Spanish threatened to bring terrible famines to new Peruvian homes, and there was no one left to work the land. To make things worse, those Peruvians who survived these terrible times were sent to work in the mines, as getting rich by selling Peruvian gold and silver was the conquerors' number one priority. This problem was solved with another problem: slaves.

African people were brought to the country to work the lands that were now empty, and with them they brought many cultural traditions, the most important being music and food. With their amazing talent in the kitchen, Africans taught Peruvians how to make ends meet by using the most humble ingredients to create what are probably the tastiest dishes of Peru's gastronomic repertoire.

Using the insides of the animals that their patrons discarded and all their leftovers, staples such as cow's heart *anticuchos*, *tacu tacu*, *picarones*, and many others were created. It is no surprise that after slavery was abolished, the streets were full of African people selling their delicious food to every passerby. And it is no surprise either that everyone who tried their creations fell in love with them immediately.

Chinatown

When slavery was abolished in the second half of the nineteenth century, Peru was once again in the critical situation of not having any hands to work the land. The solution this time was to hire labor from somewhere else. Cuba was already successfully bringing Chinese workers to the island, and Peru decided to do the same. However, the conditions under which these poor men, commonly known as "Coolies," worked were not much different from slavery, so this business relation was short-lived.

FACT

As part of their contract, Chinese workers who came to Peru to work on the land received 24 ounces of rice per day.

Eating Rice

As soon as they were free to make a living in whichever way they pleased, these enterprising Chinese immigrants started opening grocery stores on street corners or stands for selling freshly made food. What they cooked was mainly Chinese, and these little restaurants got the name of *Chifas*, which means "eating rice." *Chifas* were an immediate success, and can be found nowadays in every neighborhood of any coastal city in the country. Some neighborhoods have rows of *Chifas*, one next to the other, for several long blocks.

Chinese food stayed close to untouched by Peruvian influences, apart from a few exceptions, such as the general rule of accompanying it with a large glass of cold Inca Kola (Peru's national fizzy drink) or adding *ají* to spice it up. Peruvian dishes, however, are a different story, as many of them joyfully welcomed many Chinese ingredients, such as ginger, scallions, and soy sauce, to their preparation.

Peru's most famous stir-fry, *Lomo Saltado*, is a clear fusion of Peruvian and Chinese ingredients, cooked in a wok using Chinese techniques. Also, where do you think the Peruvian custom of eating rice to accompany every single meal comes from?

The Italian Job

Even though the fusion of native food with Spanish, Arab, African, and Chinese cuisines makes up the heart of Peruvian gastronomy, the importance of later culinary influences that have strongly influenced the way people eat today cannot be left out. One of these is the Italian influence, which began at the end of the nineteenth century, when countries all over South America were trying to attract European immigrants to populate their cities.

Thousands of Italians (mainly from Liguria) traveled to Peru to find new homes and start new lives, and as Italy is also a country where life revolves around food, they didn't have a hard time adapting to life in Peru and were welcomed with open arms by the locals. Most of these immigrants opened businesses that allowed them to share and promote their wonderful culinary heritage with Peruvians.

Pasta, lasagna, gnocchi, ravioli, gelato, panettone . . . all these delicious dishes are now part of the everyday diet in Peruvian homes and restaurants. In fact, some people say that Peru is the third largest consumer of *panetón* (Peruvian name for panettone) in the world, just behind Italy and Argentina. Another big influence was using fresh vegetables to make wonderful savory dishes, such as the famous *pastel de acelga* (chard tart), which comes from the Ligurian *Torta Pasqualina* and can now be bought in pretty much every corner store.

The popular *salsa verde* (green sauce) is nothing more than the Peruvian version of pesto, made with lots of fresh spinach, basil, and the local *queso fresco* (white cheese) instead of Parmesan cheese, and it's a regular recipe in most Peruvian homes nowadays. One of Peru's most celebrated appetizers, *conchitas a la parmesana*, also came from Italy, but has been completely adopted as a local dish.

ALERT

Even to this day, most of the best wine producers in Peru are of Italian descent. Walking around Lima, one can find trattorias and pizzerias everywhere, and there is even a whole street dedicated to these restaurants, called *la calle de las pizzas* (pizza street).

From Japan, with Love

Another influence on modern Peruvian cuisine is the Japanese culture, known as *Nikkei*. Japanese men, like many men before them, were brought to the country to work the land once the previous workers were freed from near-slavery. Young Japanese workers came by the thousands to fill that gap, with the naive illusion that they would become rich in the land of gold. But many Japanese left those hard mining jobs behind and, as many others did before, eventually focused their entrepreneurial efforts on the food industry.

The skill Japanese immigrants had with fish and seafood changed the way *cebiche* was made forever. Before them, the fish was left marinating in the citric juices for several hours, giving it an overcooked, chewy flavor and an opaque color. The vibrant *cebiche* everybody loves today was transformed in the Japanese kitchens by their tradition of eating raw fish. *Cebiche* is now made almost at the moment it's going to be eaten, and nobody nowadays would accept an old-fashioned, overcooked version. These wise cooks also taught Peruvians to use new sea species and to adapt many Japanese traditional dishes to the Peruvian taste, adding lots of sauces to it and using local ingredients.

Staple Ingredients for the Peruvian Kitchen

Markets in Peru look like rainbows, and they are a playground for any cook. The diversity of ingredients is so great that one would never finish discovering all the possible things to eat or cook with. There are a few basic ingredients, however, that will take you a long way.

Ají

Scholars say that chili peppers, or *ají* (*amarillo, rocoto, limo, mirasol, panca, charapita, mochero, pipí de mono*, etc.) are native to the highlands of Peru and that thanks to migrating birds that spread the seeds all over the continent, they grew in different countries and adapted to a variety of weathers.

There are hot chili peppers all over Peru—in the Amazon jungle, in the coastal valleys, and in the Andes—and they are used raw and cooked in countless recipes, mostly for their flavor and color, and not as much for their heat. Ancient Peruvians seasoned their food with salt and chili peppers, and had so much respect for both ingredients that when they fasted for religious purposes, they abstained from sex, chili peppers, and salt.

Beans

More than forty varieties of beans of all different sizes and colors have been found in pre-Columbian tombs all over the country, and there are records of ancient recipes prepared with native beans. Some beans were used in soups and others were toasted, stewed, dried, or ground like flour. When the Spanish set foot in Peru, they were surprised to find that beans similar to the ones found in Spain were part of the daily diet of the natives. They were called *purutus*. Now they are called *frijoles* or *porotos*, and their popularity has not diminished.

Cheese

Even though dairy consumption was taboo during the Incan Empire, as soon as the Spanish brought it to the "new" continent and introduced it into the native Incan diet, it became a success. As it turns out, the Inca's taste buds were stronger than their minds. As they realized how this simple ingredient enhanced so many of their dishes, particularly their daily soups and stews, they had a change of heart and started not only consuming it, but also producing all kinds of regional cheeses, each one more delicious than the next.

Peruvian cheeses are generally soft, but not creamy, and usually very salty. They are not aged, so they have a fresh, mild flavor, which is why they are such a great addition to so many dishes. A great selection of local, fresh cheeses can be found in any Peruvian market, and it is now hard to imagine any *papa a la huancaína*, *solterito*, *locro*, or ocopa without fresh cheese.

Cherimoya

Cherimoya is a sweet fruit that gives flavor to many desserts. This fruit is also often enjoyed on its own because of its delicious, refreshing flavor, and silky texture. Archeologists have found cherimoya seeds in pre-Columbian tombs and in *huacos* (pre-Incan vases).

Corn

As the name in English very well describes, Peruvian giant corn is gigantic compared to the types of corn found elsewhere. The kernels of Peruvian giant corn tend to be the size of a small olive, or a small cherry tomato, neutral instead of sweet, and crunchy.

It is hard to replace with other corn, because there is something really special and unique about Peruvian corn, and it adds a lot of character to any dish. Luckily, it can now be found frozen in a lot of grocery stores around the world. However, if you can't find it, you can replace it with another type of corn that is not too sweet and preferably has larger kernels.

Giant corn is not the only kind of corn consumed in Peru. Many varieties, in all the colors of the rainbow, are cultivated in the Andes. This is because even though corn appears to have originated in Mexico, in the Andes it was handled with the most agricultural skill and sophistication, and it has been able to adapt to all kinds of weather conditions.

Some corn is purple, and is used to make the famous refreshment called *chicha morada* or to prepare the Arab-inspired dessert called *mazamorra morada*. Toasted dried corn is called *cancha*, which is the favorite nibble at any Peruvian bar or restaurant, and the snack of choice of Andean farmers.

Dried and cooked corn is called *mote*, and is used to prepare soups or to have as a snack with some artisanal cheese. Corn flour is used to make breads, and ground fresh or dried corn is the ingredient of choice to make *tamales* and *humitas*.

Fish and Seafood

The Peruvian sea is one of the richest in the world. The cold water currents that come from the south produce the best-quality fish and seafood. Add to this all the rivers in the mountains and the Amazon jungle, and you have an incredible amount of excellent-quality food. In Peru, you could eat a different kind of sea creature in a different preparation every day of the year without repeating.

Lúcuma

Some say *lúcuma* is the oldest fruit used in Peru, and it's still the favorite flavor when making all kinds of desserts (ice creams, milkshakes, mousses, cheesecakes, *suspiro a la limeña*, or *manjarblanco*). Despite the wide use of it in Peru, it hasn't been exported to other countries until recently. It can now be found in health food stores and some supermarkets abroad as *lúcuma* powder, which is consumed more for health than for taste. *Lúcuma* is floury and has an earthy flavor. It is said to have anti-inflammatory, anti-aging, and skin-repairing qualities.

Onion

The onion, which was brought to Peru by the Spanish, changed Peruvian food forever. Can you imagine enjoying Peruvian dishes without crowning many of them with the omnipresent *salsa criolla*? This salsa, made with red onion, chili, lime juice, and salt, is the accompaniment of choice for virtually every Peruvian dish, giving a crunchy and citrusy freshness to any meal.

Or could you imagine visiting Peru and not trying a *cebiche*? This could very well have been the case if the onion hadn't been incorporated into the ancient Peruvian practice of eating raw fish with chili peppers. Not to mention every cooked recipe begins with an *aderezo*, which is made of sautéed onions, garlic, and *ají*.

Potato

Potatoes are of Andean origin, and archeologists have even found a prehistoric species of potato in Peru that dates back about 9,000 years. It is said that there are around 4,000 potato species that have been found and developed in Peru to this day, and 3,000 of them existed already by the time the Spanish arrived in the country.

This shows how skilled the Andean farmers were with selecting and genetically improving their crops. The potato was first rejected by the Spanish conquerors, who believed it caused leprosy. Spaniards also believed that God didn't approve of the potato because it wasn't mentioned in the Bible and because it was a sinful aphrodisiac. It wasn't until the famines hit Europe many decades later that they finally saw it for what it was: a wonderful food rich in nutritional value. Potatoes were then widely used as a possible solution to famine.

Potatoes are loaded with vitamins and antioxidants, and the more intense the color (blue, purple), the more nutritious. Natives like to eat the potatoes that have been pierced by worms, because they believe worms pick the best-tasting potatoes. Andean communities consider the potato harvest to be sacred, and they still make offerings to the *apus* (mountains which are thought to contain the souls of dead people) in gratitude for this crop.

Quinoa

Along with potatoes and corn, quinoa was a key part of the basic pre-Columbian diet. This seed originated in the Andes, and comes in different colors. Quinoa has been found in tombs that date back over 2,000 years. This superfood looks like a simple grain, but it is actually a complete protein, as it contains all eight essential amino acids.

Peruvians eat quinoa in many ways. They make a porridge with it for breakfast, just as Americans prepare oatmeal. They use quinoa as a starchy side dish instead of rice, in soups and stews, as a flour for baking, and even as baby food. Try mixing some quinoa into your juice to make it thicker, richer, and much more nutritionally powerful.

Rice

Rice in Peru is eaten not only as a side dish, but also to make tamales (*juane*), to accompany stews and meats (*cau cau, ají de gallina*), as the main course in several exquisite preparations (*arroz tapado, arroz chaufa, arroz con mariscos*), and even to make desserts (*arroz zambito, arroz con leche*). Peruvians eat rice hot, warm, or cold, straight out of the fridge. They also mix it with *choclo* (corn), vegetables, or even *salsa huancaína*.

Rice is one of those ingredients that has transcended all cultures and geographies throughout Peru. It's consumed on the coast, in the mountains, and in the Amazon jungle. And the fact that a lot of Peruvian dishes are already packed with carbohydrates doesn't diminish the consumption of rice, as dishes containing ingredients such as potatoes, quinoa, or wheat berries are happily accompanied by rice as well.

A Grape Story

Grape vines were brought to Peru because the Spanish colonizers didn't like the native *chichas*, and wanted to keep drinking the wine they were used to. Soon enough, they started yielding great results in the hot, dry weather of the southern regions of Lima, especially in Ica, a small town right in the middle of the desert.

This was quite a surprise to everyone, because grapes were not usually grown in arid weather. But luckily for all wine lovers, the results were juicy, sweet fruits, some perfect to make wine and others ideal for making a distilled liquor that became popular in Peru and then in Chile. This strong spirit was named Pisco, after the famous port where it was shipped out to other countries (*pisco* is the Quechua name for a colorful bird that was at one time abundant in this region).

It didn't take long to start exporting Peruvian wines and Pisco, and especially in Peru, the latter became the preferred drink of the masses. A series of wars and plagues put an end to this flourishing industry, which has only been revived by Peruvians in the last few decades.

There are several types of Pisco:

- **Pure Pisco** is made with nonaromatic grapes like *quebranta*, *mollar*, and *negra corriente*. This Pisco is almost odorless, and it's perfect for cocktails, especially the Pisco Sour, in which *quebranta* grapes are the shining star.
- **Aromatic Pisco** is made with perfumed grapes, like *Italia*, *torontel*, *moscatel*, and *albilla*. Aromatic Pisco is good to drink straight because its aromatic fruity and floral compounds have great complexity. Sip it slowly from a Pisco glass, designed to give you the best of each kind of Pisco.
- **Acholado Pisco** is a blend of different Piscos, combined in carefully designed proportions, and each vineyard has its own secret recipe for its production. This mix has the best of both types of Pisco: the perfume of the aromatic ones and the structure of the pure ones. Make a Pisco Sour with Acholado Pisco or drink it straight.
- **Mosto Verde Pisco** is made with young grapes. It is the most expensive of all, velvety and with good body and extraordinary flavor.

Macerados are not among the four main types of Pisco, but they are worthy of consideration. Fruits, flowers, vegetables, and spices are added to Pisco bottles and macerated for days or months. They make extraordinary Piscos to drink on their own or in cocktails. Flavors include cinnamon, pineapple, lime peel, raisins, grapes, dried apricots, dried pears, prunes, *ají limo*, *ají amarillo*, cherries, orange peel, honeycomb, and coca leaves.

Equipment for the Peruvian Kitchen

It is not necessary to have a professional kitchen to get good results with Peruvian cooking. As a matter of fact, many famous cooks rely only on a good knife, a great skillet, some pots and pans, and a blender. A wooden spoon will make your life easier, too. What else?

- **Potato ricer:** you will be working with mashed potatoes or yucca very often, so this tool will be really helpful.
- **Colander:** a medium or large one.
- **Salad spinner:** to wash lettuce, shredded cabbage, or any other greens.

- **Small saucepan:** to make small amounts of sauces and *aderezos*.
- **Medium saucepan:** this will cook potatoes and corn, make stews and soups, even rice pudding and *chicha morada*.
- **Blender:** unless you have a mortar and pestle or a *batán* (see the Appendix A), and you want to make your sauces the traditional way, you'll need a blender. A food processor is a good idea if you don't have a blender.
- **Knives:** a very sharp one is all you need.
- **Potato peeler:** this will help you peel potatoes and other vegetables the easy way.
- **Baking pan:** for *causa* or to bake a cake.
- **Cutting boards:** basic wooden or plastic boards for cutting meat or chopping vegetables.
- **Cooling rack:** if you bake often, this is a must.
- **Skillets:** at least two or three, in different sizes, to sear chicken, fish, or steak.
- **Medium wok:** okay, this is not really necessary, but it's great for *lomo saltado*, and if you like to stir-fry, you'll be addicted to it.
- **Bowls:** small, medium, and large.

Cooking Methods

Cooking in Peru is done daily, and from scratch. But don't worry! You don't have to spend your whole day in the kitchen. With the help of technology, and a handful of techniques, you will be on your way to making great Peruvian food quickly and whenever you want.

- **Raw:** Fish and seafood are marinated in lime (or other acidic fruit) juice, chili pepper, and onion.
- **Sudado:** An ancient cooking method in which fish or seafood is placed in a saucepan over a layer of onion, tomato, and chili pepper and then cooked over very low heat, steaming everything in their own juices.
- **Pachamanca:** This is a traditional cooking technique using hot stones in a pit in the ground, like an underground oven. The stones are covered with banana leaves and the seasoned meats and vegetables are

placed on top, covered with more leaves, and left to cook. The resulting food is wonderfully tender and tasty, infused with the flavors of herbs and seasonings, and of the earth.

- **Stir-Frying:** Meat, chicken, fish, seafood, or vegetables are cooked quickly in a wok over very high heat. This technique was inherited from Chinese immigrants.
- **Simmer:** Meat is cooked slowly, for hours, in a tightly closed pan on the stove or in the oven. The meat will be full of flavor and fork tender after several hours of slow cooking.
- **Grilling:** Meats and vegetables are grilled over open fire. Grilling improves the taste of anything, including *anticuchos*, steaks, chicken, corn, potatoes, and plantains.
- **Baking:** A lot of Peruvian dishes are cooked in the oven. Some small towns have communal wood ovens that make amazing bread!
- **Boiling:** Traditionally, boiling was done with heated stones added to the pot to cook the food. Now you can use the stove. This is good for cooking cereals, potatoes, and soups.

Getting Started

Are you ready to start cooking like a Peruvian? Here are some tips for a successful cooking experience:

- Read the entire recipe very carefully. This way you will make sure you have all the ingredients and equipment on hand. Also take notice of the preparation time and the cooking time.
- Before you start cooking, measure, peel, chop, dice, sift, and do all the necessary prep steps. The French call this step *mise en place*, and it's a great idea to organize your way in the kitchen.
- Above all, have fun and cook with joy. Your food will be infused with good energy and will bring happiness to all.

CHAPTER 2

Salsas, Creams, and Dips

Salsa Criolla

This salsa goes well with almost everything. Peruvians love it! They make it on the spur of the moment to accompany sandwiches, beans, lentils, rice with chicken or duck, tamales, soups, causa, and even fried eggs on toast. It has several delicious variations.

INGREDIENTS | YIELDS ¾ CUP

½ red onion, finely sliced

1 fresh ají amarillo (Peruvian yellow pepper), finely sliced (optional)

Salt to taste

Pepper to taste

Juice of 2 limes

2 tablespoons olive oil

2 tablespoons chopped cilantro leaves

In a bowl, combine onion, ají amarillo, salt, pepper, lime juice, and olive oil. Mix carefully and sprinkle with cilantro leaves. Serve immediately or refrigerate up to one hour.

All-Radish Variation

If you don't like raw onions, substitute the same amount of shredded radishes for the onion, and follow the recipe as indicated.

Bell Pepper Salsa Criolla

This is one of the many variations of Salsa Criolla.
Add a touch of color with red, yellow, and orange bell peppers.

INGREDIENTS | YIELDS ¾ CUP

½ red onion, finely sliced

½ red bell pepper, finely sliced

Salt to taste

Pepper to taste

Juice of 2 limes

2 tablespoons olive oil

2 tablespoons chopped cilantro leaves

In a bowl, combine onion, bell pepper cut in thin slices, salt, pepper, lime juice, and olive oil. Mix carefully and sprinkle with cilantro leaves. Serve immediately or refrigerate up to one hour.

Crunchy Onion

The secret for the best Salsa Criolla is this: Slice the onions and wash them under running cold water. Then transfer to a bowl with water and ice, and let rest while you prepare the rest of the salse. Drain before mixing with the other ingredients.

Scallion Salsa Criolla

Serve with beef, broiled chicken, fried fish, soups and stews, beans, or sandwiches.

INGREDIENTS | YIELDS ¾ CUP

½ red onion, finely sliced

¼ cup sliced scallions (white and green parts)

1 ají amarillo, ribs and seeds removed, finely sliced

Salt to taste

Pepper to taste

Juice of 1–2 limes

2 tablespoons olive oil

2 tablespoons chopped cilantro leaves

In a bowl combine the onion, scallions, ají amarillo, salt, pepper, lime juice, and olive oil. Mix carefully and sprinkle with cilantro leaves. Serve immediately or refrigerate up to one hour.

Scallions

To enhance the flavor of chicken soup, or any other soup, add a tablespoon of finely sliced scallions, along with lime juice and a good spoonful of chili pepper.

Parsley Salsa

This salsa goes well with grilled meats, chicken, or Sancochado (see Chapter 14), a hearty soup usually served with several salsas.

INGREDIENTS | YIELDS 1½ CUPS

1 cup parsley leaves

1 cup olive oil

3 fresh ají amarillo, seeded and deveined

Salt to taste

Pepper to taste

In a blender, process all ingredients until smooth or slightly chunky, as you wish. Serve immediately.

Huacatay Salsa

Huacatay is an aromatic leaf that tends to be overpowering. Use just a few leaves to enjoy it at its best. This salsa goes well with potatoes, corn, Sancochado (see Chapter 14), and other soups.

INGREDIENTS | YIELDS 1½ CUPS

8 huacatay (black mint) leaves
1 cup cottage cheese
½ cup evaporated milk
1 tablespoon ají amarillo paste (optional)
Salt to taste

1. In a small bowl, blanch the huacatay leaves in boiling water for 1 minute. Drain and put in a bowl with iced water until cool. Drain.

2. In a blender, process the huacatay, cottage cheese, milk, ají amarillo (if a spicy sauce is preferred), and salt. Serve immediately or refrigerate up to one hour.

Finding Huacatay

If you can't find fresh huacatay, buy huacatay paste in a Latin American grocery store, or on the Internet. If you have huacatay paste, use ½ teaspoon in place of the 8 leaves in this recipe. Remember that it should give a nice and subtle flavor to the dish, far from overpowering.

Ají Amarillo Mayonnaise

Serve with chicharrones (pork, chicken, fish, seafood fritters), beans, salads, meats, causa, potatoes, or corn.

INGREDIENTS | YIELDS 1 CUP

1 egg
1 teaspoon salt
1 teaspoon sugar
½ teaspoon pepper
1 teaspoon mustard
1 tablespoon lime juice
2 tablespoons ají amarillo paste (or to taste)
1 cup vegetable oil

In a blender, process at low speed the egg, salt, sugar, pepper, mustard, lime juice, and ají amarillo paste. Turn the speed to medium and add the oil in a thin stream until the mayonnaise is thick. Keep refrigerated and use within a couple of days.

Black Olive Mayonnaise

Serve this sauce with fried or steamed fish, squid, shrimp, and octopus.

INGREDIENTS | YIELDS 3 CUPS

1 cup chopped black olives

1 garlic clove, mashed

2 cups mayonnaise

½ cup chopped roasted red bell pepper

Salt to taste

Pepper to taste

In a food processor, process black olives and garlic clove with mayonnaise. Transfer to a bowl and add red bell pepper. Season to taste with salt and pepper, but remember that olives are already very salty.

Peruvian Black Olives

Peru produces wonderful olives, big and meaty, and they are a favorite snack among Peruvians. Besides being delicious, they provide a lot of energy and are healthy because of their antioxidants and vitamin E. Use Alphonso, Kalamata, or Gaeta olives.

Avocado Cream

Serve this sauce with fish and seafood fritters, fried yucca, salads, tequeños, and most finger food. Peruvians love to use it as bread spread, too.

INGREDIENTS | YIELDS 2 CUPS

3 avocados, peeled, seeded, and mashed

2 tablespoons lime juice

2 tablespoons scallions, chopped

3 tablespoons fresh ají amarillo, chopped (optional)

½ cup mayonnaise

Salt to taste

Pepper to taste

1 tablespoon chopped cilantro leaves

In a bowl, mix the mashed avocado with lime juice, scallions, ají amarillo, mayonnaise, salt, and pepper. Serve in a nice sauce container sprinkled with cilantro leaves, next to the food it will accompany.

Salsa Verde (Peruvian Pesto)

Inspired by Italian pesto, this sauce is always served with pasta, but you can vary the kind of pasta and use it over ravioli or gnocchi. Peruvians love to eat spaghetti with salsa verde, combined with Papa a la Huancaína (Chapter 3), all in the same dish.

INGREDIENTS | YIELDS 3 CUPS

¼ cup vegetable oil

½ cup chopped onion

2 whole garlic cloves

1 pound spinach, stems removed

1 cup basil leaves

1 cup evaporated milk

1 cup diced queso fresco (white cheese)

Salt to taste

Pepper to taste

1. Heat oil in a large skillet over medium-high heat. In the hot oil, fry the onion and garlic for 3–5 minutes, until golden brown. Add the spinach and basil leaves and cook until wilted. Drain any excess liquid.

2. Transfer to a blender and process with the milk, cheese, salt, and pepper until smooth. Use immediately.

Make It Vegan

For a vegan version of salsa verde, just replace the cheese with tofu and the milk with soymilk.

Escabeche Sauce

Try this delicious sauce over fried fish, shrimp, chicken, duck, beans, potatoes, causa, and many other dishes.

INGREDIENTS | SERVES 4

4 medium red onions, cut in thick slices

⅓ cup vegetable oil

2 garlic cloves, chopped

1 tablespoon ají panca paste

Salt to taste

Pepper to taste

½ teaspoon ground cumin

1 fresh ají amarillo, cut in long thin slices

½ cup red wine vinegar

½ cup fish or chicken stock

½ teaspoon dried oregano

1. In a saucepan with salted boiling water, blanch the onions for 3 minutes. Drain.

2. Heat the oil in a skillet over medium heat and sauté garlic, ají panca, salt, pepper, and cumin for 3 minutes.

3. Stir the sliced ají amarillo, blanched onion, and vinegar into the skillet mixture. Add the stock and bring to a boil over high heat. Sprinkle with oregano and cook for 3 minutes. Season with salt and pepper, and remove from heat. The onion should remain crunchy. Use immediately. This sauce does not reheat well.

Peanut Sauce

Serve this tasty sauce with boiled potatoes, fried yucca, or pasta.

INGREDIENTS | YIELDS 1½ CUPS

5 tablespoons vegetable oil
½ cup chopped onion
2 garlic cloves, chopped
½ cup toasted peanuts
4 tablespoons ají mirasol paste
2 tablespoons water
½ cup evaporated milk
Salt to taste
Pepper to taste

1. Heat oil in a skillet over medium-high heat. In the hot oil, fry the onion and garlic for 5 minutes. Add peanuts and ají mirasol paste, stirring for 3 minutes. Cool and process in a blender with water.

2. Return the sauce to the skillet, and heat with the milk over medium-high heat, but do not let it boil. Season with salt and pepper. If too thick, add another ¼ cup evaporated milk to thin the sauce. Serve warm.

Peanuts in Peru

Historians know for sure that peanuts have been in Peru for more than 4,000 years. They say this legume arrived from what is now Brazil and became an important crop for the Moche culture.

Ají Mirasol Sauce

This sauce was originally made using a batán, a heavy stone used to grind cereals and to make ají pastes and sauces. Serve at room temperature with potatoes, yucca, and pasta.

INGREDIENTS | YIELDS 1 CUP

3 tablespoons vegetable oil
½ cup chopped onion
2 garlic cloves, chopped
3 tablespoons ají mirasol paste
4 vanilla wafers, broken into large pieces
½ cup pecans
½ cup evaporated milk
Salt to taste
Pepper to taste

Heat the oil in a skillet over medium-high heat. Sauté the onion and garlic for 5 minutes, and then add the ají mirasol paste. After 4 minutes, add the broken cookies and pecans. Remove from heat and cool. Transfer to a blender and process with the milk, salt, and pepper. The sauce should be very creamy, and it's at its best if served immediately.

Crema de Rocoto (Fiery Rocoto Cream)

This cream is perfect as a dip for cocktail potatoes, yucca sticks, corn kernels, chicken anticuchos, and quail eggs. For a creamier texture, use cream cheese instead of queso fresco.

INGREDIENTS | YIELDS 1½ CUPS

2 tablespoons vegetable oil

½ red onion, chopped

½ rocoto, chopped

1 garlic clove, chopped

½ cup diced queso fresco

⅓ cup evaporated milk

Salt to taste

Pepper to taste

1. In a skillet heat the oil over high heat. Sauté the onion, rocoto, and garlic for 5 minutes. Transfer to a blender and process with the remaining ingredients until creamy.

2. Serve at room temperature.

Rocoto Jam

Remove the seeds and ribs from 4 pounds of rocotos, and juice them. Weigh the juice and add the same amount of granulated sugar. Cook in a saucepan over high heat, skimming the surface. When a teaspoon of jam dropped into a glass of cold water forms a soft ball, it is ready. Cool and place in jars.

Anticucho Sauce

Spicy and full of flavor, this is the perfect sauce to accompany those hearty beef, chicken, or chicken liver anticucho bites.

INGREDIENTS | YIELDS 1½ CUPS

8 ounces fresh ají amarillo, ribs and seeds removed

1 onion, chopped

3 garlic cloves, whole

1 sprig huacatay (black mint), or ½ teaspoon huacatay paste

1 sprig cilantro

Salt to taste

Pepper to taste

½ cup vegetable oil

1. Preheat broiler. Place ají amarillo, onion, and garlic on a baking sheet and broil for about 15 minutes, turning once. When some parts of the vegetables look charred, take out of the oven, clean the burned parts, and let cool.

2. Put the broiled vegetables in a blender, add huacatay and cilantro leaves, season with salt and pepper, and process until combined. Add vegetable oil in a thin stream until the cream is smooth. Taste for seasoning. Serve in a ramekin.

Rocoto and Huacatay Sauce

If you love rocoto cream and huacatay salsa, why not put them together into one power sauce?

INGREDIENTS | YIELDS ¾ CUP

½ cup plus 2 tablespoons vegetable oil, divided

1 rocoto, seeds and ribs removed

5 huacatay (black mint) leaves

½ cup diced queso fresco

Salt to taste

1. Heat 2 tablespoons oil in a skillet over medium heat. Stir-fry the rocoto until tender, about 7 minutes. Turn off the heat and cool.

2. Process in a blender with the remaining ingredients until creamy. Serve immediately or keep refrigerated up to one hour. Bring to room temperature before serving.

About Queso Fresco

In Peru, the name *queso fresco* refers to a white cheese with a mild flavor and a semi-firm texture. It does not melt, but turns soft and gooey when heated, and if properly made it has a nice, salty, neutral flavor that goes well with a variety of recipes.

Ground Rocoto Sauce

Serve this in small ramekins and put them on the table so your friends can add a teaspoon or more to their food, to taste.

INGREDIENTS | YIELDS 1 CUP

¼ cup vegetable oil

2 rocotos, blanched 3 times in boiling water (or use frozen rocotos)

1 red onion, chopped

2 garlic cloves, chopped

Salt to taste

Pepper to taste

¼ cup water

Heat the oil in a skillet over medium heat. Stir-fry the rocoto, onion, and garlic for 10 minutes. When the vegetables are cooked, turn off the heat and cool. Add salt and pepper and process in a blender with water. Serve at room temperature.

Rocoto Béchamel (White Sauce) Mini Recipe

Heat 2 tablespoons butter in a skillet over medium heat. Add 2 tablespoons all-purpose flour and, stirring quickly, cook for 3 minutes. Add 2 tablespoons rocoto paste, 2 cups hot evaporated milk, stirring rapidly to avoid lumps. Add salt and white pepper to taste. Lower the heat and simmer for 15 minutes. Serve hot with fish, chicken, beef, or pork.

Mango and Bell Pepper Chalaquita

Chalaca is the sauce served over Mussels Callao-Style, and consists of finely diced onion, ají, tomato, corn, and cilantro. This is a nice variation with a sweet touch. It can also be made with pineapple or peaches instead of mango.

INGREDIENTS | YIELDS 1 CUP

½ ripe Edward mango, finely diced

1½ tablespoons finely diced red onion

2 tablespoons finely diced red bell pepper

1 tablespoon rocoto, finely diced (optional)

Juice and zest of 1 lime

½ tablespoon cilantro

3 tablespoons olive oil

Salt to taste

Pepper to taste

Combine all the ingredients in a bowl. Serve.

Spicy Tamarillo Salsa

Sachatomate is a Quechua word meaning tree tomato, a fruit native to the Andes region. Nowadays you can find it everywhere in the world, only with different names. Tamarillo is one of them.

INGREDIENTS | YIELDS 1½ CUPS

6 fresh tamarillos, finely diced

1 fresh ají limo, seeds and ribs removed, finely diced

1 fresh, frozen, or jarred rocoto, seeds and ribs removed, finely diced

Salt to taste

Pepper to taste

Juice of 1 lime

¼ cup olive oil

¼ cup cilantro leaves

1. Place tamarillos, ají limo, and rocoto in a small bowl. Season with salt and pepper, and add lime juice and olive oil. Stir.

2. Tear half the cilantro leaves and add them to the salsa with the rest of the whole leaves. Serve at room temperature.

Ají and Tamarillo Sauce

Sachatomate (or tamarillo) is widely used in delicious sauces and other recipes, and in folk medicine as well. Here you have a pleasing recipe that goes well with chicken, beef, fish, lamb, or pork, or with legumes like lentils and beans.

INGREDIENTS | YIELDS 3 CUPS

2 tablespoons vegetable oil

3 tablespoons ají amarillo paste

1 small white onion, chopped

2 garlic cloves, minced

6 sachatomates (tamarillos)

½ cup olive oil

Salt to taste

Pepper to taste

1. Heat the vegetable oil in a skillet over medium heat. Add the ají amarillo paste and fry until it curdles, about 3 minutes. Add the onion and garlic and sauté until the onion is soft and translucent, about 3–5 minutes. Turn off the heat.

2. Fill a saucepan with water and bring to a boil over high heat. With the tip of a knife, cut an X at the base of the sachatomates; plunge them in boiling water and boil for 1 minute. Drain and transfer to a bowl of iced water. Peel when cool enough to handle.

3. Put the onion mixture, sachatomates, and olive oil in a blender, add salt and pepper, and process until chunky or smooth. Serve at room temperature.

Scallion and Egg Dip

This recipe, from the city of Moquegua in the southern part of Peru, has a surprising flavor and a spicy kick, and is delicious with Sancochado (see Chapter 14). Do not overcook it, though! You do not want scrambled eggs.

INGREDIENTS | YIELDS 1½ CUPS

1 tablespoon vegetable oil
4 tablespoons ají amarillo paste
3 cups sliced scallions, white and green parts
2 eggs, lightly beaten
Salt to taste
Pepper to taste

1. Heat the oil in a skillet over medium heat. Add the ají amarillo paste and fry it for about 3 minutes or until it curdles. Add the scallions, and stir. Cook for 1 minute.

2. Incorporate the eggs and cook for 30 seconds. Eggs need to be moist, not like scrambled eggs. Season with salt and pepper and serve immediately.

Peruvian-Style Tartar Sauce

The origin of this sauce is not Peruvian at all, but it's one of the classic sauces for fish and seafood fritters.

INGREDIENTS | YIELDS ¾ CUP

¾ cup mayonnaise
1 tablespoon chopped capers
1 teaspoon rocoto paste (optional)
1 tablespoon chopped parsley
1 garlic clove, chopped
Salt to taste
Pepper to taste

In a small bowl, combine mayonnaise, capers, rocoto paste if using, parsley, and garlic. Season to taste with salt and pepper. Serve immediately or keep refrigerated until serving time.

More Flavor

Tartar sauce gets better with the addition of more ingredients, like finely diced onion, hard-boiled eggs, pickles, chives, and even caviar!

CHAPTER 3

Appetizers

Ocopa

Don't be intimidated by the long list of ingredients for this cold potato appetizer; chances are you already have most of them in the kitchen. Traditionally, the Ocopa sauce was grinded by hand, in a stone mortar called a batán. Luckily, there are blenders nowadays, although the experts swear that the taste is compromised when modern appliances are used to prepare it.

INGREDIENTS | SERVES 4

½ cup chopped onion

2 garlic cloves, chopped

1 cup diced queso fresco, divided

3 tablespoons ají mirasol paste

½ cup peanuts, toasted

5 huacatay (black mint) leaves, or ½ teaspoon huacatay paste

½ cup animal crackers

½ cup evaporated milk

½ cup vegetable oil

Salt to taste

4 lettuce leaves

1 pound yellow potatoes, boiled, peeled, and thickly sliced

2 hard-boiled eggs, sliced

4 black olives

1. Roast the onion and garlic in a clean saucepan over medium-high heat, until soft and fragrant, about 12 minutes. (No oil in the pan.) Reserve.

2. Divide the cheese, coarsely chopping half of it and finely dicing the other half.

3. In a blender, process chopped half of queso fresco, ají mirasol, roasted onion and garlic, peanuts, huacatay, animal crackers, milk, oil, and salt until smooth.

4. Place a lettuce leaf on each dish, top with potato slices, cover with the sauce, and garnish with a hard-boiled egg slice, 1 tablespoon diced white cheese, and 1 black olive. Serve immediately.

Ají Mirasol

Ají mirasol is a sun-dried chili pepper with a unique flavor and intensity. The drying process makes it lightweight and gives it a long shelf life, while keeping its piquancy. Before using, you should remove the seeds and ribs, toast it, rehydrate it in hot water, and then blanch it to reduce its spiciness.

Papa a la Huancaína

This is the prima donna of Peruvian sauces, and it is so popular that many ready-made versions are now sold in every supermarket. Although it lasts a couple of days in the refrigerator, it does not keep well at room temperature, especially if the weather is hot.

INGREDIENTS | SERVES 4

5 fresh or frozen ají amarillo, seeds and ribs removed

¼ cup vegetable oil

½ cup evaporated milk

4 soda crackers

1 cup diced queso fresco

Salt to taste

4 leaves Bibb lettuce

4 yellow (or white) potatoes, boiled and peeled

4 black olives

2 hard-boiled eggs, peeled and cut in slices

4 parsley sprigs

1. Put the ají amarillo in a saucepan with enough salted water to cover it. Boil for 15 minutes over high heat, drain, and peel; the skin will be easy to remove. Put the ají in a blender, add oil and milk, and process with the crackers, cheese, and salt until creamy.

2. On each plate, place a lettuce leaf and some potato slices. Cover with a few tablespoons of the sauce. Garnish with black olives, hard-boiled eggs, and parsley. Serve immediately.

Uses for Huancaína Sauce

Use huancaína sauce as a side in any of these dishes: fried yucca, quail eggs, lettuce, plantain chips, tequeños, pita chips, boiled corn, fish fritters, or causa. In addition, it can be used as part of risotto, quinotto, trigotto, spaghetti, steak, arroz con pollo, or plain rice.

Lima-Style Tuna Causa

This potato terrine filled with tuna is lemony, spicy, creamy, and refreshing, all at the same time. It is so popular that Peruvian chefs are constantly creating more variations of it. In Peru, yellow potatoes are the ones to use for this dish, but other starchy varieties work well.

INGREDIENTS | SERVES 4

6 starchy yellow potatoes (or you may use Russet or Idaho potatoes)

2 tablespoons ají amarillo paste (see sidebar)

¼ cup vegetable oil

Juice of 3 limes

Salt to taste

1 (7-ounce) can tuna in olive oil

¾ cup mayonnaise

1 avocado

Pepper to taste

4 hard-boiled eggs, quartered

6 black olives, sliced

1 cup giant corn kernels, cooked (or use regular white corn)

3 parsley sprigs

Making Ají Paste

Slice 6 fresh ají amarillos lengthwise. Remove the seeds and ribs, using plastic gloves to protect your hands if possible. Place peppers in a saucepan, cover with cold water, bring to a boil, and cook over high heat for 15 minutes. Turn off the heat. Drain, peel, and process in a blender with 2 tablespoons water until creamy. Make this in advance and keep refrigerated for up to 4 days, or freeze in ice cube trays and use as needed.

1. Scrub the potatoes and cook in a pan of boiling water over high heat for 25 minutes or until soft, but not mushy. Drain. Peel them while hot and mash them immediately or pass them through a ricer.

2. Add the ají amarillo paste, vegetable oil, lime juice, and salt to the mashed potatoes. Mix well and keep tasting and adding more of any of the previously mentioned ingredients if needed, until it is tasty enough for you. This is the base for causa. The texture should not be watery at all (it's more like firm mashed potatoes). Cover with a kitchen towel and reserve.

3. Drain tuna and combine with mayonnaise in a bowl. Slice the avocado. Lightly oil a 10-inch cake pan, loaf pan, or small pastry rings. Line the base of the pan with a layer of potato. Cover with the tuna mixture, then with avocado slices, salt, and pepper. Add another layer of potatoes on top, cover, and refrigerate.

4. Unmold the causa prior to serving and garnish with eggs, olives, corn, and parsley. (You can choose any mix of these ingredients, or get creative and add your own!) Serve cold.

Chiclayo-Style Causa

Chiclayo is one of the most important cities on the northern coast of Peru, with one of the most creative and unique gastronomies. This is their version of causa, a complete dish that you may prefer to share because it is so big!

INGREDIENTS | SERVES 4

6 starchy potatoes (Russet or Idaho potatoes)

2 tablespoons ají amarillo paste

¼ cup plus ⅓ cup vegetable oil, divided

Juice of 3 limes

Salt to taste

6 small fish fillets

Pepper to taste

½ cup all-purpose flour

4 leaves Bibb lettuce

2 sweet potatoes, cooked, peeled, and thickly sliced

1 pound yucca, peeled, cooked, and cut in chunky sticks

Kernels from 2 cooked ears of corn (about 1 cup)

2 cups Salsa Criolla (see Chapter 2)

4 black olives

4 slices queso fresco

The Humble Potato Conquered the World

Potatoes are the fourth largest crop in the world, after rice, wheat, and corn. They are cultivated in more than 150 countries, and more than 320 million tons of potatoes are produced per year.

1. Scrub the potatoes and cook in a pan of boiling water over high heat for 25 minutes or until soft, but not mushy. Drain. Peel them while hot and mash them immediately or pass them through a ricer.

2. Add the ají amarillo paste, ¼ cup vegetable oil, lime juice, and salt to the mashed potatoes. Mix well and keep tasting and adding more of any of the previously mentioned ingredients if needed. Cover the causa with a kitchen towel and reserve.

3. Season the fish fillets with pepper and salt and dredge them in flour. Heat ⅓ cup oil in a frying pan and fry the fish over medium-high heat until golden, about 4 minutes per side, depending on the thickness of the fillets. Transfer to a plate and keep warm.

4. On each of four plates, place a lettuce leaf, then a thick layer of causa, cover with fried fish, and surround with sweet potato slices, yucca sticks, and corn. Top with Salsa Criolla.

5. Garnish with olives and queso fresco, and serve.

Meat-Filled Corn Pudding

The best pastel de choclo should be soft and creamy, not heavy and dry. You can change the meat filling and use chicken or vegetables instead. It is great for Sunday brunch.

INGREDIENTS | SERVES 6

⅓ cup vegetable oil, divided

1 pound ground beef

2 onions, chopped

2 garlic cloves, chopped

1 tomato, peeled, seeded and chopped

½ cup red wine

1 teaspoon ají amarillo paste (optional)

½ cup raisins

3 hard-boiled eggs, peeled and coarsely chopped

½ cup sliced black olives

½ red bell pepper, diced (optional)

4 cups white corn kernels

½ cup milk

¾ cup melted unsalted butter

4 tablespoons sugar

Salt to taste

Pepper to taste

5 eggs, whites and yolks separated, plus 2 additional yolks

3 tablespoons water

¼ teaspoon aniseed

1. In a medium skillet, heat ¼ cup oil over high heat. Add the ground beef and cook for 10 minutes. Transfer to a bowl.

2. In the same pan, heat the remaining oil over medium-high heat and add the onion and garlic, stirring a few times until onion is transparent, about 5 minutes. Add the tomato, wine, and ají amarillo paste and cook for 5 minutes. Return the beef to the pan.

3. Stir in raisins, hard-boiled eggs, olives, and red pepper and remove from heat.

4. Preheat the oven to 350°F. In a blender, process the corn kernels with milk and melted butter. Add sugar, salt, pepper, and five egg yolks. Transfer to a bowl, stirring with a wooden spoon until the mixture looks very soft. Beat the egg whites until firm, and fold into the corn mixture.

5. Have a rectangular 15" × 10" baking pan ready. Pour half the corn mixture in the pan; cover with the beef mixture and then with the remaining corn. Lightly beat remaining egg yolks with water and brush egg wash over the surface of the corn. Sprinkle with aniseed and bake 40–50 minutes, or until golden and firm. Serve immediately.

Papa Rellena (Stuffed Potato)

Traditionally this is an appetizer, but sometimes it makes
a great entrée, served with white rice.

INGREDIENTS | SERVES 10

2 pounds waxy (Red or Fingerling) potatoes

Salt

Pepper

2¼ cups vegetable oil, divided

1 onion, diced

2 garlic cloves, minced

1 tablespoon ají panca paste (optional)

1 tablespoon tomato paste

1 pound ground beef

2 hard-boiled eggs, peeled and chopped

½ cup raisins

½ cup sliced black olives

2 tablespoons chopped parsley

2 cups all-purpose flour

2 eggs

2 cups Salsa Criolla (see Chapter 2)

Adding Yucca to the Potato

Starchy potatoes do not work for this recipe because the papas will crack open when fried. To avoid this, smart cooks found that mixing potatoes with the same amount of cooked and puréed yucca provides the best texture to keep the shape of Papas Rellenas. The flavor is great, too.

1. Cook the potatoes in a saucepan with boiling water over high heat until they are tender, about 20 minutes. Peel them while hot and pass them through a ricer at once. Add salt and pepper. Keep covered while you cook the filling.

2. In a skillet, heat ¼ cup oil over high heat and add the onion and garlic. Cook, stirring constantly, for 5 minutes; then add the ají panca, if using, and tomato paste. Add the beef and cook for 3–5 minutes, then add salt and pepper to taste. Stir and cover the saucepan. Cook over low heat for about 15 minutes, stirring every now and then. Incorporate hard-boiled eggs, raisins, olives, and parsley. Turn off the heat.

3. With floured hands, knead the potatoes for a few seconds. Take a portion of the potato dough and flatten it between your hands, like a thick tortilla. With a spoon, put a portion of the beef filling in the center of the potato. Close it with your hands and form a little football. Repeat, using all of the potato and beef mixtures.

4. Put the flour in a shallow bowl and lightly beat the eggs in another bowl. Roll each stuffed potato in the eggs, then in the flour, shaking off any excess. Heat 1 cup oil in a large skillet over medium heat, and cook the papas a few at a time, turning often to make sure every side becomes golden and crisp, about 7 minutes per side. Add more oil if necessary.

5. Drain on paper towels and serve immediately with Salsa Criolla.

Rocoto Relleno (Stuffed Rocoto)

This dish is from Arequipa, where rocotos abound. Serve it with Potato Gratin Arequipa-Style (see recipe in this chapter). For a sophisticated twist, substitute chopped shrimp for the beef in the filling.

INGREDIENTS | SERVES 10

10 rocotos

¼ cup plus ¼ teaspoon sugar, divided

⅓ cup vegetable oil

6 tablespoons ají panca paste

1 pound sirloin tips, minced

2 bay leaves

2 pounds red onions, chopped

Salt to taste

Pepper to taste

2 tablespoons toasted and ground peanuts

½ teaspoon dried oregano

5 black olives, pitted

2 hard-boiled eggs, peeled and chopped

1 tablespoon chopped parsley leaves

2 tablespoons raisins

3 eggs, divided

1 (12-ounce) can evaporated milk

1. Put the rocotos in a pan with enough water to cover and 1 tablespoon sugar. Bring to a boil over high heat, turn off the heat, drain, and add more fresh water to cover and 1 tablespoon sugar. Repeat three times. Drain and cool the rocotos. Reserve.

2. Meanwhile, in a saucepan over high heat, heat the oil; add the ají panca paste, minced sirloin, and bay leaves. When the meat is cooked through, about 15 minutes, add the onion, ¼ teaspoon sugar, salt, and pepper, and turn off the heat. Add the peanuts, oregano, olives, hard-boiled eggs, parsley, and raisins.

3. Preheat the oven to 350°F. Fill the rocotos with the meat mixture. Place them in a rectangular or square baking pan, one next to the other. In a bowl, whisk one egg with evaporated milk and salt and pepper, and pour over the filled rocotos.

4. In a mixer, beat the remaining eggs until very thick and put a tablespoon over each rocoto. Cover each one with the reserved tops and bake for 15 minutes. Serve immediately with potato gratin.

What Are Rocotos?

Rocotos are fiery chili peppers native to Arequipa, in the south of Peru. They grow in the Andes, and despite the fact that they are very hot, they also have a sweet and unique aroma. As a rule of thumb, the smaller the rocoto, the hotter it is. To prepare them, cut a slice from the top, remove seeds and ribs, and blanch them three times in boiling water with 1 tablespoon of sugar, changing the water every time. You can also buy them frozen or in ready-to-use jars. Cut the top off each rocoto, reserving the tops. Using a spoon, scrape the seeds and ribs from the inside. It is wise to use gloves to protect your hands, and wash them well when you finish. DO NOT touch your eyes or your lips!

Pastel de Papa a la Arequipeña (Potato Gratin Arequipa-Style)

This hearty gratin is de rigueur for Rocotos Rellenos, but also try it plain or with a green salad. It makes a wonderful side for any meat dish.

INGREDIENTS | SERVES 6

2 pounds waxy potatoes (Red or Fingerling)
8 ounces queso fresco, cut in slices
1 teaspoon aniseed
Salt to taste
Pepper to taste
4 eggs
1 (12-ounce) can evaporated milk

1. Boil the potatoes over high heat in enough water to cover for 25 minutes or until fork tender. Drain, peel, and cut them into ½-inch slices.

2. Preheat the oven to 350°F. Butter a rectangular baking pan. Make layers with the potatoes, alternating with queso fresco and a sprinkling of aniseed, salt, and pepper. Repeat three times.

3. In a bowl, whisk the eggs until thick and add evaporated milk, salt, and pepper. Pour over the potatoes and cheese. Bake until golden, about 40 minutes. Serve immediately.

Escribano

When people working at court offices in the city of Arequipa want a quick lunch, they combine all the nibbles offered to them at restaurant and bar tables and turn them into a simple, fiery, and tasty meal.

INGREDIENTS | SERVES 2

3 potatoes, cooked, peeled, and coarsely chopped
3 tomatoes, chopped
¼ rocoto, chopped
½ cup vinegar
½ cup olive oil
½ cup chopped parsley
Salt to taste
Pepper to taste

Mix all the ingredients in a bowl and mash coarsely. Serve.

Corn, Avocado, and Pineapple Salad

Light and refreshing, this is a good salad to have ready when friends come to have lunch over the weekend. It goes well with poultry and pork.

INGREDIENTS | SERVES 4

1 (8-ounce) can chopped pineapple in juice, drained

4 cups cooked corn

3 avocados, peeled, seeded, and diced

1 red bell pepper, diced

2 cups mayonnaise

2 tablespoons ketchup

Salt to taste

Pepper to taste

3 cups lettuce leaves

1. In a bowl, combine pineapple, corn, avocado, bell pepper, mayonnaise, and ketchup. Season with salt and pepper.

2. Serve over a bed of lettuce.

Healthy Corn

Corn is good for your health. It's high in vitamin B6, which helps to metabolize protein and strengthen the nervous system.

Chicken Salpicón

For some people this is a perfect diet lunch because it is light, but at the same time very satisfying. Serve it with a green salad.

INGREDIENTS | SERVES 4

1 chicken breast, cooked and sliced

4 cups cooked vegetables, diced (potatoes, carrots, green peas, corn, green beans, or any other leftover vegetables)

2 tomatoes, seeded and diced

Juice of 2 limes

Salt to taste

Pepper to taste

2 tablespoons olive oil

Combine everything in a bowl. Serve at room temperature.

Avocado Filled with Trout and Palm Hearts

In the rivers of the Mantaro Valley there is an abundance of trout, and you can find them fresh in the markets every day. Smoked trout makes a luxurious salad.

INGREDIENTS | SERVES 4

4 avocados, halved, peeled, and seeded
Juice of 1 lime
Salt to taste
Pepper to taste
1 cup diced smoked trout
1 cup sliced hearts of palm
4 tablespoons mayonnaise
8 lettuce leaves
Parsley leaves for garnish

1. Sprinkle avocados with lime juice, salt, and pepper.

2. In a bowl, combine the trout with the hearts of palm and the mayonnaise. Fill each avocado with about ½ cup of this mixture.

3. Put 2 avocado halves on each plate over lettuce leaves. Garnish with parsley leaves. Serve immediately.

Amazonian Chonta Salad

Fresh heart of palm (chonta) is an amazing ingredient from the Amazon jungle, used to make delicious salads. It looks like a thick stick, and once peeled and shredded in long ribbons, you can enjoy its wonderful flavor and delicate texture.

INGREDIENTS | SERVES 4

¼ cup lime juice
¾ cup vegetable oil (or use half olive and half vegetable oil)
1 teaspoon salt, plus additional to taste
½ teaspoon pepper, plus additional to taste
1 teaspoon sugar
1 teaspoon mustard
1 pound fresh chonta (heart of palm)
1 tangerine, peeled and divided in pieces
½ cup chopped watercress or parsley

1. In a jar with a tight-fitting lid, combine lime juice, oil, salt, pepper, sugar, and mustard. Close the jar and shake vigorously.

2. Shred the chonta with your fingers, pulling it like ribbons. It will look like a plate of fettuccini. Add tangerine pieces, the vinaigrette you just made in the jar, and add additional salt and pepper to taste. Garnish with watercress or parsley and serve immediately.

Capchi

Cusco, with its cold weather, is the ideal place to have a rustic and comforting dish like this one. Warm and soothing, it has all the flavors of this Andean region. Serve it in clay pots for a nice touch.

INGREDIENTS | SERVES 4

2 tablespoons vegetable oil

½ cup chopped onion

2 garlic cloves, chopped

1 tablespoon ají mirasol paste

1 teaspoon cumin

1 tomato, peeled, seeded, and chopped

1 teaspoon dried oregano

1 huacatay sprig (black mint), or 1 teaspoon huacatay paste

Salt to taste

Pepper to taste

1 cup water

2 cups fresh fava beans, cooked

2 cups potato chunks, cooked

1 cup heavy cream

1 cup queso fresco, diced

2 eggs, beaten

1. In a skillet, heat the oil over medium heat and sauté the onion, garlic, ají mirasol, cumin, tomato, and oregano for about 10 minutes. Add huacatay, salt, pepper, water, fava beans, and potatoes. Cook over medium-low heat for 25 minutes.

2. Add cream and cook for 10 minutes more over low heat, but do not bring to a boil. Finally, add queso fresco and the beaten eggs, stirring until slightly thick. Turn off the heat and serve immediately in bowls.

Food in Pre-Columbian Peru

The seasonings in the ancient Peruvian diet were ají, salt, and herbs. They didn't know of any kind of oil, and for this reason they never fried their food and favored an almost vegetarian diet consisting mainly of corn, roots, quinoa, vegetables, and fruits. Occasionally, they ate fish, alpacas, or guinea pigs, which had been salted, dehydrated, or smoked.

Chard Pie

Chard pie is of Italian descent, and Peruvians have loved it since Italian immigrants brought it to the country. It is always a bestseller in every bakery or café where they make it, and it is also part of every household's baking repertoire.

INGREDIENTS | SERVES 6

2½ cups all-purpose flour
½ cup butter
½ cup vegetable shortening
1 teaspoon salt, plus additional to taste
1 teaspoon sugar
5–6 tablespoons iced water, for blending
2 cups cooked chard
2 cups cooked spinach
3 tablespoons vegetable oil
1 onion, chopped
2 garlic cloves, chopped
9 eggs, divided
¼ cup grated Parmesan cheese
Pepper to taste
¼ teaspoon ground nutmeg
6 slices white bread, soaked in water
6 slices Edam cheese
4 limes, cut in slices

1. In a food processor, combine flour, butter, vegetable shortening, 1 teaspoon salt, and sugar. Pulse the mixture until it resembles oatmeal. Add 5–6 tablespoons iced water, one at a time, and pulse until a dough forms. Wrap in plastic film or put in a plastic bag and refrigerate at least 30 minutes. (Dough can be kept in the refrigerator for up to 3 days or frozen for up to 3 months.)

2. Squeeze the chard and spinach in clean kitchen towels to remove excess moisture, then chop coarsely. In a skillet, heat the vegetable oil over medium heat and sauté onion and garlic for 5 minutes. Remove from heat. Add chard and spinach, 3 eggs, Parmesan cheese, salt, pepper, nutmeg, and squeezed bread, crumbled. Mix well and set aside.

3. Preheat the oven to 350°F. Roll half the dough on a floured kitchen counter until thin. Line a 9-inch spring-form baking pan with dough, put the cheese slices on the bottom of the pan and pour the chard filling on top, reserving 5 tablespoons. Make 5 holes on the surface of the filling, and break an egg into each one. Cover with a tablespoon of the reserved filling.

4. Roll the remaining dough. Cut a circle 1 inch bigger than the pan edge, put over the chard, and seal the edge, pressing with your fingers or with a fork. In a small bowl, beat the remaining egg with 1 tablespoon water and brush the surface of the pie. Bake for 45 minutes or until golden. Serve warm with lime slices.

Artichoke Flan

The best artichokes in Peru come from Huancayo, a beautiful and picturesque city up in the Andes. This city is a commercial emporium, too, with lots of activity and wonderful food.

INGREDIENTS | SERVES 6

6 large artichokes

3 tablespoons vegetable oil

½ cup chopped onion

2 slices bacon, chopped

Salt to taste

Pepper to taste

4 eggs

1 cup evaporated milk

3 bread slices, soaked in ¾ cup milk and squeezed

½ cup grated Parmesan cheese

Artichoke Goodness

Did you know that artichokes are great for liver problems? You may drink the cooking water to relieve any discomfort. Also, it is a slight diuretic and can help you lose weight.

1. Cook the artichokes in plenty of boiling, salted water over high heat until a leaf is easy to remove with your fingers, about 25 minutes. Remove artichokes from the water, cool, and cut each in half. Discard the fuzzy choke and the leaves. Chop the pulp coarsely. Reserve.

2. In a frying pan, heat the oil over medium heat and cook the onion until translucent, about 5 minutes. Add the bacon and continue cooking, but do not let it get crisp, about 3 minutes. Turn off the heat. Add the artichoke pulp, salt, and pepper.

3. Preheat the oven to 350°F. Have a kettle with hot water ready. Beat the eggs in a large bowl, add evaporated milk, the squeezed bread, and the reserved onion mixture. Sprinkle with Parmesan cheese. Pour into a buttered 9" × 9" dish, and put this dish in a larger baking pan with an inch of hot water in it, to make a water bath.

4. Bake for 40 minutes or until golden. Take out of the oven. Cool to lukewarm and serve with a green salad.

Pasta Salad

This salad is colorful and easy to make for lunch or dinner, and is the perfect option for the hot days of summer. It is a delicious and healthy addition to the weekly menu and goes very well with the Yogurt Dressing.

INGREDIENTS | SERVES 5

3 cups medium pasta shells
1 teaspoon salt, plus additional to taste
1 cup corn
¾ cup diced carrots
¾ cup green peas
1 cup broccoli florets
2 tomatoes, peeled and sliced
3 cups torn Bibb lettuce
1 recipe Yogurt Dressing (see sidebar)
Pepper to taste

Yogurt Dressing

Process 1 egg white in the blender, adding ½ cup olive oil in a thin stream. As the mixture thickens, it will turn white. Add ½ garlic clove. Turn off the blender and add 1 cup plain Greek yogurt, 1 teaspoon Dijon mustard, and salt and pepper to taste. Process for 15 seconds. Keep refrigerated.

1. Cook pasta in salted, boiling water over high heat for 8 minutes. Drain, rinse in cold water, and set aside.

2. Pour 3 cups water and 1 teaspoon salt in a saucepan and bring to a boil. Turn the heat to medium and add the corn and carrots; cook for 10 minutes. Add green peas during the last 5 minutes. Drain and reserve.

3. In another saucepan with boiling, salted water, cook the broccoli florets for 4 minutes. Drain and reserve.

4. When the corn kernels, carrots, green peas, and broccoli florets are cold, mix them with the pasta, tomatoes, and lettuce. Finally add the Yogurt Dressing, taste for seasoning, add salt and pepper if desired, and serve.

Homey Tuna Salad

Canned tuna in olive oil is a great ingredient to have on hand. It's useful in a large amount of recipes, like sandwiches, dips, burgers, and this refreshing salad.

INGREDIENTS | SERVES 5

1 white onion, chopped
3 cups water
1 cup green peas
1 cup corn
1 cup fresh Lima beans
2 (6-ounce) cans tuna in oil
3 tomatoes, peeled, seeded, and diced
Juice of 2 limes
3 tablespoons mayonnaise
Salt to taste
Pepper to taste
Lettuce leaves

1. Rinse the onion three times with cold water: put in a bowl, cover with iced water, and soak for 10 minutes. Drain and reserve.

2. Pour 3 cups water in a saucepan and bring to a boil over medium heat. Add peas, corn, and Lima beans and boil for about 10 minutes or until they are tender. Drain and reserve.

3. Open the tuna cans, drain, and transfer tuna to a bowl. Add tomatoes, onions, peas, corn, and Lima beans and stir. Mix in lime juice, mayonnaise, salt, and pepper. Serve over lettuce, or use this salad to fill beefsteak tomatoes.

Faux Risotto

Who says you need rice to make risotto? In this recipe, the potato is the star ingredient. Serve with beef, chicken, or fish.

INGREDIENTS | SERVES 3 (AS A SIDE DISH)

¼ cup vegetable oil
3 tablespoons chopped red onion
1 tablespoon chopped garlic
3 cups peeled and finely chopped potatoes
1 teaspoon ají amarillo paste
2 cups beef stock
Salt to taste
Pepper to taste
1 tablespoon coconut milk
1 tablespoon fennel fronds

1. In a saucepan, heat vegetable oil over medium-high heat. Add red onion and garlic, stirring until translucent, about 5 minutes. Add potatoes and ají amarillo paste. Stir until potato begins to brown, about 15 minutes.

2. Add beef stock and lower the heat to low, stirring every few minutes. Add more stock if mixture becomes too dry.

3. Season with salt and pepper, coconut milk, and fennel fronds. Serve hot.

CHAPTER 4

Nibbles and Starters

Conchitas a la Parmesana (Gratinéed Scallops)

The scallops for this recipe—and every other recipe with this ingredient—should be incredibly fresh to get the ideal flavor and texture. It would be best to avoid frozen scallops.

INGREDIENTS | SERVES 6

12 bay scallops on the half shell
Salt to taste
Pepper to taste
1 teaspoon Worcestershire sauce
Juice of ½ lime
1 teaspoon Pisco (optional)
12 tablespoons grated Parmesan cheese
6 tablespoons salted butter
6 lime slices

1. Preheat the broiler. Clean and wash the scallops in the half shell, dry with paper towels, and season with salt, pepper, Worcestershire sauce, lime juice, and Pisco. Put scallops on a baking sheet. Cover each one with 1 tablespoon grated cheese and a piece of butter.

2. Broil for about 4 minutes or until the cheese is bubbling and golden. The scallops should remain almost raw, with a clean flavor and a soft texture.

3. Serve hot with lime slices on the side.

Choritos a la Chalaca (Mussels Callao-Style)

Tasty and refreshing, these mussels are very easy to make if you have the ingredients on hand. The only cooking involved is the steaming of the mussels, and even that step takes only a few minutes.

INGREDIENTS | SERVES 4

12 mussels
½ cup white wine
⅓ cup finely diced red onion
1 tomato, peeled, seeded, and chopped
½ cup corn, cooked
1 tablespoon chopped rocoto pepper (or any other chili pepper)
Juice of 4 limes
1 tablespoon olive oil
Salt to taste
Pepper to taste
1 tablespoon chopped parsley leaves

1. Clean and scrub the mussels, removing the beards attached to the shells. Put mussels in a medium saucepan with the wine, cover, and bring to a boil over high heat. Steam for 5 minutes. Remove from heat. Discard any mussels that did not open and let cool.

2. In a bowl, combine onion, tomato, corn, rocoto pepper, lime juice, olive oil, salt, pepper, and parsley leaves.

3. Cover each mussel with a tablespoon of the salsa, and with some of the cooking juices. Serve immediately.

Pisco and Scallop Shots

Scallops and tomato make a wonderful combination in this twist on the popular Bloody Mary. Pisco gives the dish a distinctly Peruvian flavor.

INGREDIENTS | SERVES 12

2 tablespoons finely diced red onion

2 garlic cloves, diced

1½ cups ketchup

Juice of 3 limes

1 tablespoon Worcestershire sauce

1 tablespoon hot sauce

¼ cup Pisco

2 dozen sushi-grade scallops, cleaned

Salt to taste

Pepper to taste

¼ cup cooked corn

12 small celery sticks with leaves

1. In a glass bowl, combine onion, garlic, ketchup, lime juice, Worcestershire sauce, hot sauce, Pisco, and scallops. Season with salt and pepper. Refrigerate for 15 minutes.

2. In the meantime, have 12 shot glasses ready. Put 2 scallops with some of the marinade in each glass and garnish with corn and celery sticks. Serve at once, or keep refrigerated for up to an hour.

Peruvian Giant Kernel Corn

Peruvian corn is famous for the size of its kernels. They are so big that they have been given the name of Giant Kernel Corn. This variety generally comes from Cusco, and in Peru is known as "Choclo Serrano" (corn from the Andes). Its flavor is not sweet like the yellow corn usually sold in the United States, and it is crunchier.

Chicharrón de Calamar (Fried Calamari)

Summer is the best time to enjoy these delightful fritters. Peruvian fishmongers carry the freshest and tiniest squids, but frequently you can get bigger ones in the market.

INGREDIENTS | SERVES 6

1 pound squids, whole

Juice of 1 lime

Salt to taste

Pepper to taste

½ cup potato starch or rice flour

1½ cups vegetable oil

1 cup Peruvian-Style Tartar Sauce (see Chapter 2)

1. Wash the squid in a colander and rinse with cold water. Clean the insides and peel them if needed. Cut into ½-inch rings, and blanch for 30 seconds in boiling, salted water. Drain, put in a bowl, and add lime juice, salt, and pepper.

2. Combine the squid rings with the potato starch or rice flour in a shallow bowl. Shake in a colander to get rid of excess starch.

3. Heat the vegetable oil in a frying pan over high heat. Fry in batches in the hot oil and drain on paper towels.

4. Serve with tartar sauce.

Chicharrón de Pescado (Fish Fritters)

Fritters are very popular in Peru—they're also made with shrimp, squid, and chicken. Remember: The fresher the fish, the better your fritters will be!

INGREDIENTS | SERVES 4

1 pound white fish fillet, cut in 1-inch cubes

Salt to taste

Pepper to taste

Juice of ½ lime

½ cup all-purpose flour

1½ cups vegetable oil

1 cup Peruvian-Style Tartar Sauce (see Chapter 2)

1. Season the fish cubes with salt, pepper, and lime juice.

2. In a shallow bowl, toss fish with flour to coat. Put in a colander and shake off the excess flour.

3. Heat oil in a large frying pan over high heat. Fry fish in hot oil for about 4–5 minutes and drain on paper towels.

4. Serve immediately with tartar sauce.

Crispy Shrimp with Honey Sauce

The coconut gives this dish a tropical touch, while the panko helps to create an attractive golden crust. Use the largest shrimp you can find.

INGREDIENTS | SERVES 5

10 extra-large shrimp
Salt to taste
Pepper to taste
½ cup all-purpose flour
2 eggs, lightly beaten
1 cup panko
½ cup grated coconut
1½ cups vegetable oil
½ cup vinegar
2 tablespoons honey
2 cups fish stock
2 tablespoons cold unsalted butter

Crunchier Crust

Finely shredded wonton dough makes a wonderful crust for shrimp. So does cooked quinoa or amaranth. Each will add not only texture to these tasty fritters, but flavor as well.

1. Clean and peel the shrimp, leaving the tails intact. Season with salt and pepper and toss with the flour in a shallow bowl.

2. Dip the flour-coated shrimp in the beaten eggs. In another bowl, combine panko and grated coconut. Roll the shrimp over this mixture to cover completely.

3. In a frying pan, heat the oil over high heat and deep-fry the shrimp until golden, about 5 minutes. Drain on paper towels.

4. In a small saucepan, bring the vinegar to a boil over high heat, and boil for 4 minutes. Add honey and stock. Boil until it has reduced by half. Reduce heat to low and add butter cut in pieces. Stir constantly until butter melts.

5. Serve the shrimp with the honey sauce on the side for dipping.

Shrimp Cocktail Tartelettes

*A tray full of tartelettes, or hojarascas, as they are called in Peru,
is always fun and a great addition to any party.*

INGREDIENTS | SERVES 6

½ cup mayonnaise

2 tablespoons ketchup

½ teaspoon Worcestershire sauce

Salt to taste

Pepper to taste

12 baked tartelette shells

½ avocado, diced

12 cooked medium shrimp

6 pickled baby onions, diced

6 hard-boiled quail eggs

12 parsley leaves

1. In a bowl, combine the mayonnaise with ketchup, Worcestershire sauce, salt, and pepper, to make Golf Sauce.

2. In each tartelette shell, place 2 pieces of avocado, followed by 1 shrimp and a half teaspoon of pickled onion.

3. Top each tartelette with 1 teaspoon Golf Sauce, and garnish with half a quail's egg and 1 parsley leaf. Serve immediately (once assembled do not let them stand because the tartelettes will turn soggy).

Golf Sauce

This sounds like a funny name for a sauce, but in Peru it is very popular with shellfish. It is a pink and creamy sauce made with mayonnaise, ketchup, and Worcestershire sauce, but some home cooks add a little orange juice and drops of brandy. The result is very tasty, and it is truly the perfect complement for shrimp or fish.

Novoandean Chicken Fritters with Passion Fruit Sauce

Quinoa makes a crunchy crust for these fritters; use different colors of this wonderful seed for a bright presentation.

INGREDIENTS | SERVES 4

2 chicken breasts, skinned and boned
Salt to taste
Pepper to taste
¾ cup all-purpose flour
1 egg, lightly beaten
1 cup cooked quinoa
1 cup vegetable oil
Passion Fruit Sauce (see sidebar)

Passion Fruit Sauce

Put ¼ cup honey, ¼ cup orange juice, and ¼ cup passion fruit juice in a saucepan over medium-high heat. Cook until syrupy, stirring every few minutes. Turn off the heat. Add salt and pepper to taste and transfer to a bowl. Using a wire whisk or a fork, mix in 1 teaspoon finely chopped chili pepper, ½ teaspoon sesame oil, 1 tablespoon vinegar, and ½ cup olive oil, whisking until thick.

1. Cut the chicken breasts into bite-sized pieces and season with salt and pepper.

2. In a shallow bowl, toss chicken pieces with flour to coat. Put in a colander and shake off the excess flour.

3. Have the beaten egg ready in a small bowl. Drip floured chicken in egg. Taking one piece at a time, roll chicken in the quinoa; each chicken piece should be completely covered with quinoa.

4. Heat oil in a frying pan over high heat. Fry chicken for 5–6 minutes, and drain on paper towels.

5. Serve with the Passion Fruit Sauce on the side.

Fried Yucca Sticks with Peanut Sauce

*In Peruvian markets, you can buy fresh white or yellow yucca.
It's tender and buttery when cooked and has a delicate flavor.*

INGREDIENTS | SERVES 6

2 pounds yucca

4 whole garlic cloves, divided

Salt to taste

1 cup plus 1 tablespoon vegetable oil

1 onion, chopped

1 cup peanuts, roasted

4 tablespoons ají mirasol paste

Pepper to taste

⅓–½ cup evaporated milk

Freezing Cooked Yucca

As soon as you buy the yucca, you can peel it, cook it, cool it, and cut it in sticks. Place in one layer on a baking sheet or dish and freeze. Transfer to freezer bags and store until needed. To fry, take the amount of yucca sticks you need from the freezer and fry in very hot oil without thawing. This will make the yucca crispy on the outside with a soft interior. You can also freeze raw yucca.

1. Peel and chop the yucca and cut each piece in half lengthwise. Place in a saucepan with enough water to cover and 2 garlic cloves. Add salt when the yucca is halfway cooked, or when it offers a slight resistance when pierced with the tip of a knife. Turn off the heat when it is tender. If the yucca is young, this process won't take more than 20 minutes. Cool in the cooking water. Drain, cut yucca pieces into sticks, and reserve. You may refrigerate or freeze the yucca at this point.

2. To make the peanut sauce, in a frying pan over medium heat, heat 1 tablespoon oil and cook the onion and remaining garlic cloves for about 5 minutes. Add peanuts, ají mirasol paste, salt, and pepper, and cook 3 more minutes. Remove from heat and cool.

3. Transfer the onion mixture to a blender and process with the milk until smooth. Add a little water if you think the mixture is too dry. Put back in the frying pan and heat over low heat before serving.

4. To serve, heat 1 cup vegetable oil in a frying pan over high heat. Fry the yucca sticks until golden, about 7 minutes, and drain on paper towels. Sprinkle with remaining salt and serve with the peanut sauce on the side for dipping.

Quail Eggs with Quick Huancaína Sauce

These little eggs make a pleasant combination when mixed with the spicy Huancaína sauce, and are very typical as hors d'oeuvres at Peruvian dinner parties and cocktail parties. They are usually served without any decoration, but this green variation will make a pretty dish to share with family and friends.

INGREDIENTS | SERVES 6

4 tablespoons ají amarillo paste

1 tablespoon vegetable oil

⅓ cup evaporated milk

4 soda crackers

1 cup queso fresco

Salt to taste

1 teaspoon lime juice

2 dozen quail eggs

2 bunches watercress

1. In a blender, process ají amarillo paste, vegetable oil, milk, crackers, cheese, and salt until creamy. Stir in lime juice. Refrigerate until serving time.

2. In a medium saucepan, cover the quail eggs with cold water, bring to a boil and cook for 7 minutes, uncovered, over medium heat. Drain eggs and cool under cold running water. Peel eggs at once.

3. Cover a plate with watercress, simulating a nest. Over this, place the peeled quail eggs and serve the sauce in a small bowl at the side or in the center of the nest.

New Potatoes with Rocoto Cream

Explore the many varieties of gourmet new potatoes to have a plate full of colors and textures.

INGREDIENTS | SERVES 6

1 pound new potatoes

2 tablespoons vegetable oil

½ white onion, chopped

1 rocoto, seeds and ribs removed, chopped

1 garlic clove, chopped

Salt to taste

Pepper to taste

½ teaspoon dried oregano

1 cup chopped queso fresco or feta cheese

¼ cup evaporated milk

1. In a saucepan, cook the potatoes with water to cover, over high heat for about 17 minutes. Drain, peel, and reserve.

2. In a frying pan, heat the oil over medium-high heat and sauté the onion with the chopped rocoto and garlic for about 8 minutes. Remove from heat and add salt, pepper, and oregano. Transfer to a blender and process with the cheese and evaporated milk until smooth. Taste for seasoning and transfer to a nice bowl.

3. Serve potatoes with the rocoto sauce on the side.

Cheese-Stuffed Yucca Croquettes

What can you do with leftover cooked yucca? Make these scrumptious bites, of course!
Instead of cheese, you can also fill them with shrimp or crabmeat.

INGREDIENTS | SERVES 4

1 cup mayonnaise

1 tablespoon lime juice

2 tablespoons ají amarillo paste

½ pound cooked yucca

½ cup diced Mantecoso, Danbo, or firm mozzarella cheese

1 tablespoon chopped parsley leaves

1 teaspoon and ½ cup vegetable oil, divided

1 egg

1 cup flour or panko

1. Combine the mayonnaise, lime juice, and ají amarillo paste. Refrigerate until serving time.

2. Pass the cooked yucca through a potato ricer or a food mill. Sometimes you need to do this twice to get the right consistency, completely smooth without hard pieces or strings from the yucca. If you do not have a ricer, use a potato masher or a fork.

3. Knead the yucca for 2–3 minutes, and take a piece the size of a walnut. Pressing with your hands, lightly oiled with 1 teaspoon vegetable oil, form a round disk, like a mini tortilla. In the middle of each round, place a square of cheese and a little bit of parsley. Close the dough over the filling and press the edges to seal. Repeat with the entire yucca.

4. Whisk the egg lightly. Dip the yucca croquettes in the egg, and then roll them in the flour or panko. Place them on a plate or a rack.

5. Heat the ½ cup vegetable oil in a frying pan and fry the yuccas at high heat, leaving enough room between them so they do not stick to each other. Turn them all over so they get a nice golden color. Transfer to a cooling rack or a dish covered with paper towels to drain the excess oil. Serve with ají amarillo mayonnaise on the side.

Patacones

These crispy and versatile patacones make an appetizing snack or a side dish, and they are easy to make, quick, and oh so satisfying! You need very green plantains for this recipe. Avoid any signs of ripeness because they will be too soft and too sweet for patacones.

INGREDIENTS | SERVES 4

4 green plantains
1 cup vegetable oil
Salt to taste

Chifles

Here's another satisfying way to enjoy green plantains. Peel them, cut them in half, and slice thinly with a mandoline or a very sharp knife to form almost transparent round slices. Fry in hot oil until nicely golden and serve with Cancha (see recipe in this chapter). They will also look gorgeous if sliced lengthwise.

1. Cut the tips off the plantains, and cut each into 2 or 3 pieces. Make a lengthwise slash on the skin and peel. Cut into 2-inch pieces.

2. Heat oil in a sauté pan over high heat. Precook the plantains, but do not let them color. You only want to partially cook them, about 2 minutes per side. Remove from the pan and drain on paper towels. Reserve oil.

3. With the bottom of a glass, a cup, or a cleaver, press every piece of plantain to make it almost flat. Do not break them. Reserve. (You put them aside at this point, at room temperature, and fry them hours later.)

4. When ready to serve, reheat the oil and deep-fry the plantain slices until golden. Patacones should be crispy on the outside. Drain on paper towels, sprinkle with salt, and serve at once.

Cancha

In most restaurants and bars all over Peru, diners are greeted with a bowl of salty and floury cancha. It is also a side dish for some cebiches and seafood dishes. Once you start nibbling on cancha, it is hard to stop!

INGREDIENTS | SERVES 6

2 tablespoons lard
8 ounces dried corn (chulpe)
Salt to taste

Cancha Chulpe

Cancha is a staple of the Peruvian diet, especially in the Andes. There are several varieties of this corn, in all kinds of colors and sizes, but all of them are cooked the same way.

A clay pot will work perfectly for this recipe, but any saucepan will do the job. Heat the pot over medium-high heat. Add the lard, and then the dried corn and cook, stirring with a wooden spoon every few minutes, until golden and puffy. The corn should start to crack in some places and to show its starchy heart. Transfer to a bowl, add salt, and serve.

French Fries

Even though they are Belgian, Peruvians love French fries. Serve them as a side dish with Peruvian Roasted Chicken (see Chapter 10), with fried fish, or with a dip.

INGREDIENTS | SERVES 4 (AS A SIDE DISH)

2 pounds potatoes
3 cups vegetable oil
1 teaspoon salt

1. Cut potatoes into sticks (thin or thick, depending on how you like them).

2. Heat oil in a saucepan over high heat. When the oil is very hot, put some potato sticks on a slotted spoon, and carefully submerge them in the oil. When lightly golden, about 10 minutes, transfer to a plate covered in paper towels and cool. You can refrigerate them at this point. Reserve oil.

3. Before serving, heat the oil to a higher temperature and fry again for about 10 minutes or until nicely golden. Transfer to a plate with paper towels, and sprinkle with salt. Serve warm.

Tequeños with Avocado Cream

Golden, crispy, and with a creamy, melted cheese heart, tequeños are the center of many parties in Lima, and can be made in advance and fried before serving. Fill them with Lomo Saltado or seafood to make them different. They are originally from Venezuela, but Peruvians adore them.

INGREDIENTS | SERVES 8

1 avocado
½ cup mayonnaise
1 tablespoon ketchup
Juice of ½ lime
1 teaspoon Tabasco sauce
Salt to taste
Pepper to taste
1 cup diced queso fresco
½ cup grated Parmesan cheese
1 teaspoon dried oregano
1 package wonton dough
1½ cups vegetable oil

1. Peel and pit the avocado and mash it with a fork. Add mayonnaise, ketchup, lime juice, Tabasco sauce, salt, and pepper. Process in a food processor to get a smoother sauce.

2. Combine queso fresco with the Parmesan cheese and dried oregano.

3. Place a sheet of wonton dough on a chopping board and, with your fingertip or a pastry brush, wet the edges of the dough with drops of water. Add 2 teaspoons of the cheese mixture alongside one edge. Roll like a jelly roll to enclose the filling and press firmly to seal. At this point you can put the tequeños in a sealed container and keep them refrigerated until ready to use.

4. In a frying pan, heat the vegetable oil over high heat and fry the tequeños until golden, about 2 minutes per side, turning them frequently. Drain on paper towels and serve hot with the avocado sauce.

Beef Mini Anticuchos

Serve these with a flavorful sauce of roasted garlic and butter for a different flavor, and add more vegetables to make them colorful.

INGREDIENTS | SERVES 6

1 pound mushrooms

4 tablespoons olive oil, divided

Salt to taste

Pepper to taste

1 pound sirloin steak, cut into 1-inch cubes

2 garlic cloves, chopped

1 tablespoon sesame oil

⅓ cup soy sauce

2 tablespoons lime juice

1 tablespoon sugar

1 ají limo (or habanero pepper), seeded and sliced thinly

1 tablespoon cilantro leaves

1. Put the mushrooms in a bowl and season with 2 tablespoons olive oil, salt, and pepper. Place the steak in another bowl with garlic and the remaining olive oil, and salt and pepper to taste.

2. Thread on small skewers, alternating mushrooms and beef. Heat a skillet over medium-high heat without oil, and cook skewers for 3 minutes on each side or until brown. Remove from heat and set aside.

3. Combine sesame oil, soy sauce, lime juice, sugar, ají limo, and cilantro leaves in a small bowl. Stir well and serve as a sauce alongside the skewers.

Ají Limo

Ají limo is a colorful Peruvian chili pepper, which comes in red, white, purple, orange, green, and yellow colors. They are not only beautiful; they also have a very intense heat, which depends on the color. The red peppers are the hottest.

Chicken Mini Anticuchos

Asian-inspired, these mini brochettes are so tasty that they do not need any sauce at all. Make them bigger and serve them with fluffy white rice as a light lunch.

INGREDIENTS | SERVES 6

4 skinless, boneless chicken breasts, cut into 1-inch cubes
1 tablespoon honey
4 garlic cloves, chopped
1 teaspoon grated ginger
Juice of 1 lime
4 tablespoons rice vinegar
2 tablespoons chili-garlic sauce
4 tablespoons soy sauce
Parsley sprigs for garnish

1. Place chicken in a medium bowl with honey, garlic, ginger, lime juice, rice vinegar, chili-garlic sauce, and soy sauce. Cover and refrigerate for at least 4 hours (more is better).

2. Using small bamboo skewers, thread 2 chicken pieces on each one. Heat a skillet over medium-high heat without oil, and cook skewers for 3 minutes on each side. Do not let them dry. The chicken should be moist and flavorful. Remove from heat and set aside.

3. Place on a tray or on a plate. Garnish with parsley and serve immediately.

Chicken Liver Mini Anticuchos

With lightly charred edges, smoky and spicy, these brochettes are good as hors d'oeuvres or as an appetizer if you make them bigger. Be careful not to overcook!

INGREDIENTS | SERVES 8

24 chicken livers, cleaned
2 garlic cloves, mashed
1 tablespoon ají panca paste
1 tablespoon red wine vinegar
1 tablespoon olive oil
½ teaspoon ground cumin
Salt to taste
Pepper to taste
¼ cup ají amarillo paste
Juice of ½ lime
1 tablespoon diced scallion

1. Marinate the chicken livers for 30 minutes in a bowl with garlic, ají panca paste, vinegar, oil, cumin, salt, and pepper.

2. Using small bamboo skewers, thread 2 chicken livers on each one. Grill over medium heat for 3 minutes per side. They should be cooked, but remain pink in the center.

3. Combine ají amarillo paste, lime juice, and scallions in a small bowl. Serve the chicken liver brochettes on a plate with a bowl of sauce and lots of napkins.

Mini Causas with Ají Amarillo Sauce

Fill these with cheese, cooked shrimp, chicken, corn, avocado, or whatever you like.
Serve in paper candy cups if you want them to look like sweets.

INGREDIENTS | SERVES 6

¾ cup plus 1 tablespoon mayonnaise, divided

5 tablespoons ají amarillo paste, divided

1 tablespoon chopped scallion

Salt to taste

Pepper to taste

8 ounces yellow potato (or you may use Russet or Idaho potatoes)

Juice of 3 limes

2 tablespoons vegetable oil

½ cup crabmeat

1 teaspoon chives, chopped

Curly parsley leaves for garnish

1. In a small bowl, combine ¾ cup mayonnaise, 2 tablespoons ají amarillo paste, scallion, salt, and pepper. Refrigerate while cooking potatoes.

2. Boil the potatoes in plenty of water over high heat for about 25 minutes, or until tender. Turn off the heat, drain, peel them while hot, and pass through a ricer. Season the mashed potatoes with remaining ají amarillo paste, lime juice, oil, and salt.

3. In a small bowl, combine the crabmeat with 1 tablespoon mayonnaise and chives. Taste for seasoning and add salt if needed.

4. Make small balls with the potato mash, filling each ball with a teaspoon of the crabmeat mixture. Put on a plate and garnish with curly parsley leaves. Serve with ají amarillo sauce.

CHAPTER 5

Sandwiches

Olive and Raisin Mini Sandwiches

Serve these two-bite sandwiches at birthday parties or as part of a buffet table, with mini Triples (see recipe in this chapter), Chicken Mini Sandwiches (see recipe in this chapter), and some sweets.

INGREDIENTS | YIELDS 25 MINI SANDWICHES

1 cup black olives, chopped, divided
½ cup pecans, finely chopped
½ cup golden raisins, chopped
½ cup mayonnaise
Pepper to taste
12 slices sandwich bread

1. Process ½ cup olives in a food processor for 15 seconds, and transfer to a bowl with the remaining olives. Add pecans, raisins, mayonnaise, and pepper. There is no need to add salt here, because the olives are already very salty.

2. Spread this paste on each slice of bread, top with another slice of bread, and cut each sandwich into several squares, rounds, or rectangles. Put on a plate and serve.

Keeping Sandwiches Fresh

You can make these sandwiches in advance, cover them with a slightly damp kitchen cloth, and refrigerate them for up to a day.

Black Olive and Cheese Sandwich

This is one of the most delicious and easiest recipes for a sandwich, with few but flavorful ingredients. You can grill it to soften the cheese and add another layer of flavor.

INGREDIENTS | SERVES 2

2 Ciabatta or French rolls
Olive oil
6 slices queso fresco
8 black olives, cut in fourths or slices
Fresh oregano leaves for garnish

Slice the bread in half; drizzle with some olive oil. On the bottom half of the bread, add the queso fresco slices, the black olives, and sprinkle with oregano leaves. Lunch is ready!

Chicken Salad Mini Pita Breads

*The good thing about having mini pita bread sandwiches is that they are light,
and you can have more than one without feeling guilty.*

**INGREDIENTS | YIELDS 25 MINI
SANDWICHES**

¾ cup mayonnaise

1 teaspoon mustard

Juice of ½ lime

3 cups poached chicken breast, cooled
and finely chopped

2 scallions, chopped

1 tablespoon parsley, chopped

½ Granny Smith apple, chopped

½ cup finely chopped celery

¼ cup raisins

Salt to taste

Pepper to taste

25 mini pita breads

1 cup alfalfa sprouts

1. In a bowl, combine mayonnaise, mustard, and lime juice. Add the chopped chicken, scallions, parsley, apple, celery, and raisins. Season with salt and pepper.

2. Slice each mini pita in half and fill with a tablespoon of chicken salad. Garnish with alfalfa sprouts before serving.

Turkey Mini Sandwiches

*If you don't want to bake the turkey breast, buy it already baked in a deli;
this saves time and lets you have your sandwiches ready in a snap!*

**INGREDIENTS | YIELDS 25 MINI
SANDWICHES**

2 tablespoons butter

3 white onions, finely sliced

1 thyme sprig

Salt to taste

Pepper to taste

3 tablespoons sugar

3 tablespoons sherry vinegar

2 tablespoons chicken stock

1 head Bibb lettuce

1½ pounds baked turkey breast, sliced

25 mini rolls

1. In a saucepan, heat the butter over medium heat. Add the onions and the thyme sprig, turn the heat to low, and cook for 25 minutes, stirring every few minutes. Add salt, pepper, and sugar. Stir and add the sherry vinegar, cooking until it evaporates, about 5 minutes; then add the chicken stock and cook for 3 minutes.

2. In each mini roll, put a lettuce leaf and slices of turkey and cover with a teaspoon of the onion mixture. Serve warm.

Chicken Mini Sandwiches

This is another version of the ubiquitous chicken sandwich, this time for grownups. Leave the rocoto mayonnaise out if you aren't fond of spicy food.

INGREDIENTS | YIELDS 10 MINI SANDWICHES

½ cup mayonnaise

2 tablespoons rocoto paste (optional)

1 chicken breast or 4 chicken legs, cooked and shredded

½ cup finely chopped celery

2 tablespoons raisins or dried cranberries

1 tablespoon parsley, chopped

Salt to taste

Pepper to taste

10 mini rolls

10 lettuce leaves

1. In a small bowl, combine the mayonnaise with rocoto paste, if using. Set aside.

2. In a bowl, combine the chicken, rocoto mayonnaise mixture, celery, raisins or dried cranberries, parsley, salt, and pepper, stirring until creamy.

3. Slice each mini roll horizontally in half, put a lettuce leaf on the bottom half, and fill the sandwich with the chicken mixture. Serve.

Peruvian Roasted Chicken Sandwich

If you buy a Peruvian roasted chicken and have leftovers, use them to put this sandwich together.

INGREDIENTS | YIELDS 4 SANDWICHES

4 French rolls or 4 rolls Ciabatta bread

½ cup mayonnaise

4 lettuce leaves

1 tomato, sliced

½ cucumber, finely sliced

4 black or green olives, sliced

1 avocado, sliced

Salt to taste

Pepper to taste

2 cups leftover Peruvian Roasted Chicken, shredded (see Chapter 10)

1 cup Salsa Criolla (see Chapter 2)

1. Slice the bread horizontally and spread mayonnaise on one side. Build layers of lettuce, tomato, cucumber, olives, and avocado, sprinkling each one with salt and pepper.

2. Finish with shredded roasted chicken and serve with Salsa Criolla on top, or on the side.

Triple (Tomato, Egg, and Avocado Sandwich)

Peruvians love this simple and refreshing sandwich, and have it at any time of the day, all year long. It is perfect for breakfast or a quick lunch, as a snack or light dinner, and at birthday parties and other celebrations when cut in smaller portions.

INGREDIENTS | SERVES 2

2 hard-boiled eggs
1 ripe avocado
1 ripe but firm tomato
6 slices sandwich bread
1½ tablespoons mayonnaise, or to taste
Salt to taste
Pepper to taste

Variations

The original Triple has only three ingredients, besides the bread and mayonnaise. Substituting one or two of them will give you countless variations. For example: smoked salmon, egg, and avocado; chicken, avocado, and tomato; trout, tomato, and avocado; cheese, ham, and tomato; among many others. But you may find the traditional combination to be your favorite!

1. Cut the eggs, avocado, and tomato into thin slices.

2. Spread ¼ tablespoon mayonnaise, or to taste, on one side of all the bread slices.

3. For the first layer, put egg slices over the bread and sprinkle with salt and pepper. Add a slice of bread and a few tomato and avocado slices. Sprinkle with salt and pepper. Top with more bread and cut diagonally into 2 triangles, or cut in half into 2 rectangles. Serve.

Bacon and Spinach Triple

This simple sandwich has a very attractive combination of flavors, with spinach and bacon as the highlights and cream cheese to make it creamy and bring everything together.

INGREDIENTS | SERVES 2

1 pound spinach
6 bacon slices
1 cup cream cheese
Salt to taste
Pepper to taste
6 slices sandwich bread
1 tomato, sliced

1. Blanch spinach in boiling salted water for 2 minutes. Drain and squeeze out the water. Chop finely and reserve.

2. Blanch the bacon in ¼ cup boiling water for 3 minutes. Drain, chop, and cook in a frying pan without oil, over medium-high heat until crisp and golden, about 4 minutes. Transfer to a bowl and combine with half the cream cheese and all the spinach. Add salt and pepper to season.

3. Spread 1 bread slice with some of the spinach mixture. Cover with another bread slice, spread this with cream cheese, add some tomato slices, sprinkle with salt and pepper, and finish with more bread. Repeat, and then cut in half, making 2 rectangles, or cut diagonally, making 2 triangles. Serve.

Jamón del País (Country Ham for Butifarras)

Butifarras, one of Peru's most typical and popular sandwiches, are made with Jamón del País (Country Ham), and although you can buy it already cooked, it's very rewarding to make it at home.

INGREDIENTS | YIELDS 3 POUNDS

1 pork leg, boned

2 tablespoons mashed garlic

1½ tablespoons ground cumin

Salt to taste

Pepper to taste

1 tablespoon ají panca paste (optional)

3 tablespoons red wine vinegar

½ cup Achiote Oil (see sidebar)

Achiote Oil

Peruvian cooks use achiote oil to add a beautiful color to the food. The best part of this oil is that it is really easy to make: In a small saucepan over very low heat, heat 4 tablespoons achiote seeds and ½ cup vegetable or olive oil. When the oil turns a deep red color, about 15 minutes, remove from heat, cool, drain, and pour in a jar with a lid. Keep refrigerated. You can find achiote in Latin American grocery stores and in the spice aisle in large supermarkets.

1. Season the pork with garlic, cumin, salt, pepper, ají panca, and red wine vinegar, rubbing the seasonings all over the leg. Roll the meat like a jelly roll, and tie with a string.

2. Place the piece of meat in a saucepan big enough to hold it. Add water to barely cover the meat and cook, covered with a lid, on low heat for 2 hours. Transfer to a cutting board and rub with achiote oil until it has a nice reddish color.

3. Return to saucepan and continue cooking until very tender, about 45 more minutes. Cool in the cooking water, discard the string, and cut into thin slices. Serve. Keep any leftovers refrigerated.

Pan con Chicharrón
(Fried Pork and Sweet Potato Sandwich)

Chicharrón in Peru is meaty and succulent, different than the crispy pork rinds that have the same name in other countries. It is the customary Criollo breakfast every weekend, mainly on Sundays.

INGREDIENTS | SERVES 6

2 pounds pork ribs, or any other cut with a lot of fat

Salt to taste

2 sweet potatoes

1½ cups vegetable oil

6 French rolls

2 cups Salsa Criolla (see Chapter 2)

1 cup mayonnaise

1. Wash the ribs under running water, put in a saucepan with water enough to cover the meat, and salt. Bring to a boil and cook uncovered over medium heat until the water is evaporated and the meat begins to fry in its own fat, about 45 minutes.

2. Once the meat begins frying in its own fat, keep turning until completely golden, about 35 minutes. Cut into slices.

3. Meanwhile, peel the sweet potatoes, cut in ¼-inch slices, and fry in a saucepan with hot oil, over medium-high heat, until they have golden edges and are tender, about 8 minutes. Transfer to a plate covered with paper towels to drain and keep warm.

4. Slice the bread, put some fried sweet potato slices on each bottom half, add several pieces of chicharrón, and top with Salsa Criolla and mayonnaise. Serve immediately.

Lomo Saltado Sandwich

In Peru, the bread used for this sandwich is called a baguettino, a smaller version of a baguette that's still big enough to split in half and share.

INGREDIENTS | SERVES 2

½ pound sirloin steak, cut in thin slices

Salt to taste

Pepper to taste

2 garlic cloves, finely diced

3 tablespoons vegetable oil

½ red onion, cut in thick slices

2 plum tomatoes, cut in thick slices

1 seeded and ribbed ají amarillo, cut in thin slices, or 1 teaspoon ají amarillo paste

3 tablespoons soy sauce

3 tablespoons red wine vinegar

2 baguettinos or Ciabatta rolls

½ cup chopped, fresh cilantro

Make It Vegetarian

Use thick slices of portobello mushrooms instead of sirloin steak. They are meaty and have great flavor when cooked this way. You won't miss the beef!

1. Season the sirloin steak with salt, pepper, and garlic.

2. Put a wok or a pan over very high heat. Add the oil and stir-fry the meat, a few slices at a time, so they don't steam but remain golden instead (about 10 minutes, depending on how strong the flame is).

3. Add the onion, tomato, and ají amarillo, and stir-fry for 2–3 minutes. Pour the soy sauce and vinegar in from the sides of the pan and mix everything. Taste for seasoning and add more salt and pepper if needed.

4. Slice the bread horizontally and add the piping hot lomo saltado, sprinkled with cilantro. Serve immediately.

Butifarra

This sandwich is a big hit with Peruvians, and some cooks even prepare their own ham with secret recipes kept in their families for generations. Butifarras come in two sizes: large ones to have for lunch, or mini versions for birthday parties or to have with coffee.

INGREDIENTS | SERVES 4

4 Roseta rolls, or any rolls with a crispy crust

4 lettuce leaves

½ pound Jamón del País, finely sliced (see recipe in this chapter)

1 cup Salsa Criolla (see Chapter 2)

1. Slice the bread horizontally; place a lettuce leaf on the bottom half; then make a layer of several thin ham slices.

2. Top with Salsa Criolla, cover with the other half of the bread, and serve at once.

Cold Asado Sandwich

If there is a lot of sauce with your asado (roasted meat), take several napkins, roll up your sleeves, and enjoy it like a kid (finger licking is allowed).

INGREDIENTS | SERVES 6

6 French rolls

½ cup mayonnaise

½ cup chopped pickles

6 lettuce leaves

Thin Beef Asado or Creole Roast Beef slices (see Chapter 11)

2 cups Salsa Criolla (see Chapter 2)

1. Slice the French rolls horizontally in half. Spread each half with mayonnaise. Place a few pickles on the bottom half, cover with a lettuce leaf, then add a few asado slices with some of their sauce.

2. Top with Salsa Criolla if desired, or serve it on the side. Finish sandwich with another slice of bread and serve.

Sanguchón (Late-Night Hangover Sandwich)

If you are out and about in the city of Lima on a weekend night, you will most likely bump into a Sanguchón joint. This is where all the party people end their nights by eating a huge sandwich that is sure to satisfy their hunger.

INGREDIENTS | SERVES 6

6 hamburger rolls

6 lettuce leaves

2 tomatoes, sliced

6 beef burgers, already made

⅓ cup vegetable oil

6 Cheddar cheese slices

6 eggs

Salt to taste

Pepper to taste

2 cups papitas al hilo (thin potato sticks, fried)

Mayonnaise, to taste (optional)

Mustard, to taste (optional)

Ketchup, to taste (optional)

Ají amarillo sauce, to taste (optional)

Papitas al Hilo

Papitas al hilo (finely julienned—using a mandoline—fried potatoes) make all the difference in this sandwich, adding lots of crunchy texture to every bite. Substitute with yucca or sweet potatoes for a nice change and additional sweetness.

1. Slice the hamburger rolls horizontally and put a lettuce leaf and tomato slices on each bottom half.

2. Cook the burgers in hot oil or on the grill, to your liking, and place a cheese slice on top, letting it melt with the heat of the burger (and the pan). Transfer the hamburger and cheese over to the lettuce and tomato on each bun.

3. Fry an egg with a little bit of oil at medium-low heat, sprinkling it with salt and pepper and turning it halfway through. Place over the hamburger and cheese.

4. Put a handful of fried potatoes over the egg and splash all the sauces you want on top before closing the sandwich with the top half of the bread. Serve immediately.

Breakfast Bread with Fried Egg

Early in the morning, the streets of Peruvian towns are full of street vendors selling glasses of warm emoliente to people on their way to work. Along with emoliente, they have huge stacks of these sandwiches, one of the favorites for a breakfast on the go. The Peruvian bagel, if you will.

INGREDIENTS | SERVES 4

2 tablespoons vegetable oil for frying
4 eggs
Salt to taste
Pepper to taste
4 French rolls
1 cup Salsa Criolla (see Chapter 2)

1. Heat the oil in a frying pan at medium-low heat and fry the eggs, turning midway through, trying not to break the yolk. Sprinkle with salt and pepper.

2. Have the rolls ready, horizontally sliced, and put a fried egg on each bottom half. Top with Salsa Criolla and dig in!

Hot Caprese Sandwiches

Italian flavors, anyone? What's a better combo than bread, tomatoes, mozzarella, and basil?

INGREDIENTS | YIELDS 5 SANDWICHES

5 pita breads, white or whole wheat
10 thinly sliced pieces of mozzarella
3 tomatoes, sliced
Salt to taste
Pepper to taste
15 basil leaves
5 tablespoons olive oil

1. Preheat the oven to 350°F. Slice the pitas in half. In each one, place mozzarella, tomato, salt, pepper, 3 basil leaves, and a drizzle of olive oil. Cut in halves or fourths.

2. Place on a baking sheet and bake for 6–8 minutes, until heated through and the cheese is melted. Serve at once.

CHAPTER 6

Tamales, Empanadas, and Bread

Humitas

Humita comes from the Quechua word huminta, *the name for a sweet paste of corn, cooked with raisins and wrapped in corn husks. These sweet tamales can also become savory by filling them with cheese or chicken. Or you can make them extra sweet by filling them with raisins and manjarblanco.*

INGREDIENTS | YIELDS 15 HUMITAS

3 pounds fresh white corn kernels

¾ cup shortening

½ cup sugar

2 teaspoons salt

1 (2-pound) package green corn husks (or dry husks)

2 cups boiling water

1 cup Salsa Criolla (see Chapter 2)

Basic Aderezo

Instead of sugar, add an extra layer of flavor to the tamales with an aderezo: Cook 1 chopped onion, 2 chopped garlic cloves, and 2 tablespoons ají amarillo paste in 4 tablespoons hot vegetable oil over medium heat. When the onion is very soft (approximately 5–7 minutes), add this aderezo to the processed corn and continue with the recipe.

1. Process the corn in a food processor. Transfer to a bowl; beat with a wooden spoon, adding the shortening until the mixture is soft and creamy. Add sugar and salt, and taste for seasoning.

2. Have the corn husks ready, and proceed to make the tamales: Working with 2 corn husks at a time, place them on the table with the wide sides overlapping. Put 2 tablespoons of the corn mixture in the middle, but do not spread it. Fold the leaves from all four sides toward the center, overlapping and forming a rectangle enclosing the filling completely. Tie the tamale with a string, or make your own string with a thin slice of corn husk.

3. In a wide, large saucepan, make a thick layer of corn husks, accommodate the humitas over this, and put more corn husks on top. Add 2 cups boiling water, cover tightly with a lid, and steam for about 40 minutes over high heat. Serve with Salsa Criolla on the side.

Manjarblanco-Filled Humitas

Very fresh corn provides a wonderful flavor to these sweet humitas,
or to savory ones made without the manjarblanco.

INGREDIENTS | YIELDS 15 HUMITAS

1 pound white corn kernels

1 cup sugar

1 cinnamon stick

½ teaspoon aniseed

¼ teaspoon salt

1 cup vegetable shortening

1 package green corn husks (or dry husks)

½ cup Manjarblanco (see Chapter 16)

¼ cup raisins

1 teaspoon ground cinnamon

2 cups boiling water

Tamales and Humitas

Tamales and humitas are widely consumed all over Mexico, and in Central and South America. The main difference among them is the variety of corn used. Corn used for humitas is always fresh, and corn used for tamales is always dried. The resulting flavor depends on which seasonings are used and which chili peppers are used (these give tamales their beautiful colors ranging from pale yellow to reddish tones).

1. Grind the corn in a grain grinder, or process in a food processor. Set aside. Meanwhile, put the sugar in a saucepan with water to cover, add cinnamon stick, aniseed, and salt. Bring to a boil over medium heat and cook for 7 minutes, or until a teaspoon of the sugar mixture forms a very soft ball when dropped in a glass of cold water. Add the reserved corn and stir to combine.

2. Add shortening, stirring with a wooden spoon, and cook for 5 more minutes. Turn off the heat.

3. Have the corn husks ready, and proceed to make the tamales: Working with 2 corn husks at a time, place them on the table with the wide sides overlapping. Put 1 tablespoon of the corn mixture in the middle, but do not spread it. Add 1 teaspoon of Manjarblanco, 1–2 raisins, and sprinkle with a dash of ground cinnamon. Fold the leaves from all four sides toward the center, overlapping to form a rectangle enclosing the filling completely. Tie the humitas with a string or kitchen twine, or you can make your own string with a piece of husk.

4. In a large, wide saucepan make a thick layer of corn husks, put humitas over them, and cover with more corn husks. Add 2 cups boiling water, cover tightly with a lid, and steam for about 1 hour over high heat. Serve immediately.

Savory Humitas

These humitas are from Huánuco, in the central region of Peru. Serve them as appetizers with ají amarillo sauce, or as a snack with a steaming cup of coffee.

INGREDIENTS | YIELDS 18 HUMITAS

40 green corn husks (use dried if you can't find them fresh)

7 cups white corn kernels

2 eggs

⅓ cup butter, softened

⅓ cup evaporated milk

1½ cups queso fresco, diced

Salt to taste

1. Clean the green husks with a wet cloth or under hot running water. Fresh husks are usually flexible, so it is not necessary to blanch them in boiling water. If you only find dry husks, put them in a saucepan with boiling water for 3–4 minutes to soften. Drain and dry well before using.

2. Process the corn kernels in a food processor. Transfer to a bowl. In another bowl, beat the eggs with the butter. Mix with the ground corn, and add the milk. It is important to keep the texture thick and creamy, like coarse mashed potatoes. Add queso fresco and salt.

3. Working with 2 corn husks at a time, place them on the table with the wide sides overlapping. Place 2 tablespoons of the mixture in the middle. Fold the long sides inward first, and then the short sides. Tie with string to enclose the filling.

4. Have a kettle with boiling water ready. Place the humitas standing side by side, vertically in a saucepan, and add the boiling water halfway up the humitas. Put the lid on and boil for 35 minutes over high heat.

5. Turn off the heat and let cool in the saucepan. Serve.

Egg Yolk Tamales

These tamales are from Huánuco and are soft and sweet, ideal for tea time or as part of a big breakfast. The preparation is quick compared to other tamales, and the flavor is delicious. If you don't find corn husks, use aluminum foil to wrap them. This applies to every tamale in this book!

INGREDIENTS | YIELDS 18 TAMALES

4¼ cups white corn flour
1 teaspoon baking powder
½ teaspoon salt
12 egg yolks
1 cup sugar
1¼ cups shortening, melted
¼ cup Port wine
1 teaspoon ground cinnamon
1 cup golden raisins
36 green corn husks (or dried)

1. Sift the flour, baking powder, and salt. In a mixer, beat the egg yolks with the sugar at high speed, until white and creamy.

2. Turn the speed to low and add the shortening and the flour with the baking powder by tablespoonfuls. Beat for 10 minutes more at medium speed. Add the Port wine, cinnamon, and raisins.

3. Place 2 tablespoons of the mixture in the middle of two overlapping corn husks. Fold one of the long sides inward first, and then the short sides. The top end remains open for the tamale to grow. Tie loosely with string.

4. Place the tamales standing vertically in a saucepan and add boiling water halfway up the tamales. Put the lid on and boil for 25 minutes over high heat.

5. Turn off the heat and let them cool in the pan without the lid. Serve warm.

Garbanzo Bean Tamales

These tamales have a creamy texture, and the garbanzo beans give them a unique flavor, different from the typical corn tamales.

INGREDIENTS | YIELDS 15–20 TAMALES

2 cups dried garbanzo beans

1 cup lard or vegetable shortening

3 garlic cloves, chopped

2 tablespoons ají amarillo paste (optional)

2 cups chicken stock

6 sprigs cilantro

Salt to taste

Pepper to taste

8 ounces pork loin

2 tablespoons vegetable oil

1 cup chopped onion

2 ají amarillo, chopped (optional)

1 (2 pound) package green corn husks (or dry husks)

15 small black olives, pitted

6 hard-boiled eggs, sliced

2 cups boiling water

2 cups Salsa Criolla (see Chapter 2)

1. Put the garbanzo beans in a bowl, cover with water, and soak overnight. In the morning, drain and process in a blender or food processor until creamy.

2. Melt the lard in a saucepan, add garlic, ají amarillo paste if using, and the processed garbanzos, and cook at medium heat, stirring often. Add chicken stock, cilantro, salt, and pepper. When the mixture thickens and looks shiny (about 20 minutes), turn off the heat and reserve.

3. In another saucepan over high heat, cook the pork loin with enough water to cover, and add salt and pepper to taste. Turn the heat to medium, put the lid on, and continue cooking until the meat is very tender (about 40 minutes). Turn off the heat, transfer the meat to a chopping board, and dice it.

4. In the same saucepan where you cooked the meat, heat the oil and sauté the onion and the chopped ají amarillo, stirring constantly until very soft, about 10 minutes. Add the diced pork loin and turn off the heat.

5. Working with 2 corn husks at a time, place them on the table with the wide sides overlapping. Put 2 tablespoons of the garbanzo mixture in the center, but do not spread it. Top with 1 teaspoon of the pork mixture, 1 olive, and 1 egg slice. Fold the leaves from all 4 sides toward the center, overlapping to form a rectangle enclosing the filling completely. Tie the tamale with a string.

6. To steam, make a thick layer of corn husks at the bottom of a wide saucepan, and place the tamales over this, covering with more husks. Add 2 cups boiling water, cover tightly with a lid, and bring to a boil, steaming the tamales for 40 minutes over high heat. Serve warm with Salsa Criolla.

Tamalitos Verdes (Corn and Cilantro Tamales)

From Piura, in the northern region of Peru, these tender and creamy tamales are part of the daily diet in most households. They are eaten as a snack, as bread, as a light meal, and sometimes fried or soaked with the juices of the day's stew.

INGREDIENTS | YIELDS 20 TAMALITOS

2 pounds fresh white corn kernels

2 cups cilantro leaves

1 cup spinach leaves

1½ cups vegetable oil

Salt to taste

Pepper to taste

1 (2 pound) package green corn husks (or dry husks)

2 cups boiling water

2 cups Salsa Criolla (see Chapter 2)

Green Corn Husks

Peruvian fresh corn tamales of every variety are almost always wrapped in green corn husks. These do not need to be blanched because they are tender, but you can do it to make sure they will be very pliable when using. It is wise to clean them with a wet cloth or under running water before using. Green corn husks give tamales a wonderful flavor.

1. Process corn, cilantro, and spinach in a food processor or a grain grinder until it looks like cooked oatmeal. You can use the blender, but the texture could be too liquid, which will affect the resulting tamales.

2. Transfer the processed corn to a bowl. Add oil, stirring gently with a wooden spoon or a spatula, until smooth, about 15 minutes. Add salt and pepper.

3. Have the corn husks ready, and proceed to make the tamales: Working with 2 corn husks at a time, place them on the table with the wide ends overlapping. Put 2 tablespoons of the corn mixture in the middle, but do not spread it. Fold the leaves inward, overlapping and forming a rectangle that encloses the filling completely. Tie the tamale with a string, or make your own string with a thin slice of the corn husk.

4. Make a layer of husks in the bottom of a wide saucepan. Place the tamales and cover with more husks. Add 2 cups boiling water, put the lid on, and bring to a boil. Steam for 35 minutes over high heat. Turn off the heat. You can eat the tamales at once, but they will hold their shape better if you open them after a few minutes, when they begin to cool a little.

5. Serve 2 tamales on each plate with Salsa Criolla on the side.

Lima-Style Tamales

Here's a little secret: Some cooks put a large unpeeled potato on top of the tamales before steaming, and then they know the tamales are ready when the potato is tender.

INGREDIENTS | YIELDS 15 TAMALES

1 pound dried white corn

1 pound dried yellow corn

2 pounds pork loin

8 ounces chicken thighs

Salt to taste

2 tablespoons vegetable oil

5 garlic cloves, chopped

1 teaspoon ground cumin

Pepper to taste

1 cup lard

½ cup toasted and ground peanuts

⅓ cup toasted and ground sesame seeds

1 tablespoon ají panca paste

1 tablespoon ají mirasol paste

1 tablespoon ají amarillo paste

1 (2 pound) package banana leaves

15 small black olives

1 tablespoon whole peanuts

4 hard-boiled eggs, cut in slices

3 cups boiling water

2 cups Salsa Criolla (see Chapter 2)

1. In a bowl, combine white and yellow corn, add water to cover, put a lid on, and soak overnight.

2. The following day, cook the pork and chicken in a saucepan over medium heat, with salt and 4 cups water, until the meats are fork tender, about 45 minutes. Turn off the heat and let cool in the water. Reserve cooking water.

3. Transfer the pork and chicken to a chopping board and dice. Heat the oil in a skillet over medium heat, sauté the diced meats with garlic, cumin, salt, and pepper, for 10 minutes. Turn off the heat and set aside to cool.

4. Drain and rinse the corn, put in a saucepan, cover with water, and bring to a boil. Boil for 20 minutes over high heat. Drain, spread on a kitchen counter over a cloth to dry, and finely grind in a grain grinder or a food processor.

5. To make the dough, in a saucepan, add the lard to the ground corn, stirring with a wooden spoon, and add peanuts, sesame seeds, ají panca, ají mirasol, ají amarillo, and 3 cups of the pork's cooking water. Cook over medium-low heat, stirring continuously until the dough is thick and shiny and you can see the bottom of the pan. Turn off the heat.

6. Clean the banana leaves and cut them in 15-inch squares. Place two on a table and make sure they are overlapping. In the center, place about 1 cup corn dough, add 1 tablespoon pork and chicken, 1 olive, 1 peanut, and 1 slice hard-boiled egg. Cover with a little portion of dough. Wrap the tamale, folding the

Banana Leaves as Tamale Wrapping

Traditionally, banana leaves are the preferred wrapping for tamales, because the leaves are easy to handle and they infuse the dough with a subtle and delicious scent. To make the leaves pliable without tearing them, they need to be blanched in boiling water. Some people sun-dry the leaves so they last longer, or cook them over an open fire. Buy them fresh at specialty markets, or frozen at Latin American grocery stores. Several chefs also use aluminum foil instead of banana leaves.

sides over the dough and overlapping to form a rectangle. If more wrapping is needed, double wrap with more banana leaves. Tie lengthwise and widthwise with a string.

7. In a large and wide saucepan, put a thick layer of banana leaves, put tamales on top, and cover with more banana leaves. Add 3 cups boiling water, cover tightly with a lid, and steam for 1 hour, over high heat, adding more boiling water as needed. Serve warm with Salsa Criolla.

Baked Tamalitos Verdes

You should use the freshest corn when making this dish for the most delicate texture, but a mixture of young and ripe corn will work perfectly, too. Serve with Salsa Criolla or Huancaína Sauce.

INGREDIENTS | SERVES 6

5 cups fresh corn kernels

1 cup cilantro leaves

½ cup water

5 eggs

¾ cup evaporated milk

1 cup coarsely grated queso fresco

Salt to taste

Pepper to taste

2 teaspoons sugar

1 tablespoon butter

½ cup bread crumbs

2 cups Salsa Criolla (see Chapter 2)

2 cups Papa a la Huancaína (see Chapter 3)

1. Preheat the oven to 325°F. In a blender, process the corn kernels with cilantro leaves and water.

2. In a bowl, whisk the eggs; add the corn mixture, evaporated milk, cheese, salt, pepper, and sugar.

3. Using the butter, grease an 8" × 8" baking pan, and dust with the bread crumbs. Scrape the corn mixture into the baking pan and bake for 1 hour, or until firm and lightly golden. Serve with Salsa Criolla, Huancaína Sauce, or both.

Chapanas (Sweet Yucca Tamales)

These dark, sweet, and semitranslucent tamales are a specialty of Cañete, a small town south of Lima. They are served as dessert or as a snack, at any time of the day.

INGREDIENTS | **YIELDS 12 CHAPANAS**

2½ pounds yucca, peeled (about 3 cups grated)

1 cup sugar

1 (2 pound) package dried banana leaves

1. Grate the yucca with the finest side of the grater. Put in a bowl and combine with sugar.

2. Blanch the banana leaves in boiling water for 1 minute to soften. Drain. Make a rectangle with a leaf by folding edges over, and put 3 tablespoons yucca in the center, near the edge. Fold the straight edge over the yucca, fold both sides of the leaf toward the center, and fold again to enclose completely. Repeat with another leaf to make a double wrap, and tie with a string. Repeat with the entire yucca mixture.

3. In a wide saucepan, make a layer of banana leaves, place the chapanas over the leaves, cover with more leaves, and add 3 cups boiling water. Cover tightly with a lid and steam for 2 hours over high heat, adding more boiling water as needed. Make sure they keep steaming all the time.

4. Let them cool completely on wire racks and serve at room temperature. Keep refrigerated up to a week.

Juanes

A juane is an Amazonian tamale, and its name honors Saint John the Baptist. It is wrapped like a bun instead of in a rectangle, and it's one of the most popular dishes in the jungle.

INGREDIENTS | YIELDS 6 JUANES

1 (2-pound) hen, cut in pieces (substitute with chicken, but the flavor will be milder)

Salt to taste

Pepper to taste

1 cup lard, divided

2 cups white rice

4 cups reserved hen stock

1 cup diced onion

3 garlic cloves, chopped

1 tablespoon grated fresh turmeric (or 1 teaspoon dried)

2 bay leaves

1 teaspoon oregano

1 teaspoon powdered cumin

1 cup grated yucca

6 whole eggs

1 (2 pound) package plantain leaves, or bijao leaves, soaked in boiling water and dried

3 hard-boiled eggs

12 black olives

Ají charapita (optional)

Coriander leaves (optional)

Variations

Juane has as many variations as there are people of the Amazon jungle. They include: arroz juane (rice and hen), avispa juane (with minced beef), chuchulli juane (hen innards and rice), nina juane (chicken and eggs), sara juane (corn, guinea pig, and peanuts), uchu juane (fish, egg, and ají), and yucca juane (yucca).

1. In a heavy saucepan, cook the hen pieces in enough water to cover with salt and pepper to taste, over high heat for 45 minutes. When tender, take out of the saucepan and reserve. Strain the stock and reserve.

2. In the same saucepan over high heat, melt ½ cup lard, add rice and salt to taste, and stir for a few minutes. Add 4 cups of the reserved stock. Lower the heat to medium-low and cook the rice, covered, until tender, about 25 minutes. Transfer to a bowl and let cool.

3. In the same saucepan over high heat, melt the remaining lard, add onion and garlic, and cook until translucent, about 4 minutes. Add turmeric, bay leaves, oregano, cumin, pepper, and the hen, stirring. It is ready when it has a golden color, about 10 minutes.

4. Remove the meat, put aside, and add the rice to the pan full of spices. Put the grated yucca in a kitchen cloth and strain to get rid of its moisture. When the yucca is dry and fluffy add it to the rice. Add 6 well-beaten eggs and mix carefully.

5. To form the juanes: Make a square of two layers of plantain leaves, one next to the other and overlapping. Add 2 cups rice, a hen piece (usually a leg), ½ hard-boiled egg, and 2 black olives. Cover with ½ cup of rice. Close the package, wrapping the leaves upwards around the filling, and tie with a string.

6. Place juanes in a saucepan with boiling water, cover tightly with a lid, and cook for 45 minutes over high heat. When ready, take out of the saucepan and cool.

7. Serve lukewarm or cold, if possible with ají charapita and coriander leaves.

Beef Empanadas

Everyone loves an empanada at any time of the day. They make an excellent snack or a light meal on the go. . . . They are even good for breakfast! Make them smaller to pass as finger food at your next gathering, and just add a few drops of lime juice for a tangy surprise.

INGREDIENTS | SERVES 6

⅓ cup vegetable oil, divided
1 pound ground beef
3 onions, chopped
3 garlic cloves, chopped
1 teaspoon paprika
1 teaspoon ground cumin
1 tomato, peeled, seeded, and chopped
2 tablespoons red wine
½ cup raisins
Salt to taste
Pepper to taste
3 hard-boiled eggs, peeled and chopped
½ cup chopped black olives
1 batch Empanada Dough (see recipe in this chapter)
1 egg
1 tablespoon water
Lime slices for garnish

1. Make the filling: Heat half the oil in a skillet over medium heat; add the beef and cook, stirring often, for 15 minutes. Transfer to a bowl. In the same pan, heat the remaining oil over medium heat, add the onion and garlic, and sauté until the onion is very soft, about 8 minutes. Add paprika and cumin, then the tomato and the wine. Put the beef back in the pan, stir, and add raisins, salt, and pepper. Turn off the heat; add hard-boiled eggs and olives. Cool completely.

2. Preheat the oven to 350°F. Take a portion of the dough and, using a rolling pin, roll it on a lightly floured table to ¼-inch thick. With a large cookie cutter, cut 4-inch rounds, spoon 1 tablespoon of the filling in the center, and close the empanadas. Seal the borders by pressing with the tines of a fork. Place on an ungreased baking sheet.

3. In a small bowl, lightly beat the egg and water, and brush the empanadas with this mixture. Bake for 20 minutes or until golden. Garnish with lime slices and serve immediately.

Chicken Empanadas

Serve these empanadas with a fresh squeeze of lime juice and some ají sauce. Make veggie fillings like chard, spinach, or artichoke to suit vegetarian tastes.

INGREDIENTS | SERVES 6

½ cup vegetable oil, divided

2 chicken thighs, minced

Salt to taste

Pepper to taste

2 onions, chopped

1 bay leaf

¼ cup chicken stock

1 tablespoon ají amarillo, chopped

1 teaspoon dried oregano

1 recipe Empanada Dough (see recipe in this chapter)

1 egg

1 tablespoon water

1. Heat half the oil in a skillet over high heat. Add the minced chicken, season with salt and pepper, and sauté until golden, about 10 minutes. Transfer to a plate, cover, and reserve. In the same skillet, add the remaining oil and cook the onion over medium heat for 7 minutes. Add the reserved chicken, bay leaf, and chicken stock and cook for 10 more minutes. Turn off the heat and add ají amarillo and dried oregano. Cool.

2. Preheat the oven to 350°F. Take a portion of the dough and, using a rolling pin, roll it on a lightly floured table to ¼-inch thick. With a large cookie cutter, cut 4-inch rounds, spoon 1 tablespoon of the filling in the center, and close the empanadas. Seal the borders by pressing with the tines of a fork. Place on an ungreased baking sheet.

3. In a small bowl, lightly beat the egg and water, and brush the empanadas with this mixture. Bake for 20 minutes or until golden. Serve immediately.

Fried Seafood Mini Empanadas

These crispy and appetizing empanadas are easy to make, and can be served at any occasion. Avocado cream or guacamole is a great accompaniment.

INGREDIENTS | YIELDS 15 EMPANADAS

3⅓ cups all-purpose flour

1 teaspoon salt

4 eggs

1 dozen scallops, cleaned and chopped

½ cup raw shrimp, shelled, deveined, and chopped

Salt to taste

Pepper to taste

Juice of 1 lime

2 cups vegetable oil, divided

1 cup chopped red onion

4 garlic cloves, chopped

1 tablespoon ají panca paste (optional)

1 ají amarillo, diced (optional)

¼ teaspoon ground cumin

1 teaspoon oregano

2 tablespoons chopped parsley

Substitution: Wonton Dough

Wonton dough is a great substitution for fried empanadas and dumplings. It also makes wonderful Italian ravioli on the run. Best of all, it keeps well when refrigerated and can be frozen, but there is no need to do this because you can find it fresh at all times in the refrigerated section of most grocery stores. If you haven't tried it yet, what are you waiting for? It is very handy and a real timesaver in the kitchen.

1. Combine flour, salt, and eggs on a kitchen counter. Knead lightly until a smooth and pliable dough is formed. Cover with a kitchen towel and let rest while you prepare the filling.

2. Combine scallops and shrimp in a bowl. Season with salt, pepper, and lime juice. Heat 2 tablespoons oil in a skillet over medium heat. Sauté the scallops and shrimp for 3 minutes. Transfer to a bowl and reserve.

3. In the same skillet, over medium heat, sauté the onion and garlic until transparent (about 3 minutes). Add, if using, ají panca paste and diced ají amarillo. Add the cumin, oregano, and parsley. Add to the scallop mixture and let cool.

4. Roll the dough on a floured kitchen surface until very thin, using a rolling pin. Cut 4-inch circles and fill each one with 1 tablespoon of the filling. Fold in half, forming half-moons, and press the borders with your fingers or the teeth of a fork. Heat the rest of the oil in a frying pan and fry the empanadas over medium heat, until golden, about 3 minutes per side. Remove with a slotted spoon and place on paper towels to drain. Serve at once.

Empanada Dough

Good pastry dough is a cook's best friend. It is quite useful in savory cooking as well as in pastry baking.

INGREDIENTS | YIELDS 1 POUND

1 pound all-purpose flour
1 teaspoon salt
4 ounces cold vegetable shortening
⅓–½ cup iced water

1. Combine flour and salt in a bowl. Make a well in the center and add the shortening.

2. Working quickly with your fingertips or a pastry blender, cut the shortening into the flour until it resembles oatmeal.

3. Add iced water, a tablespoon at a time, kneading mixture lightly until it no longer sticks to your hands. Wrap the dough in plastic film, or put in a plastic bag, and refrigerate up to 20 minutes.

Fried Corn and Cheese Mini Empanadas

The perfect nibble for any time, if you have the ingredients at home, these empanadas will be ready in a matter of minutes.

INGREDIENTS | YIELDS 10 EMPANADAS

1 cup sweet corn, cooked and drained (canned is fine)
½ cup finely diced queso fresco (or any other cheese)
3 tablespoons grated Parmesan cheese
1 tablespoon chopped parsley
Salt to taste
Pepper to taste
½ (6 ounce) package wonton dough
2 cups vegetable oil
1 cup Ají Amarillo Mayonnaise (see Chapter 2)

1. In a bowl, combine corn, queso fresco, Parmesan cheese, parsley, salt, and pepper.

2. Put 2 teaspoons of the corn mixture in the center of a wonton dough sheet. Run your fingertip with a drop of water along the edge, fold the dough to form a triangle or a rectangle, and press the edges to seal.

3. Heat the oil in a saucepan over medium heat and fry the empanadas until golden, about 3 minutes per side. Transfer to a plate covered with paper towels to drain. Serve immediately with Ají Amarillo Mayonnaise.

Spinach Empanadas

Leave the bacon out of this recipe and these will become vegetarian empanadas. A mixture of spinach and chard is a great idea, and you may want to add some sliced and sautéed mushrooms to the filling.

INGREDIENTS | YIELDS 16 EMPANADAS

2½ pounds spinach, or 2 (8-ounce) packages frozen spinach

4 slices bacon, blanched and chopped

2 garlic cloves, chopped

1 cup onion, chopped

⅛ teaspoon grated nutmeg

Salt to taste

Pepper to taste

½ cup water

1 cup coarsely grated Fontina cheese

2 tablespoons all-purpose flour

½ (6-ounce) package wonton dough

2 cups vegetable oil

Lime wedges for garnish

1. In a saucepan with salted, boiling water, blanch the fresh spinach for 2–3 minutes. Drain. When cool enough to handle, squeeze out the water from the leaves and chop them. Set aside. If using frozen spinach, thaw it, discard the stems, chop the leaves, place them in a colander, and squeeze out all the water. Set aside.

2. To blanch the bacon, place in a pan with boiling water and cook for 3 minutes. Drain and chop up. In a skillet without any oil, sauté the bacon over medium heat until it has released most of its fat (about 5 minutes). Add the garlic and stir. Add the onion, nutmeg, salt, and pepper, and stir occasionally until the onions start to get golden (about 7 minutes). Add ½ cup water, turn the heat to low, and continue cooking until the water has evaporated (about 5 minutes). Remove from the heat and set aside to cool. Just before assembling the empanadas, mix in the cheese and spinach and season with salt and pepper to taste.

3. Put 1 tablespoon spinach filling in the center of a wonton square, previously dusted with a little flour. Brush the edges with water and fold a corner of the dough over the filling, diagonally, to make a triangle. Press the edges together with your fingertips or the tines of a fork to seal. Repeat until all the empanadas are assembled.

4. Heat the oil in a saucepan over medium-high heat and gently drop the empanadas (a few at a time, do not crowd them) into the hot oil and fry them on both sides until golden brown (about 6 minutes total). Remove from the pan and drain on paper towels. Serve immediately, accompanied by lime wedges.

Apple Mini Empanadas

These sweet morsels are an apple pie in the form of a turnover.
The house will be filled with their wonderful and delicious aroma.

INGREDIENTS | YIELDS 10 EMPANADAS

3 tablespoons unsalted butter

¾ cup brown sugar

4 Granny Smith apples, or any other tart apples, peeled and diced

3 cinnamon sticks

¼ teaspoon ground cloves

¼ teaspoon grated nutmeg

¼ teaspoon salt

Zest and juice of 1 lime

1 package puff pastry (store-bought)

1 teaspoon flour

Confectioners' sugar, for sprinkling over the empanadas

Freezing Empanadas

Once assembled, place the uncooked empanadas on a baking sheet and freeze. Transfer to freezer bags and use within 3 months. To bake or fry, put them in the oven or drop them in the hot oil without thawing.

1. Heat a saucepan over medium heat; add butter and brown sugar and cook until the sugar melts. Add apples, cinnamon sticks, cloves, nutmeg, salt, lime zest, and lime juice, stirring every few minutes. The apples will start to release their juices. Continue cooking, stirring every few minutes, until the apples are cooked and the juices are reduced and syrupy (but do not let them dry completely), about 20 minutes. Turn off the heat and cool.

2. Preheat the oven to 350°F. Place puff pastry on a lightly floured kitchen counter and roll with a rolling pin until it is ⅛-inch thick. Cut into 4-inch squares. Put 1 tablespoon apple filling in the center of each square and fold to form a triangle or a rectangle. Press the edges with your fingertips and place the empanadas on a baking sheet. Sprinkle with confectioners' sugar before baking to glaze them in the oven, and bake for 25 minutes, or until golden. Cool to room temperature before serving.

Chaplas (Andean Bread)

Chapla is one of the most popular breads in the Peruvian Andes. Usually homemade, it is served as part of breakfast, lunch, and dinner. Andeans often eat chaplas with artisanal cheese, and this bread goes amazingly well with Brie, Jarlsberg, and queso fresco, just to name a few.

INGREDIENTS | YIELDS 40 CHAPLAS

5 cups all-purpose flour
¼ cup melted shortening
1 teaspoon aniseed
1 cup water, divided
⅓ cup brown sugar, divided
Salt to taste
1 teaspoon dry yeast
1 teaspoon vegetable oil

1. On a baking sheet, divide the flour into two parts. One part should be twice the size of the other. Make a well in the center of each one.

2. In the larger one, add the shortening, aniseed, ½ cup water, 2 tablespoons sugar, and salt. Mix everything with your hands and knead lightly for 3 minutes.

3. In the small one, put the dry yeast and the remaining sugar, ½ cup water, and salt. Mix everything with your hands and knead for 3 minutes.

4. Gather both dough portions and knead together, pushing the dough against the table until it is elastic and shiny.

5. Grease a bowl with oil; place the dough in the bowl and cover with a cloth. Let rest, undisturbed, for 40 minutes. When done, take the dough from the bowl and punch it down to release the air.

6. Cut the dough into 40 pieces and shape them into flattened rounds, like pita bread. Cover with a cloth and let them rest for 40 minutes on the kitchen counter.

7. Preheat the oven to 450°F. With a rolling pin, roll each piece of dough on a floured surface until they are ¼-inch thick.

8. Put the chaplas on a baking sheet and bake for 4 minutes until lightly golden. They should be puffed like pita bread. Serve warm.

CHAPTER 7

Cebiches and Tiraditos

Classic Fish Cebiche

When the fish is completely fresh, the quality of your cebiche will be unrivaled.
Try to find the juiciest limes available, crisp red onions, and a good chili pepper as well.

INGREDIENTS | SERVES 4

1½ pounds fish, cut in bite-sized pieces
(sole, flounder, sea bass)

1 red onion, cut in thin slices, lengthwise

Salt to taste

½ ají amarillo, finely diced, or 1
tablespoon ají amarillo paste

5 ice cubes

1 cup lime juice

1 tablespoon iced water

2 tablespoons cilantro leaves

½ red ají limo, or ½ chile habanero,
finely sliced

4 leaves Bibb lettuce

2 sweet potatoes, cooked and cut in
thick slices

1 cob giant kernel corn, boiled, and cut
in four rounds

1. In a stainless steel or glass bowl, combine fish and onion. Wash under running water. Drain. Season with salt and ají amarillo. Add ice cubes, lime juice, and iced water. Let rest for 5 minutes. Before serving, discard the ice cubes and sprinkle with cilantro leaves and ají limo slices.

2. On one side of each plate, put a lettuce leaf. Place 2 slices sweet potato and corn over the lettuce leaf. Place cebiche in the center of the plate. Serve immediately.

Five-Ingredient Cebiche

Peru's famous cooks say that great cebiche does not need more than five ingredients: fish, lime juice, chili pepper, onion, and salt. Many variations have appeared in the culinary world, giving birth to unique and creative flavors. Add a few drops of celery juice, finely grated garlic, chili pepper pastes in different colors, or even evaporated milk and grated Parmesan cheese.

Fish Cebiche

Limes in Peru are so acidic that they need to be tamed with ice cubes or fish stock. A few tablespoons of soda water also work great. This will give cebiche a superb flavor without being too harsh on the taste buds.

INGREDIENTS | SERVES 3–4

⅔ cup lime juice

2 tablespoons ají amarillo paste

¾ cup fish stock

1 pound white-fleshed fish, cut in 1-inch pieces

Salt to taste

Pepper to taste

¼ teaspoon sugar

2 tablespoons finely grated celery

1 tablespoon finely chopped cilantro

1 teaspoon grated garlic

1 tablespoon finely sliced ají limo (or chile habanero)

1 medium red onion, finely sliced lengthwise, divided

1 cup giant kernel corn, cooked

2 sweet potatoes, cooked, peeled, and cut in thick slices

4 Bibb lettuce leaves

How to Spell Cebiche

Maybe you noticed that *cebiche* has different spellings, and guess what? All of them are correct. *Cebiche, ceviche, seviche,* or *sebiche* are all accepted, and the scholars are still discussing which one is right. For now, you are free to choose your favorite.

1. Wait until you are just about to serve the dish before preparing. First, squeeze limes, but not too strongly to avoid the bitter taste of the lime peel.

2. In a small bowl, combine ají amarillo paste with ½ cup fish stock. Strain and reserve.

3. Place fish in a bowl; add salt, pepper, sugar, celery, cilantro, and garlic.

4. Add lime juice and stir with a metal spoon. Add 4 tablespoons of the ají amarillo mixture and keep tasting. It should have a nice kick from the ají, but this does not have to be overwhelming.

5. Incorporate the diced ají limo or habanero, along with ⅓ of the sliced onion. Stir carefully.

6. Add 1 tablespoon fish stock to tame the acidity of the limes. Add more if necessary.

7. Place cebiche on a serving dish with its juice. Top with the remaining onion, and more ají limo if desired.

8. Serve with corn and sweet potato slices placed on lettuce leaves.

Fish Cebiche with Parmesan Cream

Using the best quality Parmesan cheese in this cebiche will surprise your palate.

INGREDIENTS | SERVES 2

2 tablespoons finely chopped white-fleshed fish fillet

1 tablespoon fish stock

½ tablespoon vegetable oil

1 tablespoon ají amarillo paste

2 teaspoons finely grated Parmesan cheese

Salt to taste

Pepper to taste

1 pound white-fleshed fish, cut in bite-sized pieces

Juice of 10 limes

½ onion, thinly sliced lengthwise, washed

1 sweet potato, cooked and peeled, cut in thick slices

1 cup cooked Peruvian giant corn kernels (or any white corn)

2 sprigs cilantro

1. In a blender, process the finely chopped fish, fish stock, oil, ají amarillo paste, Parmesan cheese, salt, and pepper.

2. Place the cubed fish in a bowl, add salt and lime juice, and cover with the Parmesan cheese mixture. Stir, transfer to 2 plates, and top with onion.

3. Serve with sweet potato slices and corn kernels on the side. Garnish with cilantro leaves.

Fish Cebiche with Fried Calamari

There are some cebiches served "en dos tiempos," meaning two preparations with different flavors, textures, or temperatures. This is a good example. Serve in cups and do not use corn or sweet potatoes.

INGREDIENTS | SERVES 8

1 recipe Classic Fish Cebiche (see recipe in this chapter)

1 recipe Fried Calamari (see Chapter 4)

2 tablespoons chopped cilantro leaves

Have the recipes for Classic Fish Cebiche and Fried Calamari ready. Working quickly, serve the cebiche in glasses, and top with the fried calamari. Sprinkle with cilantro leaves. Serve immediately.

Cebiche Mixto

It is believed that this dish is an aphrodisiac and a magical cure for hangovers, among other things. Use any kind of seafood to your liking: octopus, clams, crabs, and so on. Top with seaweed, called yuyos in Peru, and you will be addicted. As a variation, use this cebiche to fill avocado halves and serve as an appetizer.

INGREDIENTS | SERVES 4

8 ounces medium-sized shrimp, peeled and deveined

Bowl of iced water

1 cup squid, cut in ⅓-inch rings

1 cup small scallops, cleaned

1 cup mussels, steamed and shelled

Salt to taste

Pepper to taste

2 garlic cloves, grated

1 tablespoon ají limo (or chile habanero), finely sliced

½ cup lime juice

¼ cup olive oil

1 tablespoon chopped parsley

1 tablespoon chopped cilantro, plus a few leaves for garnishing

2 sweet potatoes, cooked, peeled, and cut in thick rounds

1 cup giant corn kernels, cooked

1. Cook shrimp in boiling, salted water over high heat for 2 minutes or until they turn pink. Transfer to a bowl with iced water. In another pan, cook squid in boiling, salted water for 3 minutes over medium heat. Cool in iced water.

2. Transfer shrimp and squid to a bowl along with the raw scallops and steamed mussels. Season with salt, pepper, garlic, ají limo, lime juice, and olive oil. Add parsley and cilantro. Stir and marinate for 3 minutes.

3. On 4 plates, place the seafood mixture. Garnish with sweet potato, corn kernels, and cilantro leaves. Serve cold or at room temperature.

Steaming Mussels

To clean, scrub the shells with a sturdy brush to get rid of any sand. Pull the beard and discard. Throw away any that feel too heavy, because they could be full of sand. To cook, place in a saucepan, add 1 cup water or white wine, cover tightly with a lid, bring to a boil, lower the heat, and steam for 5 minutes or until their shells open. Discard the ones that remain closed and reserve the flavorful cooking water to use in soups and sauces.

Scallop Cebiche

This refreshing and light cebiche should be made with the freshest scallops you can find in the market. Do not even think of trying it with frozen ones.

INGREDIENTS | SERVES 2

8 ounces small scallops, cleaned

½ cup diced red onion

1 tablespoon finely diced ají limo (optional)

2 tablespoons chopped parsley

1 teaspoon chopped garlic

Salt to taste

Pepper to taste

Juice of 4 limes

¼ cup olive oil

2 Bibb lettuce leaves

1 cup giant kernel corn, cooked

1. Combine the scallops, onion, ají limo, and parsley in a bowl. Add garlic, salt, and pepper and stir well.

2. Add lime juice and olive oil. Let rest for 5 minutes. Serve in glasses lined with a lettuce leaf, and with some corn kernels on top.

Cebiche de Camarones a la Piedra (Hot Stone Shrimp Cebiche)

This is a slightly cooked cebiche, just enough to let the shrimp turn pink. A pound of boiled yucca could take the place of glazed sweet potato if you prefer the flavor.

INGREDIENTS | SERVES 3

1 tablespoon vegetable oil

1 teaspoon chopped garlic

3 tablespoons ají amarillo paste

1 red onion, cut in medium thick slices

1 pound medium-sized shrimp, peeled and deveined

Salt to taste

Pepper to taste

6 tablespoons lime juice

1 tablespoon finely sliced ají limo (or chile habanero)

1 tablespoon chopped cilantro

2 tablespoons fish stock (optional)

1 Glazed Sweet Potato (see recipe in this chapter)

1. Heat the oil in a skillet over medium heat. Sauté garlic, ají amarillo paste, onion, and shrimp for 3 minutes. Working quickly, add salt, pepper, lime juice, and ají limo. Add cilantro, and a couple of tablespoons of fish stock if needed.

2. Serve immediately with Glazed Sweet Potato.

Glazed Sweet Potatoes

Sweet potatoes and corn are always served with cebiches, to balance the heat of the fish. There are orange, purple, and in some countries white sweet potatoes, the orange one being the favorite in Peruvian kitchens because of its candy-like flavor. Glazed potatoes can substitute plain boiled ones for a more polished look.

INGREDIENTS | YIELDS 4

4 medium-sized sweet potatoes

2 cups orange juice

2 tablespoons granulated sugar

2 cinnamon sticks

2 cloves

Benefits of Sweet Potatoes

Even though their origin is uncertain, it is said that sweet potatoes have been well known in Peru for more than 6,000 years. They are delicious and nourishing, and because of their high sugar content, they are energizing and help to regulate high blood pressure and soothe stress. It has also been said that one sweet potato a day gives you bright and shiny hair!

1. Peel the sweet potatoes and cook over medium high heat in enough water to cover for 10 minutes. Drain and cook again over medium heat in a mixture of orange juice, sugar, cinnamon sticks, and cloves, until tender, about 25 minutes. Add boiling water as needed if the liquid in the pan is evaporating.

2. When sweet potatoes are tender, take them out of the pan and continue cooking the juices until slightly thick, about 10 minutes. Turn off the heat and put the sweet potatoes back in the pan until ready to use. Serve at room temperature.

Rocoto Cream Cebiche

Rocoto cream and ají amarillo cream became fashionable several years ago. They bring beautiful colors to cebiches and tiraditos, and wonderful flavors characteristic of each ají.

INGREDIENTS | SERVES 4

2 tablespoons finely chopped white-fleshed fish fillet

1 tablespoon fish stock

½ tablespoon vegetable oil

3 tablespoons rocoto paste

Salt to taste

Pepper to taste

10 ounces octopus, cooked and sliced

10 ounces white-fleshed fish, cut in bite-sized pieces

Juice of 10 limes

½ onion, thinly sliced and washed

1 sweet potato, cooked and peeled, cut in thick slices

1 cup cooked giant kernel corn

2 sprigs cilantro

1. In a blender, process the finely chopped fish, fish stock, oil, rocoto paste, salt, and pepper.

2. Combine octopus slices and fish pieces in a bowl, add lime juice, and cover with the rocoto mixture. Stir, transfer to 4 plates, and top with onion.

3. Serve with sweet potato slices and corn kernels on the side. Garnish with cilantro leaves before serving.

Red Onion

This is one of the basic ingredients of cebiche, along with lime and chili peppers. Finely sliced and washed well, onion combines perfectly with fish, but be careful to wash it thoroughly and to soak it in iced water. This way it will be crunchy, adding a nice textural accent to the cebiche.

Asian Cebiche

Asian flavors—Japanese or Chinese—are present in many cebiches. Soy sauce, sesame oil, and ginger, among other ingredients, give this Peruvian dish an exotic and mouthwatering taste.

INGREDIENTS | SERVES 4

1½ pounds salmon fillet

Salt to taste

Pepper to taste

1 tablespoon toasted sesame oil

1 tablespoon chopped cilantro leaves

¾ cup lime juice

3 tablespoons orange juice

2 tablespoons soy sauce

1 teaspoon ají limo (or chile habanero), finely sliced

1 tablespoon honey

1 tablespoon black sesame seeds

1 cup vegetable oil

4 sheets wonton dough, finely sliced, like angel hair pasta

4 Glazed Sweet Potatoes (see recipe in this chapter)

2 sprigs cilantro

1. Cut the salmon fillets into 1-inch dice. Place in a bowl and season with salt and pepper.

2. In another small bowl, combine sesame oil, cilantro, lime juice, orange juice, soy sauce, ají limo or habanero, honey, and sesame seeds. Add to the fish and marinate, refrigerated, for about 2 minutes.

3. In the meantime, heat the oil in a small saucepan and fry the sliced wonton dough until golden, about 1 minute. Drain on paper towels.

4. Serve the cebiche, top with fried wonton, garnish with cilantro, and accompany with a Glazed Sweet Potato on the side.

Tiradito Style

Transform this cebiche into a beautiful tiradito (a dish made with thinly sliced raw fish instead of cubed fillets) by cutting the fish into thin slices and placing them on plates. Cover with the lime mixture and top with fried wonton dough.

Chinguirito (Dried Fish Cebiche)

This is a classic recipe from Lambayeque, in the northern part of Peru. It is made with finely shredded dried fish called guitarra *instead of fresh fish. This gives the dish a crunchy texture.*

INGREDIENTS | SERVES 2

8 ounces dried fish (cod, for example)

1 medium red onion, thinly sliced

Salt to taste

Juice of 6 limes

1 tablespoon ají amarillo (or any other chili pepper), finely diced

2 tablespoons fish stock

8 ounces yucca, peeled, cooked, and cut in thick slices

1 sweet potato, cooked, peeled, and cut in thick slices

1. Place the dried fish in a bowl with enough water to cover and soak for 10 minutes. Drain and shred with your fingers. Place in dry bowl.

2. In another bowl, soak the sliced onion in iced water. Drain and dry. Add to the shredded fish with salt, lime juice, ají amarillo, and fish stock.

3. Serve with boiled yucca and sweet potato.

Mango Cebiche

Serve this vegetarian delight, with its tropical and fruity flavor, in martini glasses. Mango is a great ingredient in cebiche, and with the addition of cooked shrimp and passion fruit juice, you can transform this recipe into something glamorous.

INGREDIENTS | SERVES 4

3 mangoes, ripe but firm

1 red onion, finely sliced lengthwise

1 tablespoon ají limo (or chile habanero), finely diced

⅓ cup lime juice

⅓ cup orange juice

1 tablespoon olive oil

Salt to taste

Pepper to taste

4 Bibb lettuce leaves

1 tablespoon chopped cilantro

1. Peel the mangoes and dice or cut into fine slices. Place in a bowl with onion, ají limo, lime juice, orange juice, olive oil, salt, and pepper. Marinate for 10 minutes in the refrigerator or at room temperature.

2. Serve in glasses lined with a lettuce leaf and sprinkle with cilantro.

North-Style Tiradito

The difference between cebiche and tiradito is in the cut of the fish. Tiradito uses very thin slices of fish that are placed on the plates like a delicate carpaccio. It also does not have onion.

INGREDIENTS | SERVES 2

9 ounces fresh white-fleshed fish

2 tablespoons ají amarillo paste

1 tablespoon vegetable oil

Salt to taste

Pepper to taste

1 garlic clove, finely chopped

Juice of 4 limes

1 cup cooked giant corn kernels

2 tablespoons finely sliced parsley

1. Cut the fish in almost transparent slices and divide over 4 cold plates. Cover with plastic wrap and refrigerate.

2. In a bowl, combine ají amarillo paste, vegetable oil, salt, pepper, and garlic. Add the lime juice. Pour over the fish to cover completely.

3. Serve immediately with corn kernels, garnished with parsley.

Mushroom and Artichoke Cebiche

Adding artichokes to this cebiche is a clever way to use the delicious vegetable. You can use only mushrooms if you want, or add a few tiny cherry tomatoes for a nice color.

INGREDIENTS | SERVES 2–4

1 pound small mushrooms, cut in halves or quarters

½ pound artichoke hearts, cooked and cut in quarters

⅔ cup lime juice

4 tablespoons olive oil

Salt to taste

White pepper to taste

2 garlic cloves, finely chopped

1 tablespoon chopped cilantro leaves

½ red onion, finely sliced lengthwise

1 sweet potato, cooked, peeled, and cut in thick slices

1 cup giant corn kernels, cooked

1. Blanch the mushrooms in boiling, salted water for 1 minute. Drain and put in a bowl with artichokes, lime juice, olive oil, salt, pepper, garlic, and cilantro leaves. Marinate for 10 minutes at room temperature or in the refrigerator.

2. Put the onion in a bowl, add cold water, and soak for 10 minutes. This will help to remove the pungency of raw onions.

3. When ready, drain well and add the onion to the mushroom and artichoke mixture. Let marinate for 5 more minutes.

4. Serve with a few slices of sweet potato and corn kernels on the side.

Creamy Tiradito

Is evaporated milk really one of the ingredients of a tiradito? Of course! There are numerous cebiche and tiradito recipes in Peru, and it's not possible (or recommended) to stick only to traditional ones.

INGREDIENTS | SERVES 3

1 pound white-fleshed fish, cut in thin slices

3 tablespoons celery

2 tablespoons leek

2 tablespoons white-fleshed fish fillet, finely chopped

1 tablespoon fish stock

½ tablespoon olive oil

2 tablespoons ají amarillo paste

1 tablespoon evaporated milk

1 teaspoon grated ginger

1 tablespoon chopped onion

1 garlic clove

Juice of 6 limes

Salt to taste

Pepper to taste

1 cup cooked giant corn kernels

2 sprigs cilantro

1. Divide the fish onto 3 plates. Cover with plastic wrap and refrigerate.

2. Blanch celery in boiling, salted water for 3 minutes. Drain and reserve. In the same pan, blanch leeks for 5 minutes in boiling, salted water. Drain and reserve.

3. In a blender, process the finely chopped fish, fish stock, oil, ají amarillo paste, evaporated milk, ginger, onion, garlic, lime juice, celery, leek, salt, and pepper. Taste for seasoning.

4. Cover the fish with this sauce and garnish with corn and cilantro. Serve immediately.

Tiger's Milk

Leche de Tigre or Tiger's Milk is the marinating juice of cebiche. In cebicherías, you may ask for a shot or two of this flavorful and very spicy mixture, which is believed to have aphrodisiac and invigorating powers. Some brave people also add a shot of Pisco or more chili to this drink.

Creole Tiradito

When making tiradito, slice the fish with the sharpest knife and, with the side of the blade, give a quick smack to each slice to flatten it. Serve as an appetizer.

INGREDIENTS | SERVES 4

1 pound white-fleshed fish fillets

Salt to taste

Juice of 6 limes

1 teaspoon ají amarillo paste, or to taste

1 teaspoon ají limo (or chile habanero), finely diced

1 garlic clove, grated

½ teaspoon grated ginger

1 tablespoon olive oil

Pepper to taste

2 sweet potatoes, cooked, peeled, and cut in thick slices

1 cup baby arugula for garnish

1. Slice the fish fillet very thinly. Place on 4 cold plates. Sprinkle with salt.

2. In a bowl, combine lime juice with ají amarillo paste, ají limo, garlic, ginger, olive oil, salt, and pepper. Using a spoon, pour this juice over the fish to cover.

3. In the center of the fish, place sweet potato slices and then cover with greens to garnish. Serve cold.

Passion Fruit Tiradito

The star of this recipe isn't the fish; it's the passion fruit juice. Its acidity gives tiradito or cebiche a fantastic flavor, which can be enhanced with a few drops of lime juice. This fruit gives you a new, delicious tiradito to impress your family and friends.

INGREDIENTS | SERVES 2

4 passion fruits

1 tablespoon ají limo (or chile habanero), finely diced

Juice of 1 lime

1 garlic clove, grated

Salt to taste

Pepper to taste

8 ounces white-fleshed fish, cut in thin slices

1 tablespoon chopped cilantro

2 Bibb lettuce leaves

1 cup cooked giant corn kernels

1. Cut passion fruits in half. Place the pulp in a colander over a bowl and press with a spoon to release most of the juice.

2. Combine juice with ají limo, lime juice, garlic, salt, and pepper.

3. Divide fish slices onto 2 plates. Pour the passion fruit mixture over the fish and sprinkle with cilantro.

4. Garnish each plate with a lettuce leaf and corn. Serve immediately.

Octopus Tiradito

Octopus can be tender if it is cooked properly, or chewy and inedible if overcooked.

INGREDIENTS | SERVES 4–6

1 medium-sized octopus, clean
Salt, as needed
1 medium potato, unpeeled
1 tablespoon lime juice
1 tablespoon olive oil
Pepper to taste
1 cup baby arugula
4 tablespoons vinaigrette
2 sweet potatoes, cooked, peeled, and cut in thin slices

For a Stunning Presentation

Flavio Solorzano, one of the best Peruvian chefs, cools octopus inside an empty can of evaporated milk. Then he takes the octopus out and cuts it into thin slices with a mandoline. The presentation is gorgeous, and a beautiful way to turn a simple dish into a masterpiece.

1. Scrub the octopus with plenty of salt to get rid of the viscous secretion. Rinse several times under running water and tenderize meat by pounding it with a mallet. Put in a saucepan with boiling, salted water and the potato. Boil over high heat, uncovered, until the potato is tender (about 25–30 minutes). Cool completely.

2. In a bowl, combine lime juice, olive oil, salt, and pepper.

3. Cut the octopus into very thin slices and place on plates, forming a nice pattern. Drizzle with the lime juice mixture.

4. In the center of the plate, place a mound of arugula leaves dressed with vinaigrette. Serve immediately with sweet potato slices.

CHAPTER 8

Rice, Beans, and Grains

Basic Peruvian Rice

This garlicky white rice is a daily side dish in Peru, and it's so fluffy when it is perfectly cooked that you could probably count every grain.

INGREDIENTS | SERVES 4

2 tablespoons vegetable oil

3 garlic cloves, mashed

2 cups white rice

Salt to taste

3 cups boiling water

Arroz con Choclo (Rice with Corn)

To make a "special" variation of this rice (because Peruvians eat rice every single day), try Arroz con Choclo: Boil 1 cup of giant corn kernels in water with 1 tablespoon sugar. Drain and sauté with 2 tablespoons butter. Add to the basic rice.

1. Heat the oil and garlic in a medium saucepan over medium heat, about 3 minutes. Do not let the garlic turn golden because that makes it bitter. Stir in the rice and salt, and add the boiling water.

2. Cover tightly, reduce heat to low, and cook undisturbed until the liquid is absorbed, about 20 minutes. Fluff with a fork and serve.

Arroz a la Cubana (Cuban-Style Rice)

There is nothing Cuban about it, but this is one of the simplest and most satisfying dishes in any cook's recipe book. Organic eggs are a must!

INGREDIENTS | SERVES 4

½ cup vegetable oil, divided

8 eggs

Salt to taste

Pepper to taste

4 bizcochito bananas (or ripe plantains)

3 cups Arroz con Choclo (see sidebar in this chapter)

1 cup Salsa Criolla (see Chapter 2)

1. Heat half the oil in a skillet over medium-high heat. Fry the eggs sunny side up (this means without turning). Remove from pan and season with salt and pepper. Keep warm.

2. Peel the bananas and fry them in the remaining oil, whole or sliced, on both sides until nicely golden, about 4 minutes. If you are using plantains, cut thick slices and fry until golden.

3. Serve a portion of Arroz con Choclo on a plate, covered with 2 fried eggs and 1 fried banana, or some plantain slices. Add Salsa Criolla and serve immediately.

Purple Rice

The beautiful purple color of this rice and the amazing flavors of pineapple and spices contained in the purple water make this a great side dish for poultry and pork.

INGREDIENTS | SERVES 4

3 tablespoons vegetable oil

2 garlic cloves, mashed

2 cups white rice

Salt to taste

3 cups unsweetened purple corn water, heated to just boiling

½ red bell pepper, cut in thin slices

Purple Corn Water

Made with dried purple corn, this water is the base for a popular dessert called Mazamorra Morada and a delicious beverage, Chicha Morada. To make the drink, put 1 pound dried purple corn in a saucepan with 6 cups water, 2 cinnamon sticks, 4 cloves, 4 allspice, the peel of ½ pineapple, and 1 chopped Granny Smith apple. Boil for 45 minutes over high heat until the water has turned purple and is perfumed. Strain and discard the solids.

1. Heat the oil with the garlic in a saucepan over medium heat. When the garlic is fragrant and slightly golden (about 3 minutes), add the rice and stir. Add salt and the purple water. Bring to a boil.

2. Cover tightly with a lid, turn the heat to low, and cook for about 10 minutes. Uncover, add the red bell pepper and stir with a fork, cover again, and continue cooking for 10 more minutes or until the liquid has been absorbed. Fluff with a fork and serve.

Arroz al Olivar (Rice with Purple Olives)

There is a park in Lima called El Olivar that has olive trees that date back to colonial times, and still yield olives. Serve this dish with shrimp or poultry, or eat it alone.

INGREDIENTS | SERVES 4

¾ cup pitted purple olives

6 ounces bacon, chopped

2 garlic cloves, chopped

3 cups water

2 cups white rice

Salt to taste

Pepper to taste

½ cup raisins

½ cup chopped pecans

½ red bell pepper, cut in thin slices

3 hard-boiled eggs, peeled and sieved

Salt and Olives

Be careful when adding salt to this dish because the olives are already salty. You may want to rinse them in fresh water before adding them to the dish in order to get rid of some of their salt.

1. Process the olives in a food processor or a blender until finely chopped, but not liquid.

2. Heat a large skillet over high heat and fry the bacon without oil. Add the olive paste and garlic cloves and cook them in the bacon fat for about 5 minutes. Add the water, bring to a boil, and then add the rice, salt, and pepper.

3. Turn the heat to low, cover the rice with a tight-fitting lid, and cook until all the water has been absorbed. Add raisins, pecans, and the red pepper, stir with a fork, and turn off the heat.

4. Transfer the rice to a bundt pan; then unmold onto a plate and sprinkle with sieved hard-boiled eggs.

Rice with Artichokes

This rice has two delicious elements: the delicate and sophisticated flavor of the artichokes, and their creamy texture. This recipe is a great side dish for fish, chicken, pork, lamb, and beef.

INGREDIENTS | SERVES 8

6 artichokes

Salt to taste

¼ cup vegetable oil

1 small white onion, chopped

2 garlic cloves, minced

3 cups jasmine rice (or any long-grain rice)

1 cup light cream

1 cup Gruyère cheese

1. Place the artichokes in a saucepan. Add enough water to cover, add salt, and turn the heat to medium. Boil for about 35 minutes, until the artichokes are cooked through. The artichokes are ready when you pull a leaf and it comes easily; this means the artichoke is tender. Transfer artichokes to a bowl, reserving the cooking water.

2. Heat the oil in a skillet over high heat and sauté the onion and garlic. When the onion is soft and translucent (about 5 minutes), add rice, 4½ cups of the artichoke cooking water, and salt (the water is already salted). Bring to a boil, cover with a lid, and turn the heat to very low. Cook for about 20 minutes, until the rice is fluffy.

3. Remove all the artichoke leaves, one by one, and scrape the flesh off each leaf with a spoon. Mash this pulp and dice the artichoke hearts.

4. When the rice is ready, fluff with a fork and add the mashed artichokes and the diced artichoke hearts. Stir with a fork to combine.

5. Prior to serving, add cream and cheese. Serve hot.

Arroz con Mariscos (Rice with Seafood)

Choose any combination of seafood according to your preference.
Make sure it's really fresh to get the best flavor.

INGREDIENTS | SERVES 4

¼ cup vegetable oil, divided

¾ cup diced onion

1 tablespoon garlic, chopped

2 plum tomatoes, peeled, seeded, and chopped

1 red bell pepper, diced

1 tablespoon ají amarillo paste (optional)

1 teaspoon dried oregano

3 tablespoons achiote oil

½ cup white wine

1 pound raw, mixed seafood (shrimp, squids, scallops)

4 cups Basic Peruvian Rice (see recipe in this chapter)

¼ cup chopped cilantro

Salt to taste

Pepper to taste

4 lemon slices

1. In a skillet, heat the oil over medium-high heat. Add the onion and garlic and cook until the onion is transparent and very soft, about 7 minutes. Add tomatoes, bell pepper, ají amarillo paste, oregano, and achiote oil and continue cooking for 5 minutes.

2. Add the wine to the skillet and bring to a boil. Add seafood and cook for 3 minutes.

3. Stir in the hot rice very gently with a fork. Taste for seasoning and sprinkle with chopped cilantro, salt, and pepper.

4. Serve with a slice of lemon on the side.

Rice with Shrimp

The best Peruvian shrimp comes from the rivers in Arequipa.
They are a freshwater species and very much appreciated for their size and flavor.
Do not confuse them with langoustines, which are found in the ocean.

INGREDIENTS | SERVES 4

⅓ cup vegetable oil

½ cup diced onion

4 garlic cloves, chopped

4 tomatoes, peeled, seeded, and chopped

1 teaspoon paprika

1 bay leaf

1 teaspoon oregano

1 cup white wine

2 pounds medium shrimp, peeled and deveined

2 cups shrimp stock (see sidebar)

1 red bell pepper, diced

3 cups Basic Peruvian Rice (see recipe in this chapter)

3 tablespoons chopped cilantro

Cilantro sprigs for garnish

4 limes, cut in half

1. Heat the oil in a large saucepan over high heat. Add onion and garlic, stirring for 5 minutes. Add tomatoes, paprika, bay leaf, and dried oregano and continue cooking for 5 minutes. Incorporate the wine and bring to a boil. Discard the bay leaf.

2. Add the shrimp to the saucepan, stir, then add the stock and diced pepper. The shrimp should be ready in 3–4 minutes. Do not overcook or they will be rubbery and tough. As soon as the shrimp is cooked, add the rice to the pan and sprinkle with the chopped cilantro. Taste for seasoning and turn off the heat.

3. Serve with sprigs of cilantro and lime halves.

Shrimp Stock

Make your own stock with shrimp shells. Fry shells in a saucepan in 1 tablespoon olive oil; then add 1 teaspoon tomato paste, 1 tablespoon chopped onion, 1 chopped garlic clove, and 1 tablespoon chopped carrot. Stir and after 5 minutes, add ½ cup white wine and bring to a boil over high heat. Add water to barely cover the shells and vegetables. Bring to a boil, turn down the heat to medium-low, and cook for 30 minutes, or until you have a flavorful stock. Strain and reserve.

Rice with Scallops

The sweetness of the scallops is what makes this recipe so delicious.
This dish is also very colorful thanks to the vegetables and the scallop's roe.

INGREDIENTS | SERVES 4

¼ cup vegetable oil

1 cup diced onion

2 garlic cloves, chopped

2 tablespoons ají amarillo paste

1 cup white corn kernels

1 cup diced carrot

1 cup green peas

½ cup white wine

2 cups fish stock

Salt to taste

Pepper to taste

3 cups Basic Peruvian Rice (see recipe in this chapter)

½ cup diced red pepper

½ cup diced yellow or orange pepper

2 cups scallops (with or without the roe)

2 tablespoons chopped cilantro

4 lemon slices

1. Heat the oil in a skillet over medium heat and sauté the onion and garlic until translucent, about 10 minutes. Add the ají amarillo paste, stirring well.

2. Add corn, carrot, green peas, white wine, stock, salt, and pepper. Cook for 10 minutes or until the vegetables are tender. Add the cooked rice and the peppers.

3. Add the scallops, stir, and cover the pan with a tight-fitting lid. Turn off the heat and let steam for 5 minutes; the scallops will be tender and juicy. If cooked too long, they will be rubbery and tough.

4. Sprinkle with cilantro and serve with slices of lemon on the side.

Eating the Roe

In Peru, it is common to buy and eat scallops with the roe attached. Many people find this to be a delicacy and love it, but health-conscious cooks are very aware of the high amount of cholesterol contained in the little, bright orange morsels. Whatever the case may be, they always add texture and color to the dish.

Arroz Árabe (Arab Rice)

For many years, this rice has been an important part of every banquet table in Lima, accompanying turkey and other meats. It is a favorite for Christmas and other celebrations.

INGREDIENTS | SERVES 4

⅓ cup vegetable oil

1 cup angel hair pasta, broken into 1-inch pieces

2 garlic cloves, chopped

2 cups rice

Salt to taste

Pepper to taste

3 cups cola

½ cup raisins

½ cup sliced almonds

Rice with Soda?

The sweetness of the soda brings a very distinct taste to this dish, without being overwhelming. If you season carefully with salt and pepper, the flavors will be balanced.

1. Heat the oil in a large saucepan over medium heat. Add the broken angel hair pasta and cook, stirring until it turns a nice golden color, about 3 minutes.

2. Add the garlic and cook for 2 minutes; then add the rice, salt, pepper, and the cola. Turn the heat up to high and bring the mixture to a boil. Cover tightly with a lid, lower the heat to very low, and cook until the rice is al dente, about 20 minutes.

3. Add the raisins and almonds. Cover again and continue cooking until all liquid is absorbed. Turn off the heat, let rest a few minutes, and fluff with a fork before serving.

Lima-Style Rice with Pork

Peruvians love pork, and they use it in many ways; this is only an example. Tasty and satisfying, Arroz Limeño (the Spanish name for this dish) is always a good dish for an informal party.

INGREDIENTS | SERVES 4

3 tablespoons vegetable oil

1 pound pork loin, cut in bite-sized pieces

½ cup diced onion

1 tablespoon ají panca paste (optional)

2 garlic cloves, chopped

1 teaspoon dried oregano

½ red bell pepper, diced

2 tomatoes, peeled, seeded, and chopped

½ cup green peas

¾ cup chicken stock

Salt to taste

Pepper to taste

2½ cups Basic Peruvian Rice (see recipe in this chapter)

8 black olives, pitted and sliced

½ cup raisins

½ cup chopped pecans

¼ cup grated Parmesan cheese

2 hard-boiled eggs, peeled and chopped

3 tablespoons chopped parsley

1. Heat the oil in a large skillet over high heat. Add the pork and stir-fry until golden, about 7 minutes. Transfer to a plate and reserve, covered.

2. In the same pan, cook the onion, ají panca, and garlic over high heat, stirring a few times. When the onion is very soft, about 5–7 minutes, add oregano, bell pepper, tomatoes, green peas, chicken stock, salt, and pepper. Return the pork to the skillet. Cover pan and reduce heat to low, cooking until the pork is tender, about 20 minutes. Taste for seasoning.

3. Add the cooked rice to the mixture, along with olives, raisins, and pecans. Stir and let the flavors meld.

4. To serve, sprinkle with Parmesan cheese, hard-boiled eggs, and parsley.

Rice with Duck

Cooking duck over low heat for a long time makes it incredibly tender. Plan in advance and start the preparation of this dish with enough time to have it ready for lunch.

INGREDIENTS | SERVES 4

4 duck legs or thighs
1 (12-ounce) can dark beer
½ cup vegetable oil
1 cup chopped red onion
4 garlic cloves, chopped
½ cup ají mirasol paste
1 teaspoon ground turmeric
1 teaspoon ground cumin
1 cup cilantro leaves
1 cup spinach leaves
½ cup water
8 cups duck stock, divided
Salt to taste
Pepper to taste
3 cups long-grain white rice
1 red bell pepper, diced
1 cup green peas
2 cups Salsa Criolla (see Chapter 2)

1. In a bowl, combine duck legs with beer; cover and refrigerate at least 8 hours. Take them out of the marinade before cooking and dry the pieces with paper towels.

2. In a saucepan, heat the oil over medium heat, add the duck, and sear until golden, about 15 minutes. Transfer to a plate, cover the pieces, and keep warm.

3. In the same pan, add the onion and garlic, cooking for 5 minutes over medium heat. Add ají mirasol, turmeric, and cumin. Stir and cook for 5 more minutes.

4. In the meantime, process cilantro and spinach leaves with water in a blender until very smooth. Add to a saucepan with the duck stock and the reserved seared duck. Season with salt and pepper and cover tightly. Reduce the heat to low and cook for 1½ hours or until the duck is falling from the bone. Taste for seasoning. Transfer to a bowl with some of the liquid.

5. Measure the liquid in the pan. You will need 4½ cups of the stock to cook the rice. Pour the cooking stock into a large saucepan and add the rice, bell pepper, and green peas. Bring to a boil, cover, and cook for 20 minutes over low heat. Turn off the heat, let sit for 5 minutes, and then stir the rice with a fork.

6. Serve the rice with a piece of duck on top and Salsa Criolla on the side.

Peruvian-Style Green Rice with Chicken

This is a more "homey" version of Arroz con Pato (Rice with Duck). This dish is very easy to make, and you will be delighted by the green color and the intense cilantro flavor.

INGREDIENTS | SERVES 4

¾ cup cilantro leaves

4 spinach leaves

2 tablespoons water

4 chicken legs with thighs

¼ cup vegetable oil

Salt to taste

Pepper to taste

1 cup diced onion

1 tablespoon chopped garlic

½ cup diced ají amarillo (optional)

1 cup light beer

1½ cups chicken stock

¼ cup green peas

¼ cup diced carrots

½ red bell pepper, sliced

1 cup corn kernels

3 cups Basic Peruvian Rice (see recipe in this chapter)

2 cups Salsa Criolla (see Chapter 2)

1. Process the cilantro and spinach leaves in a blender with 2 tablespoons water. Reserve.

2. Dry the chicken with paper towels. Heat the oil in a skillet over high heat, add the chicken, and sear until it has a beautiful golden color, about 10 minutes. Add salt and pepper. Transfer to a plate, cover, and reserve.

3. In the same pan, sauté the onion, garlic, and ají amarillo, stirring for 5 minutes over medium heat. Add the cilantro mixture, beer, chicken stock, and the seared chicken pieces.

4. Bring to a boil and cook for 15 minutes over medium heat. Season with salt and pepper. Add peas, carrots, bell pepper, and corn and cook for 15 more minutes until the chicken and vegetables are tender. The liquid should be reduced, but not dried out completely.

5. Add the rice, stir very well, and serve with Salsa Criolla.

Cook a Rainbow

Arroz con Pollo has different colors, depending on the region where it is originally from. The green version is one of the most popular, but for those who do not like cilantro, yellow, white, orange, and red versions are great as well. These are made with Peruvian saffron and other spices to give them color.

Arroz Tapado (Meat-Filled Rice Terrine)

You should consider this a quick meal, as it cooks in a matter of minutes if you have all the ingredients prepared. Try it with chicken, seafood, or, for a vegan version, vegetables.

INGREDIENTS | SERVES 4

¼ cup vegetable oil

1 red onion, chopped

2 garlic cloves, chopped

1 tablespoon tomato paste or ají panca paste

1 pound ground beef

Salt to taste

Pepper to taste

½ cup diced carrot

⅓ cup raisins

⅓ cup sliced black olives

2 hard-boiled eggs, peeled and chopped

2 tablespoons chopped parsley

3 cups Basic Peruvian Rice (see recipe in this chapter)

Parsley sprigs for garnish

1. Heat the oil in a skillet over high heat and sauté the onion and garlic, stirring a couple of times. When the onion is soft and translucent, about 5 minutes, add the tomato paste or ají panca, stir for 2–3 minutes, and then add the ground beef. Cook for 15 minutes over medium-low heat, stirring every now and then. If the mixture looks dry, add some water to make it moist (about ½ cup).

2. Season with salt and pepper, add the carrot, and cook for 5 minutes. Stir in raisins, olives, eggs, and parsley. Remove from heat.

3. For each portion, in an oiled (6-ounce) ramekin, make a layer of rice, pressing with a spoon. Over the rice put a layer of ground beef, and cover with more rice. Put a plate over the ramekin and turn upside down. Remove the ramekin, garnish the Arroz Tapado with parsley sprigs, and serve.

Chicken Arroz Chaufa (Fried Rice)

Peruvians love Chinese stir-fried rice. Some recipes are extremely simple and others are very complex, depending on the preparation. Here you have an easy version that can be made in a few minutes.

INGREDIENTS | SERVES 2

2 chicken breasts, skinned and boned

4 tablespoons vegetable oil, divided

2 eggs, lightly beaten

1 cup diced cooked ham

2 garlic cloves, chopped

2 teaspoons grated ginger

½ cup sliced snow peas

2 cups unsalted cooked white rice, chilled

½ cup bean sprouts

2–3 tablespoons light soy sauce

1 teaspoon sesame oil

½ cup sliced scallions, white and green parts

2 tablespoons toasted sesame seeds

Unsalted Rice

To make good stir-fried rice, you need cold, unsalted rice. Cook it the day before and keep it refrigerated until ready to use. Choose a long-grain rice, but nothing fancy like basmati.

1. Cut the chicken breasts into bite-sized pieces. Heat 1 tablespoon oil in a wok or skillet over medium heat, add the eggs, and cook to make a thin omelet. Because the omelet is thin, it will be ready in a few minutes. You can turn it if you want, but do not let it dry too much. Transfer to a cutting board and cut into small pieces.

2. In the same wok, heat the remaining oil over high heat and stir-fry the chicken, stirring until well cooked, about 6 minutes. Add the ham and stir quickly. Make a well in the center of the chicken and ham and add garlic, ginger, and snow peas. Mix in the cold rice and stir-fry until hot, 3–4 minutes, and add bean sprouts.

3. Season with soy sauce and sesame oil. Turn off the heat and sprinkle with chopped scallions and sesame seeds. Serve immediately.

Cebiche Mixto (Chapter 7)

Arroz Tapado (Chapter 8)

Passion Fruit Sour (Chapter 17)

Lima-Style Tuna Causa (Chapter 3)

Prickly Pear Juice (Chapter 17)

Olive and Raisin Mini Sandwiches (Chapter 5)

Alfajores with Manjarblanco (Chapter 16)

Choritos a la Chalaca (Chapter 4)

Tequeños with Avocado Cream (Chapter 4)

Chicken Empanadas (Chapter 6)

Bean Escabeche (Chapter 13)

Rice with Shrimp (Chapter 8)

Garden-Style Quinoa (Chapter 9)

Pan con Chicharrón (Chapter 5)

Tres Leches Cake (Chapter 15)

Cherimoya Alegre (Chapter 13)

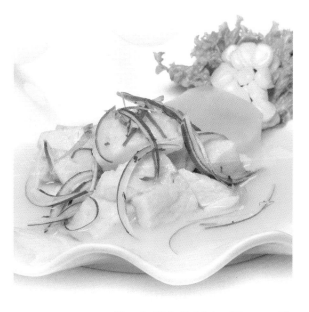

Classic Fish Cebiche (Chapter 7)

Rosquitas de Manteca (Chapter 16)

Avocado Filled with Trout and Palm Hearts (Chapter 3)

Crema Volteada (Chapter 15)

Maná (Chapter 16)

Shrimp Chupe (Chapter 14)

Humita (Chapter 6)

Suspiro Limeño (Chapter 15)

Lima Bean Purée

Silky and creamy, this purée is the perfect side dish for meat entrées. It can also be enjoyed just with rice, a fried egg on top, and some Salsa Criolla, as many Peruvians love to do.

INGREDIENTS | SERVES 4

1 pound dried Lima beans
2 sprigs thyme
2 tablespoons vegetable oil
½ onion, diced
3 garlic cloves, diced
1 tomato, peeled, seeded, and chopped
Salt to taste
Pepper to taste
3 cups Basic Peruvian Rice (see recipe in this chapter)

Lima Beans with Cheese

If you want to give the purée more depth of flavor, add 1 cup of the grated cheese of your choice (try Gouda or Edam). If you have leftovers, use them in Lima Bean Tacu Tacu (see recipe in this chapter).

1. Cover Lima beans with water and soak for 8 hours or overnight. Drain and then peel, slightly squeezing with your fingertips to release the beans. Discard the peels.

2. Put the beans in a heavy saucepan, add thyme sprigs, water to barely cover the beans, and cook at medium heat until very soft, 30–40 minutes, adding more water if needed.

3. Meanwhile, heat the vegetable oil over medium-high heat in a skillet and cook onion and garlic until very tender (7–8 minutes), stirring a few times. Add tomato and continue cooking over medium-high heat for 5 minutes. Add this mixture to the pan with the Lima beans, stirring continuously with a wooden spoon until very creamy. If you want a silky texture, use an immersion blender or pass the mixture through a food mill.

4. Season with salt and pepper. Serve with rice.

Lima Bean Tacu Tacu

Lima beans, canary beans, black beans, lentils . . . you can use any of these. Tacu Tacu is one of those earthy dishes that can be prepared with whatever ingredients you have on hand. Serve with a fried egg, fried bananas, a breaded steak, or any other way you like.

INGREDIENTS | SERVES 4

6 tablespoons vegetable oil, divided

⅓ cup chopped red onion

2 garlic cloves, finely chopped

1 tablespoon chopped ají amarillo (or to taste)

½ teaspoon dried oregano

2 cups cooked Lima beans

Salt to taste

Pepper to taste

1 cup Basic Peruvian Rice (see recipe in this chapter)

2 cups Salsa Criolla (see Chapter 2)

1. Heat 3 tablespoons oil in a skillet over medium heat. Cook the onion, garlic, ají amarillo, and oregano until the onion is soft and translucent (about 10 minutes). Stir in the beans, mashing them with a wooden spoon. Season with salt and pepper.

2. Add the rice and continue stirring and mashing until the mixture is thick like a paste. Remove from skillet and divide into four portions. Fry each one separately in remaining hot oil, about 5 minutes, trying to form a log and moving the pan back and forth with a firm but light movement. The outside of the Tacu Tacu must be slightly crispy while the inside remains soft.

3. Serve with Salsa Criolla.

Garbanzo Beans and Chard Stew

Middle Eastern in origin, like many ingredients used in Peru, garbanzos—or chickpeas—are cooked in soups and stews. This recipe is a tradition during Lent, but it can be enjoyed all year round.

INGREDIENTS | SERVES 3–4

2 (16-ounce) cans garbanzo beans (chickpeas)

3 tablespoons vegetable oil

½ medium red onion, chopped

2 garlic cloves, chopped

1 tomato, chopped

½ chili pepper, chopped

1 small sprig rosemary

4 cups water

1 bunch chard leaves

Salt to taste

Pepper to taste

2 cups Basic Peruvian Rice (see recipe in this chapter)

1. Rinse and drain the chickpeas. Heat the oil in a skillet over high heat and sauté the onion, garlic, tomato, and chili for about 5 minutes, stirring a few times.

2. Add the garbanzo beans and rosemary. Cook, stirring, for 2–3 minutes more, and then add water and bring to a boil. Cook for 10 minutes.

3. On a chopping board, separate the chard's stem and leaves. Chop the stems coarsely and slice the leaves. Add the chard stems to the skillet and season with salt and pepper, cooking for 10 more minutes. When ready, turn the heat off and add the chard leaves. Stir until leaves are wilted.

4. Serve with rice.

Canned Garbanzos

In Peru, everything is cooked from scratch, but to make things easier, this recipe calls for canned garbanzo beans. This is a shortcut that Peruvian cooks don't usually take, but it is very convenient.

Mashed Canary Beans

Canary beans are native to Peru, and they are the most frequently used beans in Peruvian cooking. Peruvians simply love the creaminess and subtle flavor of canary beans, and they serve them as both a side and as the main dish.

INGREDIENTS | SERVES 6

2 pounds canary beans

1 bay leaf

2 thyme sprigs

1 small onion

4 cloves

1 garlic head

1 bouquet garni (see sidebar)

Salt to taste

Pepper to taste

3 cups Basic Peruvian Rice (see recipe in this chapter)

What Is a Bouquet Garni?

It is a little bundle of herbs and spices you add to soup or stew to give it an amazing flavor. Open a piece of leek, take the outer layer of leek, and in the middle, put parsley sprigs, thyme sprigs, 2 sage leaves, a bay leaf, oregano, 2 garlic cloves, and 2 cloves. Roll tightly like a jelly roll and tie with string. Make the bouquet before cooking, using herbs that go with the dish you are going to prepare. Take it out when the food is ready.

1. In a large saucepan, add the canary beans, cover with water, and soak overnight. The next day, drain the beans, change the water, and bring to a boil over high heat, adding bay leaf and thyme sprigs.

2. Pierce the onion with the cloves and add to the pan with the beans. Cut the top from the head of garlic. Add the head of garlic to the pan along with the bouquet garni. Turn the heat to medium-low and cook for 2 hours, or until the beans are very soft. Add salt and pepper.

3. When the beans are done cooking, you may want to process them in a food processor, or just half of them. Alternatively, use an immersion blender to process until the beans are smooth or chunky. The texture is up to you.

4. Serve with rice, or as a side dish for meats or stews.

Corn Pepián

This dish is creamy and tasty, with the flavor of green tamales.
It's the perfect companion for Duck Escabeche (see Chapter 10).

INGREDIENTS | SERVES 4

3 tablespoons vegetable oil

¾ cup chopped white onion

3 tablespoons ají amarillo paste

4 tablespoons cilantro paste

1½ cups blended white corn

2 cups chicken stock

Salt to taste

Pepper to taste

1 teaspoon sugar

1. Heat the oil in a saucepan over medium heat. Add onion and ají amarillo; stir and cook until soft, about 7 minutes. Add the cilantro paste, cook 3 more minutes, then add the blended corn, stirring frequently. Pour in 1 cup chicken stock and keep stirring. When the liquid evaporates, add more as needed. Add salt, pepper, and sugar.

2. Pepián is ready when the corn loses its raw taste, about 25 minutes. Serve.

Pepián

In Peru, there are several dishes called pepián, all made with different ingredients. The best known is the corn pepián, but it is also made with rice and with garbanzo beans. Sometimes it has the name of "espesado" (thickened) because its texture is very thick, like porridge.

CHAPTER 9

Super Powerful Quinoa

Breakfast Quinoa

Quinoa is a seed native to the Andes, valued as gold by the Incas, and considered a superfood. It makes a wonderful breakfast because it helps keep your energy levels high throughout the day.

INGREDIENTS | SERVES 2

½ cup quinoa

2 cups water

1 cinnamon stick

3 cloves

1 teaspoon grated ginger

1 apple, chopped (you can also use pear, pineapple, or peach)

2 tablespoons ground flaxseed

1 tablespoon grated dried coconut

1 tablespoon goji berries

Honey, to taste (optional)

1. Cook the quinoa in a medium saucepan with water, cinnamon stick, cloves, ginger, and apple for 20 minutes on medium heat. When it is ready, you will see a white ring around each seed. If there is water left, drain it.

2. Add flaxseed, dried coconut, goji berries, and honey. Serve warm.

Quinoa Tabbouleh

Many cooks in Peru have started using quinoa to make Peruvian versions of dishes like this Middle Eastern tabbouleh. In this dish, quinoa takes the place of bulgur.

INGREDIENTS | SERVES 2

1 cup quinoa

2 cups water

Salt to taste

⅓ cup finely diced red onion

½ cup finely diced red bell pepper

½ cup peeled and finely diced cucumber

2 plum tomatoes, seeded and chopped

1 bunch parsley leaves, chopped

½ cup chopped mint leaves

1 tablespoon chopped cilantro

Juice of 4 lemons

¼ cup olive oil

Pepper

1. In a saucepan, cook the quinoa in 2 cups boiling water over high heat for 15 minutes, adding salt in the last 5 minutes. Drain and cool.

2. Combine with red onion, bell pepper, cucumber, tomato, parsley, mint, and cilantro. Add lemon juice, olive oil, salt, and pepper. Serve at room temperature.

Quinoa Salad

Quinoa has a very neutral taste, which makes it extremely versatile to use with all kinds of ingredients. It is the perfect replacement for couscous and rice when you want to make salads sturdier.

INGREDIENTS | SERVES 2–4

1 cup quinoa

2 cups water

Salt to taste

1 Granny Smith apple, coarsely grated

2 tablespoons golden raisins

⅓ cup dried golden berries (or ½ cup fresh)

2 tablespoons chopped almonds

2 tablespoons chopped pecans

4 tablespoons Apple Cider Vinaigrette (see sidebar)

2 cups baby arugula

3 tablespoons toasted almonds

Apple Cider Vinaigrette Mini Recipe

In a glass jar, combine ½ cup vegetable oil, 2 tablespoons apple cider vinegar, 1 teaspoon sugar, 1 teaspoon lime juice, salt, and pepper. Put the lid on and shake vigorously. Keep refrigerated up to 3 days.

1. In a saucepan, cook the quinoa in 2 cups water for 15 minutes at medium-high heat, adding salt in the last 5 minutes. Spread on a plate and let cool.

2. In a bowl, combine cooked quinoa with apple, raisins, golden berries, almonds, pecans, and vinaigrette to taste.

3. Put baby arugula in a bowl and dress with 2 tablespoons vinaigrette. Make a layer of greens on each plate and top with quinoa salad.

4. Sprinkle with toasted almonds before serving.

Quinotto with Green Peas

Quinotto is the quinoa version of the Italian risotto, and it works very well. Serve it with steak, shrimp, chicken, or just like the following recipe (with some roasted vegetables and a green salad on the side).

INGREDIENTS | SERVES 2

1 cup quinoa

2 cups water

Salt to taste

1 tablespoon olive oil

½ white onion, diced

2 small garlic cloves, chopped

1½ cups green peas

1 cup light cream

Pepper to taste

½ cup diced queso fresco

½ cup grated Parmesan cheese

2 tablespoons chopped parsley

1. In a saucepan, cook the quinoa in 2 cups water at high heat, uncovered, for 15 minutes, adding salt toward the end of cooking (last 5 minutes). At this point the quinoa is cooked but the grains retain their shape. Drain and transfer to a bowl.

2. In the same pan, heat oil at medium-high heat and sauté onion and garlic until transparent, about 7 minutes, stirring a few times. Add cooked quinoa, green peas, and gradually pour in the cream, stirring constantly. Season with salt and pepper.

3. Add queso fresco and before serving, sprinkle with Parmesan cheese and parsley. Serve immediately.

Divine Quinoa

Even though this seed was almost forgotten for many decades, nowadays it is famous everywhere for its health benefits, versatility, and how easy it is to cook. You can make every imaginable dish with it, from breakfast to dinner, even beverages, desserts, and breads.

Tamale-Style Quinoa Stew

This is a great vegetarian dish full of vegetable protein that is eaten on a regular basis in Andean homes. No wonder Andean people are so strong! Serve with rice or with cooked diced potatoes.

INGREDIENTS | SERVES 4–6

2 cups quinoa

4 cups water

Salt to taste

Pepper to taste

2 tablespoons vegetable oil

1 small onion, chopped

2 garlic cloves, chopped

2 tablespoons ají amarillo paste (optional)

2 medium-sized potatoes, peeled and diced

2 cups vegetable stock

½ cup evaporated milk

1 fresh ají amarillo, cut in small dice (optional)

1 cup diced queso fresco

½ cup parsley leaves

1. In a saucepan, put quinoa with 4 cups water and bring to a boil over high heat. Lower the heat to medium and cook for 15 minutes. Season with salt and pepper.

2. In another pan, heat the oil with onion, garlic, and ají amarillo (if using) and sauté over medium heat. When the mixture is well cooked, add to quinoa along with potatoes and stock. Turn the heat to low and stir every few minutes to keep the quinoa from scorching on the bottom of the pan.

3. When potatoes are tender, about 15 minutes, add evaporated milk, fresh ají amarillo (if using), queso fresco, and parsley. Taste for seasoning and serve.

Ever-Present Aderezo

Most dishes in Peru begin with a basic step known as aderezo. This is a sautéed mixture of onion, garlic, and some kind of ají; it is the first step for flavorful stews, soups, sauces, or any other savory dish. Some cooks call it ahogado.

Parmesan Cheese Quinoa

The Incas considered quinoa the mother of all grains because it was the basic ingredient of most of their dishes. This recipe is creamy, warm, and a little spicy; a delicious way to eat this nutritious grain. You can serve it on its own or with rice.

INGREDIENTS | SERVES 8

2 cups quinoa

6 cups water

¼ cup vegetable oil

2 garlic cloves, minced

1 small white onion, chopped

3 tablespoons ají amarillo paste

½ teaspoon dried oregano

1 cup evaporated milk

1½ cups diced queso fresco

Salt to taste

Pepper to taste

1 cup grated Parmesan cheese

¼ cup olive oil

1. Wash quinoa three or four times in a bowl under running water. Cook in a saucepan with 6 cups water over medium-high heat for 20 minutes. Turn off the heat, drain, and cool.

2. Heat the oil in a skillet over medium heat and add garlic and onion. Cook about 10 minutes until they are very soft and almost transparent. Add ají amarillo paste, then add dried oregano, and keep cooking for 5 minutes.

3. Transfer the onion mixture to a blender and process with evaporated milk. Pour over quinoa and turn on the heat to medium. Add queso fresco, salt, and pepper. Stir for 3 minutes and turn off the heat. If it is too thick, add a bit of hot water.

4. To serve, sprinkle with Parmesan cheese and drizzle with olive oil. Serve immediately.

Garden-Style Quinoa

This recipe resembles vegetarian paella because of its cheerful colors and taste. It's ideal to have as an appetizer, a vegetarian entrée, or a side dish.

INGREDIENTS | SERVES 4

2 cups quinoa

3 cups water

Salt to taste

⅓ cup vegetable oil

½ cup diced onion

2 garlic cloves, chopped

2 tablespoons ají amarillo paste (optional)

½ teaspoon ground turmeric

½ cup diced red bell pepper

½ cup chopped green beans, boiled

½ cup cooked corn kernels

½ cup diced carrots, cooked

½ cup shelled baby fava beans, cooked

½ cup green peas, cooked

2 tablespoons chopped parsley

1. In a saucepan, combine quinoa with 3 cups water. Bring to a boil over high heat, turn the heat to medium, and cook for 17 minutes, adding salt toward the end of cooking. The grains of quinoa will be cooked but not mushy. If there is water left in the pan, drain it.

2. In a saucepan over medium heat, put the oil, add onion and garlic and sauté until tender (about 10 minutes). Add ají amarillo paste, if using, and turmeric. Stir for 5 minutes; then add bell pepper, green beans, corn kernels, carrots, fava beans, and green peas and cook until heated through, about 10 minutes.

3. Add the cooked quinoa, taste for seasoning, and sprinkle with parsley before serving.

Tip for Cooking Quinoa

Start cooking quinoa in cold, unsalted water and always add salt toward the end of cooking. If you add the quinoa to boiling or salted water, it will take longer to soften.

Quinoa Fritters

Peruvians have the tendency to try to make the most out of the simplest ingredients. Vegetable, fish, and cereal patties are some of the most obvious examples. Peruvians will use whatever they have on hand to make this tasty fried food that goes well over rice, or next to a salad or a piece of meat.

INGREDIENTS | SERVES 6

2 cups cooked quinoa

1 cup diced ham

1 cup coarsely grated queso fresco

2 cups finely chopped steamed broccoli

2 scallions, finely chopped

1–2 eggs

Salt to taste

Pepper to taste

½ cup vegetable oil

3 cups Basic Peruvian Rice (see Chapter 8)

1. In a bowl, combine quinoa, ham, cheese, broccoli, scallion, 1 egg, salt, and pepper. If it holds together and forms little patties, it has the right texture. If it is a little loose, add another egg to the mixture.

2. Heat 2 tablespoons oil in a frying pan over medium heat and start frying the quinoa patties until golden, about 3 minutes per side, turning them halfway through. Repeat with all of the quinoa mixture.

3. Serve with white fluffy rice or with a nice green salad. Or make delicious mini burgers with lettuce and tomato over bread.

Quinoa Chupe

Chupe is a hearty soup from the Andes, made with all kinds of native ingredients. The most famous chupe is made with shrimp and egg, but using quinoa is equally energizing.

INGREDIENTS | SERVES 6

¼ cup vegetable oil

1 onion, chopped

2 garlic cloves, chopped

2 tomatoes, peeled, seeded, and chopped

1 cup quinoa

4–6 cups water

3 cups potatoes, peeled and diced

1 cup shelled baby fava beans

1 cup corn kernels

Salt to taste

Pepper to taste

1 cup diced queso fresco

1 cup evaporated milk

3 tablespoons coarsely chopped parsley leaves

1. In a saucepan, heat the oil over medium heat; add onion and garlic and sauté until translucent, about 10 minutes. Add tomatoes and cook for 5 more minutes. Add quinoa and 4–6 cups water, bring to a boil, cover partially with a lid, turn the heat to low, and cook for 45 minutes.

2. Add potatoes, fava beans, corn, salt, and pepper and cook until all the vegetables are tender, about 15 minutes, adding more water if needed. Taste for seasoning.

3. Add queso fresco, evaporated milk, and parsley and heat through without boiling. Turn off the heat and serve immediately.

Mango Quinoa Pudding

Quinoa pudding is a wonderful alternative to the world-famous rice pudding. It gives the dish a delicious and crunchier texture, and you can feel good about eating it because of all the great health benefits of quinoa. The mango is optional, but it provides an exotic, fruity twist.

INGREDIENTS | SERVES 8

1 cup quinoa, washed

2½ cups water

2 cinnamon sticks, divided

3 cloves

1 lemon peel

¼ teaspoon salt

1 (14-ounce) can sweetened condensed milk

1 (12-ounce) can evaporated milk

½ teaspoon ground cinnamon

2 tablespoons unsalted butter

2 cups chopped ripe mango

2 tablespoons sugar

8 mint leaves

1. In a saucepan over medium-high heat, cook quinoa with water, 1 cinnamon stick, cloves, lemon peel, and salt, until it is very soft and the water has evaporated, about 20 minutes from the moment the water boils.

2. Reduce the heat to low. Add sweetened condensed milk and evaporated milk and continue cooking, stirring every now and then, until it has a creamy consistency. Turn off the heat, transfer the cooked quinoa to a large bowl, sprinkle with ground cinnamon, let cool, and put in the fridge—covered—until ready to serve.

3. When you are about to serve the dessert, melt the butter in a sauté pan over high heat. Add chopped mango, 1 cinnamon stick, and sugar. Cook for 5 minutes or until everything is juicy and heated through. Turn off the heat.

4. In martini glasses, alternate layers of quinoa and mango. Finish with mango and garnish with a mint leaf. Serve.

Quinoa and Maca Flan

Maca is a root from the Andes, known as "the natural Viagra of the Incas" because of its reputation of giving potent sexual strength to the person who consumes it. Adding it to this already nutritious quinoa flan turns the dessert into a health food.

INGREDIENTS | SERVES 6

⅓ cup quinoa

1½ cups plus 2 tablespoons water

1 cup sugar

4 eggs

1 (14-ounce) can sweetened condensed milk

1 (12-ounce) can evaporated milk

1 teaspoon vanilla essence

2 teaspoons ground maca

More about Maca

Being of the Cruciferae family, just like carrots, celery, and mustard, these little bulbs are great for everyone, even for the elderly and the ill. Maca has revitalizing powers and strengthens the immune system. If you are lucky enough to get fresh maca, keep in mind that its bitter flavor is a bit overwhelming, and that just a little maca goes a long way. If ground maca is your only option, use it in small quantities, a teaspoon at a time, and combine well with other ingredients. Add to your morning smoothie for an energy boost that will keep you going all day long. To cook the bulbs, wash them carefully, chop them, and cook; there is no need to peel them.

1. Cook quinoa with 1½ cups water, over medium heat, for 20 minutes or until soft. Let cool. Drain, reserving the cooking liquid, and measure 1 cup of quinoa to use for the flan.

2. Preheat the oven to 355°F. In a saucepan, put sugar with 2 tablespoons water and cook over high heat until lightly golden, about 10 minutes. It should have a nice golden color (it is now caramel), but do not let it brown too much because it becomes bitter.

3. Turn off the heat and pour the caramel into a 10-inch round baking pan, moving it quickly so that the entire inner surface is covered with the caramel. Be careful because this is extremely hot and may burn badly if it gets on your skin.

4. In a blender, process quinoa, eggs, sweetened condensed milk, evaporated milk, vanilla, maca, and ¾ cup of the reserved cooking liquid. Pour in the pan that has the caramel, and put that pan in a larger baking pan with 1 inch of hot water so the flan can bake in a water bath.

5. Bake for 40 minutes. Turn off the oven, take out the flan, and let it cool at room temperature. Then put the flan in the refrigerator and let it rest overnight so the caramel becomes liquid.

6. When ready, run a knife around the edge of the flan, cover with a large plate, and turn upside down. When serving the flan, pour several spoonfuls of caramel on top.

Quinoa Champuz

*Quinoa takes the place of dried corn in this easy and simple version of champuz.
It is perfect for cold winter days.*

INGREDIENTS | SERVES 4

1 cup quinoa
4 cups water
½ pineapple, peeled and chopped
4 cloves
1 cinnamon stick
1 fig leaf (optional)
1½ cups dark brown sugar

1. In a heavy saucepan, cook quinoa with 4 cups water over medium heat for 20 minutes. Add pineapple, cloves, cinnamon stick, and fig leaf. Cook for 25 minutes more, adding more water if necessary.

2. Add the dark brown sugar and continue to cook for 15 minutes, or until thick and creamy.

3. Serve warm in medium glasses or cups.

The Fig Leaf

When making syrups for traditional dishes, add a fig leaf to infuse its wonderful fragrance. If you do not have a fig tree, look for leaves when figs are in season where you live.

Apple and Quinoa Beverage

This power drink will make you feel relaxed (thanks to the apples) and invigorated (thanks to the quinoa), all at the same time. Substitute sugar with honey, maple syrup, molasses, or agave nectar for different sweetness levels and tastes.

INGREDIENTS | SERVES 4

1 cup white quinoa
1 pound baking apples, chopped
2 cinnamon sticks
4 cloves
4 allspice
5 cups water
1 cup sugar (or to taste)

1. In a saucepan, put quinoa, apples, cinnamon sticks, cloves, and allspice. Add 5 cups water, bring to a boil over high heat, partially cover the pan with a lid, turn the heat to low, and cook for 45 minutes.

2. Sweeten with sugar, stirring until dissolved, turn off the heat, and cool.

3. Take out the spices and process the mixture in a blender to make it smooth. Serve hot or cold.

Gluten-Free Chocolate Quinoa Cake

Who doesn't like chocolate cake? And it is even better when you eat it without guilt, by substituting wheat flour with quinoa flour! This cake is thin and very light, because it does not have the structure given by the gluten.

INGREDIENTS | SERVES 6

4 ounces quinoa flour
½ cup sugar
2 tablespoons cocoa powder
¼ teaspoon baking soda
¼ teaspoon salt
⅓ cup vegetable oil
⅔ cup buttermilk
1 egg
1 teaspoon vanilla essence
Vanilla ice cream
Strawberry Sauce (see sidebar)

1. Preheat the oven to 350°F. In a bowl, sift quinoa flour, sugar, cocoa powder, baking soda, and salt. In another bowl, combine vegetable oil, buttermilk, egg, and vanilla essence. Add the liquid ingredients to the dry ingredients and stir gently with a spatula.

2. Scrape into an 8-inch round greased and floured baking pan and bake for 30 minutes, or until a toothpick inserted in the center of the cake comes out clean.

3. Cool on a cooling rack. Serve in slices with vanilla ice cream and Strawberry Sauce.

Strawberry Sauce

Blend 2 cups strawberries with 3 tablespoons sugar and the juice of ½ lime in a blender. Serve immediately, or put in a saucepan and boil for 5 minutes over high heat to thicken it slightly. Keep refrigerated. If you want a smoother sauce, pass it through a sieve.

CHAPTER 10

Chicken, Turkey, and Duck

Chicken Escabeche

This spicy escabeche sauce can be used over beans, fried fish, and other meats.
It keeps very well in the refrigerator.

INGREDIENTS | SERVES 4

4 chicken breasts, skinned and boned

Salt to taste

Pepper to taste

Juice of 1 lime

1 tablespoon Worcestershire sauce

½ cup vegetable oil, divided

½ cup water

4 red onions, peeled and cut in thick slices, from top to root

1 tablespoon chopped garlic

1 tablespoon ají panca paste

½ teaspoon ground cumin

2 bay leaves

½ cup red wine vinegar

½ cup chicken stock

1 sweet potato, boiled, peeled, and cut in thick slices

Chickens from Abroad

Along with limes, onions, garlic, oranges, lentils, goats, pork, lamb, cows, and many other ingredients, the Spanish brought chickens to Peru (a then unknown ingredient in America). Ancient Peruvians did not eat eggs or dairy, but with these new products, a new cuisine emerged from the combination of both worlds.

1. Season the chicken breasts with salt, pepper, lime juice, and Worcestershire sauce. Heat ⅓ cup oil in a large sauté pan over medium heat and sear the chicken breasts, turning once to cook evenly. Add water, cover tightly with a lid, turn the heat to low, and cook for 15 minutes or until done. Remove from pan and keep warm.

2. Put the cut onions in a saucepan of boiling water for 30 seconds. Drain. Heat a saucepan over medium heat, add the remaining oil, and then add the garlic, ají panca paste, cumin, bay leaves, and salt and pepper. Stir for 2 minutes, and then add the reserved onion and the vinegar. Bring to a boil and add the chicken stock. Taste for seasoning and turn off the heat. Discard the bay leaves. The onion should remain crunchy.

3. Cut the chicken breasts in slices and place on 4 plates. Pour the escabeche sauce over the chicken. Garnish with sweet potato slices. Serve warm or at room temperature.

Duck Escabeche

*Duck has been part of the Peruvian diet since pre-Columbian times,
and there are countless ways to cook and enjoy its savory meat.*

INGREDIENTS | SERVES 4

1 medium-sized duck (about 3½ pound)

Salt to taste

Pepper to taste

1 teaspoon ground cumin

Zest and juice of 2 oranges

½ cup vegetable oil, divided

1 head of garlic, cut in half, plus 1 tablespoon chopped garlic

1 cup white wine

½ cup water

4 red onions, peeled and cut in thick slices, from top to root

1 tablespoon ají panca paste

½ teaspoon ground cumin

2 bay leaves

½ cup red wine vinegar

2 cups Corn Pepián (see Chapter 8)

1. Preheat the oven to 350°F. Place the duck in a roasting pan, rub with salt, pepper, ground cumin, orange zest and juice, and 3 tablespoons vegetable oil. Put the garlic inside the bird. Pour the wine in the roasting pan and bake the duck for 2½ hours.

2. Take the duck out of the oven, cool, and bone, reserving the meat and the head of garlic. Add water to the roasting pan and deglaze it over medium heat, reserving the flavorful juices.

3. Put the cut onions in a pan of boiling water for 30 seconds. Drain. Heat a saucepan over medium heat. Add the remaining oil, and then add the reserved garlic, ají panca paste, cumin, bay leaves, and salt and pepper. Stir for 2 minutes; then add the reserved onion and the vinegar. Bring to a boil and add ½ cup duck juices from the roasting pan. Taste for seasoning and turn off the heat. Discard the bay leaves.

4. Cut the duck meat in slices. On each plate, put ½ cup Corn Pepián, cover with duck meat, and top with escabeche sauce. Serve warm.

Chicken Anticuchos

Anticuchos or brochettes have a place in Peruvian hearts because they are satisfying, delicious, and there are countless ways to enjoy them all year round.

INGREDIENTS | SERVES 4

6 chicken breasts, boned and skinned
Salt to taste
Pepper to taste
2 garlic cloves, chopped
2–4 tablespoons ají mirasol paste, or to taste
2 tablespoons vegetable oil, divided
1 teaspoon dried oregano
¼ teaspoon cumin
6 potatoes, boiled and peeled

A Replacement for Ají Mirasol

If you can't find ají mirasol, you can substitute it with chile pasilla. Cut 12 chiles in half, lengthwise, and take out seeds and ribs. Soak them in hot water for about an hour. Peel them and process in a blender with a little water and oil.

1. Cut the chicken breasts into 2-inch pieces. Season with salt and pepper; add garlic, ají mirasol paste, 1 tablespoon vegetable oil, oregano, and cumin. Cover and marinate in the refrigerator for 2 hours.

2. Thread the chicken pieces onto bamboo skewers and cook in a hot sauté pan or on the grill, turning after 4–5 minutes or when golden. Do not overcook the chicken.

3. Meanwhile, cut the potatoes into ½-inch slices and cook in a pan with 1 tablespoon oil, on medium heat, until golden.

4. To serve, put two skewers on every plate with golden potatoes on the side.

Ají de Gallina

This dish has been popular in Peru since colonial times.
Back then the main ingredient was hen, not the chicken that is used in modern cooking.

INGREDIENTS | SERVES 4

1 skinless chicken breast, bone-in

3 cups water

Salt to taste

Pepper to taste

2 parsley sprigs

1 bay leaf

3 slices white bread

2 cups chicken stock, divided

¼ cup vegetable oil

½ red onion, finely chopped

2 garlic cloves, finely chopped

1 tablespoon ají amarillo paste

½ teaspoon dried oregano

½ cup finely chopped pecans

½ cup grated Parmesan cheese

½ cup evaporated milk

2 potatoes, boiled and peeled

2 cups cooked white rice

2 hard-boiled eggs, peeled and cut into fourths

4 black olives

4 parsley sprigs

Three Quick Variations

To make ají de gallina empanadas: Fill empanada pastry dough with leftover ají de gallina. Bake as usual. Serve warm. To make hors d'oeuvres: Fill ready-baked tart-elette shells with warm ají de gallina and garnish with half of a hard-boiled quail egg and a curly parsley leaf. Serve immediately. For tequeños: Instead of cheese, fill won-ton dough with ají de gallina. Fry as usual and serve hot.

1. In a large, heavy saucepan over medium heat, cook the chicken breast in 3 cups water with salt, pepper, parsley sprigs, and bay leaf for about 20 minutes.

2. Remove the chicken from the water, let cool slightly, and shred the meat with two forks or with your fingers. Set chicken aside. Strain the stock, discarding the solids.

3. Put the bread slices in a bowl and add 1 cup of the stock. After 7 minutes, process in a blender to make a paste. Reserve.

4. In the same saucepan you used for the chicken, heat the oil and cook the onion and garlic over medium heat, about 7 minutes, until the onion is very soft and almost transparent. Stir continuously and do not let them brown. Add the ají amarillo paste and dried oregano. Cook for 5 more minutes.

5. Incorporate the bread and 1 more cup of chicken stock into the saucepan, always stirring, for 3 more minutes or until the mixture starts to thicken.

6. Add and stir in the shredded chicken, pecans, and cheese. Season with salt and pepper, but be careful because the cheese is already salty.

7. Incorporate the evaporated milk, stir, and turn off the heat. If the sauce looks too thick, thin it with more chicken stock. The sauce should be creamy.

8. Cut the cooked potatoes into thick slices and put 2 pieces on every plate. Serve ají de gallina on top of the potatoes, with white rice on the side.

9. Garnish with eggs, olives, and a parsley sprig. Serve immediately.

Chicken Saltado

When you come home from work and want to have something delicious on the table in less than 30 minutes, the chicken version of Lomo Saltado is your best bet.

INGREDIENTS | SERVES 2

1 pound chicken breast, skinned, boned, and cut in thin slices

Salt to taste

Pepper to taste

3 tablespoons vegetable oil

2 garlic cloves, finely diced

1 red onion, peeled and cut in thick slices

2 tomatoes, cut in thick slices

1 seeded and ribbed ají amarillo, cut in thin slices (or any chili pepper)

3 tablespoons soy sauce

3 tablespoons red wine vinegar

½ cup chopped fresh cilantro

2 cups French Fries (see Chapter 4)

1 cup Basic Peruvian Rice (see Chapter 8)

1. Season the chicken with salt and pepper.

2. Put a wok or a pan over very high heat. When it is very hot, add the oil and then sauté the chicken, a few slices at a time so they remain golden (about 10 minutes, depending on how strong the flame is).

3. Add garlic, onion, tomato, and ají amarillo and stir for a couple of minutes. Add the soy sauce and vinegar to the sides of the pan and mix in with everything. Season with salt and pepper as needed.

4. Take off the heat, add chopped cilantro, and serve at once with French Fries and rice.

Chicken Tallarin Saltado

Here is a delicious way to serve pasta: Cook spaghetti in a saucepan with boiling, salted water. In the meantime, cook the Chicken Saltado, adding ½ cup chicken stock along with the soy sauce. Drain the pasta, combine with the chicken, sprinkle with chopped cilantro, and serve piping hot.

Peruvian Roasted Chicken

Serve this scrumptious chicken with French Fries (see Chapter 4) and a salad made with lettuce, tomato, onion, and avocado. Dress with a creamy vinaigrette.

INGREDIENTS | SERVES 2

1 tablespoon chopped garlic
1 cup beer
¼ cup vegetable oil
4 tablespoons soy sauce
Salt to taste
Pepper to taste
1 teaspoon ground cumin
1 tablespoon ají panca paste
1 (2-pound) chicken

1. In a bowl, combine garlic, beer, vegetable oil, soy sauce, salt, pepper, cumin, and ají panca paste. Rub the chicken with this mixture and marinate up to 12 hours in the refrigerator.

2. Drain and grill, preferably over a wood or charcoal fire, until it is crispy on the outside and juicy on the inside, about 40 minutes. Serve with your favorite dipping sauce (examples include mayonnaise, ají amarillo sauce, or huacatay sauce).

Oven Roasted Chicken

Serve with fluffy white rice and mashed potatoes, or with sweet potato croquettes and a nice green salad.

INGREDIENTS | SERVES 6

1 chicken, cut in 6 pieces (about 2½ pounds)

Juice of 1 lime

3 tablespoons mustard

6 tablespoons soy sauce

1 tablespoon honey

2 tablespoons butter

2 garlic cloves

Potatoes: For Health and Beauty

While the chicken roasts, pamper yourself with a spa treatment at home. Grab a medium potato and slice it thinly. Turn on some music, place the potato slices over your forehead and your eyelids, and relax. Leave them on for 15 minutes, and then rinse with warm water. Potatoes make your eyes look brighter, and alleviate headaches as well. Boiling them for a few minutes and drinking the cooking water during the day will help to get rid of kidney stones, thanks to their diuretic properties. One table-spoon of raw potato juice before breakfast is a great way to calm gastritis.

1. Place the chicken in a baking pan. In a bowl, mix lime juice, mustard, soy sauce, honey, and butter. Rub the chicken with this mixture and marinate for 1 hour in the refrigerator.

2. Preheat the oven to 350°F. Place the garlic cloves in the baking pan with the chicken and bake until the chicken is golden and cooked through, about 45 minutes. Baste with the juices every 15 minutes. Add ½ cup hot water to the pan if chicken is dry. Serve immediately.

Roasted Chicken with Vegetables

This dish consists of two recipes: a juicy roasted chicken and a vegetable stir-fry. Combining them creates a great dish for a delicious lunch.

INGREDIENTS | SERVES 8

1 chicken, cut in 8 pieces (about 2½ pounds)

Salt to taste

Pepper to taste

4 garlic cloves, chopped, divided

½ cup soy sauce, divided

3 medium onions, cut into fourths

2 bay leaves

½ cup olive oil, divided

1 cup hot water

12 ounces mushrooms, cut in half

4 cups broccoli

1 red bell pepper, sliced

1 tablespoon sesame oil

Open Sesame

Sesame is known in Peru as the seed of joy. It is an excellent addition to your diet because it helps to get rid of nervousness and fatigue, and some even say it is good for insomnia and depression. The sesame seed contains a healthy dose of B vitamins, iron, and calcium. As a dietary supplement, take 1–2 tablespoons daily.

1. Preheat the oven to 350°F. Season the chicken with salt, pepper, 2 garlic cloves, and 2 tablespoons soy sauce. Place in a roasting pan and surround with onions and bay leaves. Drizzle with ¼ cup olive oil and 2 tablespoons soy sauce. Add 1 cup hot water.

2. Bake for 30 minutes. Lower the temperature to 300°F and bake 30 minutes more. Add more water as needed. Chicken should remain juicy.

3. In the meantime, prepare the vegetables. Heat the remaining oil in a skillet over medium heat. Add remaining garlic. Add mushrooms and cook until golden (approximately 5–8 minutes); add broccoli and bell pepper and cook for 5 minutes. Remove from heat. Season with the remaining soy sauce, sesame oil, salt, and pepper.

4. Take the chicken out of the oven, discard the bay leaves, and serve with the vegetables.

Slow-Cooked Duck

Since you will be using a technique similar to the one used to cook Beef Asado (see Chapter 11), this duck remains succulent and fork tender. Add some white rice on the side for texture.

(see Chapter 11)

INGREDIENTS | SERVES 4

Salt to taste

Pepper to taste

4 garlic cloves, crushed

2 tablespoons ají panca paste

1 teaspoon paprika

1 teaspoon ground cumin

½ cup red wine vinegar

1 cup red wine

4 duck legs and thighs, about 4 pounds

2 tablespoons vegetable oil

1 bay leaf

4 small whole potatoes, peeled

1. In a large dish, mix salt, pepper, garlic, ají panca paste, paprika, cumin, red wine vinegar, and red wine. Marinate duck in this mixture for at least 2 hours in the refrigerator. Drain and dry the duck legs and thighs. Reserve marinade.

2. Heat a sauté pan over medium heat. Add the oil and when hot, sear the duck pieces until golden, about 5 minutes. Add reserved marinade and bay leaf. Cover tightly, reduce heat to low, and cook for 1½ hours. If the liquid is evaporating, add hot water to keep chicken moist and juicy. Add the potatoes and cook until tender, approximately 15 minutes. Serve hot.

Bay Leaf

Have you noticed that bay leaf is used in many recipes? Bay leaf gives a delicious yet subtle aroma and flavor to dishes, especially to soups and stews. It is even used in baked dishes and in pickles. In natural medicine, it has countless uses, mainly to alleviate stomach aches, as a digestive, and as a natural antiseptic.

Chiclayo-Style Duck Risotto

This is a party dish! Everybody loves this meal because it has the intense flavor of duck combined with the creamy texture of risotto.

INGREDIENTS | SERVES 4

4 duck legs with thighs, about 4 pounds

3 cups beer, divided

½ cup vegetable oil, divided

1 red onion, chopped

2 garlic cloves, chopped

3 tablespoons ají amarillo paste

Salt to taste

Pepper to taste

1 teaspoon ground cumin

½ teaspoon turmeric

½ cup cilantro paste

4 cups water

½ cup diced carrot

½ cup chopped white onion

2 cups Arborio rice

1 cup white wine

1 cup green peas

1 red bell pepper, roasted, seeded, and sliced

1. In a nonmetallic bowl, combine duck legs and 2 cups beer. Cover and refrigerate up to 12 hours. Drain and dry with paper towels.

2. Heat ¼ cup oil in a saucepan over medium heat and sear the duck legs until golden, about 5 minutes. Transfer to a plate and keep covered. In the same saucepan, sauté the red onion, garlic, and ají amarillo paste for 10 minutes. Add salt, pepper, cumin, turmeric, and cilantro paste and cook for 5 minutes longer.

3. Put the duck legs back in the saucepan; add the water and remaining beer. Bring to a boil, cover tightly with a lid, and reduce heat to low. Cook for 1½ hours, until the duck legs are very tender. Add the carrots for the last 15 minutes of cooking.

4. In another saucepan, heat the remaining oil over medium heat, add the chopped white onion, and cook for 5 minutes. Add the rice, stirring until well covered with the oil, add the wine, and boil until evaporated.

5. Add stock from the duck pan as the duck legs are cooking, a ladle at a time, stirring into the rice. When the rice has absorbed the liquid, add more, cooking like this until the rice is tender, but not mushy, about 25 minutes. The rice will absorb as much as twice the amount of liquid. After 15 minutes, add the green peas and the roasted pepper. Continue cooking and adding stock.

6. Turn off the heat. Bone the duck legs and on each plate, serve risotto with the duck meat on top.

Turkey with Garbanzo Bean Pepián

Turkey is not an everyday dish in Peru, but if properly seasoned, it is delicious and can be used in countless preparations. Leftovers make sandwiches and salads, and with the bones you can make flavorful stocks and soups, like Aguadito de Pavo.

INGREDIENTS | SERVES 6

½ cup vegetable oil, divided
3 turkey thighs, about 3 pounds
Salt to taste
Pepper to taste
½ teaspoon paprika
3 cups water, divided
1 pound garbanzo beans
¼ cup peanuts
1 cup dried corn (chulpe)
1 cup chopped onion
2 garlic cloves, chopped
1 tablespoon ají amarillo paste
2 plum tomatoes, peeled, seeded and chopped

1. Heat ¼ cup oil in a large skillet over medium heat. Season the turkey pieces with salt, pepper, and paprika. Fry in the hot oil until golden, about 10 minutes. Add 2 cups water, reduce the heat to low, cover, and simmer until tender, about 45 minutes. Transfer to a bowl.

2. In the meantime, toast garbanzo beans in a skillet over medium heat, for 7 minutes. Add peanuts and corn, being careful to not burn them. Grind the bean, corn, and peanut mixture in a grain grinder or a food processor. Combine this with 1 cup cold water and stir until dissolved.

3. Heat the remaining oil in a skillet over medium heat; add onion, garlic, and ají amarillo and sauté until the mixture looks lightly golden, about 5 minutes. Add tomatoes and stir.

4. Add the garbanzo mixture and the cooking liquid from the turkey to the skillet. Stir continuously, adding water as needed, until you get a slightly thick purée. Season with salt and pepper to taste.

5. To serve, bone the turkey thighs and slice them; place a portion of garbanzo pepián on each plate, and top with turkey slices and some of the cooking juices.

Pollo Sabroso

This flavorful dish is pure comfort food. It is especially delicious with white fluffy rice or even pasta.

INGREDIENTS | SERVES 6

6 chicken thighs (about 1 pound)

Salt to taste

Pepper to taste

3 tablespoons vegetable oil

1 medium onion, chopped

1 teaspoon ají panca paste (optional)

2 tomatoes, peeled, seeded, and chopped

1 bay leaf

½ cup green beans, cut in 1-inch pieces

½ cup corn kernels

½ cup shelled, fresh beans

½ cup diced carrot

6 small red potatoes, peeled

1 cup Port wine (or any sweet wine)

1 cup water

½ cup green peas

1. Season the chicken thighs with salt and pepper. Heat the oil in a skillet over medium heat and sear the chicken until golden, about 7 minutes. Transfer to a bowl and keep warm.

2. In the same pan over medium heat, cook onion until golden (about 5 minutes), and then add ají panca, tomatoes, and bay leaf.

3. Add green beans, corn kernels, fresh beans, carrot, and potatoes to the skillet. Return the chicken to the pan, along with the wine and 1 cup water.

4. Cover the pan and lower the heat to medium-low. Simmer until the chicken is very tender, about 40 minutes. Add the peas for the last 10 minutes of cooking time. Serve.

Bouillon Cubes

Many cooks rely on the ubiquitous bouillon cube to add instant flavor to their dishes. Use them to make a quick bouillon, but you will need to adjust the amount of salt in your recipe because they tend to be very salty. For a great-tasting stock, use 1 bouillon cube, 2 cups water, 1 celery rib, ½ small onion, 2 garlic cloves, and ½ carrot. Boil for 10 minutes. Drain and use as indicated.

Chicken Stew

*Peruvians have more than one recipe for chicken stew, sometimes with fresh or dried fruits.
Serve it with white, fluffy rice to soak up the flavorful juices.*

INGREDIENTS | SERVES 6

⅓ cup vegetable oil

6 chicken thighs and legs, about 1½ pounds

Salt to taste

Pepper to taste

1 medium onion, chopped

2 garlic cloves, chopped

3 tablespoons tomato paste

1 cup water

2 bay leaves

6 whole medium yellow potatoes, peeled

½ cup dried apricots, cut in fourths (or raisins)

1 cup green peas

1. Heat the oil in a skillet over medium heat. Season the chicken with salt and pepper, add it to the pan and cook until golden, about 7 minutes. Transfer to a plate and keep warm.

2. In the same skillet over medium heat, sauté onion, garlic, and tomato paste for 5 minutes, stirring frequently. Put the chicken back in the pan; add 1 cup water and the bay leaves. Cover tightly with a lid, reduce the heat to low, and simmer for 40 minutes or until the chicken is tender.

3. Add potatoes, apricots, and green peas, and cook 15 minutes.

4. Turn off the heat and serve immediately.

Duck in Soy Sauce

Duck and soy sauce are a perfect pairing.
You can add some fruits, like roasted figs or plums, to round out the dish.

INGREDIENTS | SERVES 2

1 duck breast, boneless, about 8 ounces
Salt to taste
2 tablespoons soy sauce
2 tablespoons vegetable oil
2 tablespoons honey
2 tablespoons Dijon mustard
1 star anise
1½ cups beef stock
1 teaspoon grated ginger

1. Season the duck breast with salt and soy sauce. Heat oil in a skillet over medium heat. Fry duck breast in the hot oil, 3 minutes per side. Transfer to a plate, cover and keep warm.

2. Add the remaining ingredients to the skillet. Simmer over medium heat until reduced by half. Transfer the breast to the pan, turn the heat to low and cook for 6 minutes, until it is tender and juicy. Slice the duck and serve with the sauce.

Honey

Honey's characteristic flavor has nothing to do with bees, and everything to do with the flowers they got their nectar from. Because of this, there are a wide range of colors, textures, and flavors of honey, and you may choose your favorites. Feel free to experiment until you find the one that you like best. It is not only used as a sweetener; it has a place in savory cooking as well. If honey crystallizes, melt it in a hot water bath. Do not combine it with water unless you want it to ferment and turn into an alcoholic drink known as hidromiel. (Of course, this needs a special procedure, but you get the idea.)

Chicken with Pineapple

This recipe is innovative and delicious. Considering how good fresh fruits are in Peru, including them in everyday meals is a huge advantage. Mashed potatoes make a great side for this dish.

INGREDIENTS | SERVES 6

5 big slices of fresh pineapple
¼ cup sugar
1 cinnamon stick
6 cloves
6 dried mushrooms
1 cup white wine
6 chicken breasts, skinned
Salt to taste
Pepper to taste
¼ cup vegetable oil
2 garlic cloves, chopped
2 small onions, chopped
6 prunes

1. In a saucepan over medium heat, put pineapple, sugar, cinnamon, and cloves; pour water to cover and boil for 15 minutes or until the pineapples are tender.

2. Cut the dried mushrooms with a knife or scissors and soak in the wine.

3. Season the chicken with salt and pepper.

4. Heat the oil in a saucepan over medium heat and fry the chicken until it is golden, about 3 minutes per side. Remove from the pan and reserve.

5. In the same saucepan, add the garlic and onions and sauté over medium heat (add oil if needed) until the onions caramelize, about 15 minutes.

6. Transfer the onion mixture to a blender; add 3 pineapple slices and the pineapple cooking liquid. Process until smooth.

7. Put chicken back in the saucepan; pour the pineapple sauce over the chicken, along with the wine and dried mushrooms. Cut the remaining pineapple into 1-inch pieces and add to saucepan. Simmer over low heat until the chicken is cooked through, about 15 minutes.

8. Garnish plates with the prunes. Serve immediately.

Pasta with Chicken Tuco

In Lima, people love experimenting with delicious homemade pasta sauces.
This one has become the tomato sauce to make on lazy weekends.

INGREDIENTS | YIELDS 5 CUPS

½ cup vegetable oil

2 pounds red onions, chopped

2 pounds tomatoes

5 bay leaves

1 tablespoon allspice

6 dried mushrooms

2 tablespoons brown sugar

Salt to taste

4 cups water

2 pounds chicken thighs

1 pound hot cooked pasta

Ligurian Tuco

Tuco is an intense and tasty tomato sauce that can be flavored with chicken—as in this recipe—or with beef, or you can leave it plain so it bursts with tomato flavor. This sauce is an Italian recipe of Ligurian origin, which Peruvians have adopted as their own. It is perfect when combined with any kind of pasta.

1. Heat the oil in a skillet over medium-low heat, add the onions, and cook for 30 minutes until caramelized. Shake the pan often to prevent scorching.

2. Wash tomatoes under running water and cut each one into four parts. Transfer to a blender and process. Strain to remove the seeds and skin, and combine with the caramelized onions; process one more time in a blender.

3. Pour the mixture in a large saucepan or Dutch oven over medium heat and add the bay leaves, allspice, dried mushrooms, brown sugar, and salt. Add 4 cups water and bring to a boil. Turn the heat to low, cover, and simmer for 2 hours. Check the sauce often and add water if the sauce looks dry.

4. Add the chicken and cook for an additional 30 minutes, or until the chicken is cooked through.

5. The sauce is ready when the fat from the fried onions and chicken rises to the surface, after 2½ hours. Remove the bay leaves, dried mushrooms, and allspice.

6. Serve over pasta.

CHAPTER 11

Succulent Meats

Pork Sirloin with Pink Peppercorns

Molle, the fruit of a Peruvian tree, is a wild pink peppercorn with a delicious perfume and sweet flavor similar to allspice. It grows in clusters and is used in cooking and in natural medicine. This pepper is also used in artisanal wine, vinegar, and chicha.

INGREDIENTS | SERVES 3

1 pound pork loin

6 slices smoked bacon

Salt to taste

2 tablespoons vegetable oil

4 tablespoons sugar

4 tablespoons red wine vinegar

1 cup orange juice

1 tablespoon pink peppercorns

1 teaspoon ground black pepper

½ cup finely chopped onion

1 cup beef stock

2 tablespoons butter

Squash Mashed Potatoes (see sidebar)

Squash Mashed Potatoes

Loche is a squash from Lambayeque, in the northern part of Peru, used for sweet and savory dishes. Grate it with a peeler and add it to soups and stews. To make mashed potatoes for this recipe, cook 4 Yukon potatoes and ½ pound peeled butternut squash. When tender, mash with ½ cup light cream, salt, white pepper, and a sprinkling of grated nutmeg. Serve hot.

1. Clean the pork loin and cut into 6 slices, about 1-inch thick. Wrap each piece with 1 slice bacon and secure with toothpicks. Season with salt.

2. Heat vegetable oil in a skillet over medium heat and sear the pork slices, turning once until golden, about 4 minutes per side. Remove the toothpick.

3. In the meantime, in a saucepan over medium heat, combine sugar, vinegar, and orange juice. Bring to a boil and reduce until slightly thick. Add pink peppercorns, black pepper, onion, and beef stock. Boil until it has reduced by half. Turn off the heat, add butter, and stir. Taste for seasoning.

4. Serve 2 pork slices per portion, cover with the sauce, and add mashed potatoes.

Meat-Filled Zucchini

The texture of zucchini is complemented perfectly by this meat filling. The flavors are balanced and the mozzarella gives a delicate and special touch.

INGREDIENTS | SERVES 6

¼ cup vegetable oil
2 garlic cloves, minced
1 medium red onion, chopped
2 tomatoes, peeled and chopped
1 pound ground beef
3 tablespoons soy sauce
Salt to taste
Pepper to taste
½ cup raisins
½ cup sliced black olives
2 tablespoons chopped parsley
6 medium zucchini, cut in half lengthwise
½ pound shredded mozzarella

Other Vegetables to Stuff

Instead of zucchini, use bell peppers, chili peppers, eggplant, roasted onions, blanched cabbage leaves, potatoes, artichokes, etc. Follow the recipe as directed.

1. Heat the oil in a pan over high heat and sauté garlic and onion. When the onion is soft and translucent (about 5 minutes), add tomatoes, stir for a few minutes, and add the ground beef and soy sauce. Cook for 15 minutes over medium-low heat.

2. Season with salt and pepper and cook for 5 more minutes. Add raisins, black olives, and parsley. Turn off the heat and cool.

3. Preheat the oven to 350°F.

4. Put water in a saucepan and bring to a boil over high heat. Add salt and blanch the zucchini for 3 minutes. With a slotted spoon, remove the zucchini from the saucepan and cool.

5. Using a tablespoon, remove the seeds and some flesh from the zucchini to make room for the meat filling (you can add this chopped zucchini flesh to soups or omelets).

6. Fill the zucchini with the meat mixture, making a mound, and top with mozzarella. Place side by side in a baking pan and bake for 10 minutes, until the cheese is bubbling and lightly golden. Serve.

Beef Asado

The epitome of slow cooking, the longer you cook this asado, the better it gets. Serve with an option of mashed potatoes, Lima bean purée, yucca purée, fluffy white rice, steamed vegetables, or pasta.

INGREDIENTS | SERVES 6

6 garlic cloves, chopped

Salt to taste

Pepper to taste

½ teaspoon ground cumin

1 teaspoon dried oregano

½ cup red wine vinegar

4 pounds rib eye steak

⅓ cup vegetable oil

1 cup onion, chopped

2 cups red wine

1 pound medium-sized potatoes, peeled (optional)

1 carrot, peeled and cut in slices

4 cups Basic Peruvian Rice (see Chapter 8)

Leftovers

Leftover asado works well in sandwiches, salads, or as filling for ravioli. You can also freeze individual portions in small containers with some of its sauce; just thaw to reheat, and serve.

1. In a bowl, combine garlic, salt, pepper, cumin, oregano, and vinegar. Pour over the beef. Marinate in the refrigerator for at least 2 hours, but overnight will be better.

2. Heat the oil in a saucepan big enough to accommodate the steak. Drain the beef from the marinade and sear in the hot oil over medium heat, turning to seal in the juices, about 4 minutes per side. When the beef has a nice brown color, add onion and stir for 5 minutes. Pour in the marinade and wine, cover tightly, turn the heat to low, and simmer for 2 hours, adding water or beef stock if beginning to get dry.

3. Add potatoes and carrot and continue cooking until the vegetables are tender, about 15 minutes. Cut the rib eye in slices and serve immediately with the vegetables, rice, and sauce.

Creole Roast Beef (Asado)

*Leftover asado is one of the best ingredients to build a sandwich
with on the spur of the moment. The sauce is a great addition to enhance the flavor
and the texture, with extra bread used to mop up every last drop.*

INGREDIENTS | YIELDS 10 SLICES

2 pounds of eye round roast, clean

1 tablespoon chopped garlic

⅓ cup soy sauce

2 tablespoons ají panca paste (optional)

2 cups red wine

2 tablespoons Worcestershire sauce

3 tablespoons vegetable oil

2 bay leaves

5 dried mushrooms, rehydrated (see sidebar)

Salt to taste

Pepper to taste

1 tablespoon potato starch

Rehydrating Dried Mushrooms

Dried mushrooms bring a wonderful earthy flavor to any dish. They are easy to use, but should be rehydrated before cooking. Place them in a bowl and pour 1 cup of boiling water over them. Cover and let rest for at least 20 minutes. When the water is lukewarm, take out the mushrooms and chop them coarsely. Strain the water using a cheesecloth or paper napkins; save the water but discard the sediments.

1. Put the meat in a bowl, and season with garlic, soy sauce, ají panca, red wine, and Worcestershire sauce. Cover tightly and marinate overnight, refrigerated.

2. The next day, take the meat out of the marinade and dry with paper towels, reserving the marinade. Heat the oil in a saucepan over medium heat, add the meat, and sear all over. Pour the marinade over the meat and add 1 cup of water, the rehydrated mushrooms, and the bay leaves. Put on the lid and cook covered over low heat for 1½ hours.

3. Remove the meat and cut it into ¼-inch slices (an electric knife will do this job beautifully in seconds).

4. Transfer the slices back into the pan and taste for seasoning, adding salt, pepper, or more soy sauce as needed. Continue cooking over low heat until the meat is very tender, about ½ hour more. If necessary, add more water.

5. Dissolve the potato starch in 2 tablespoons water and add it to the pan, stirring constantly. The sauce will thicken and cover the spoon slightly. Serve immediately.

Ollucos with Beef

This Andean dish is made with charqui, which is dried llama meat. Sometimes it is easier and just as delicious to substitute the llama meat with sirloin steak.

INGREDIENTS | SERVES 6

2 pounds ollucos

3 tablespoons vegetable oil

1 pound sirloin steak, cut in thin slices

1 onion, diced

2 garlic cloves, chopped

2 tablespoons ají panca paste (optional)

1 cup beef stock

½ teaspoon dried oregano

Salt to taste

Pepper to taste

5 tablespoons chopped parsley

4 cups Basic Peruvian Rice (see Chapter 8)

1. Wash ollucos in cold water. Drain and, without peeling them, cut into thin and long sticks, like matchsticks. Reserve.

2. Heat the vegetable oil in a saucepan over high heat and stir-fry the beef until nicely golden, but not dry, about 5 minutes. Do this in batches (you do not want the beef to steam). Transfer to a plate, cover, and reserve.

3. In the same pan, cook onion, garlic, and ají panca paste over high heat for 7 minutes. Shake the pan and stir constantly.

4. Add ollucos; stir and cook for 5 minutes. Put the sirloin back in the saucepan, add the stock, dried oregano, salt, and pepper, and cook over medium-low heat, covered, for 30 minutes. Taste again and season with more salt and pepper if desired.

5. Add parsley and serve immediately with Basic Peruvian Rice.

Sirloin Anticuchos

Anticuchos have a long history in Peru. Because of their similarity to shish kebabs, some historians say anticuchos were brought to Peru by Spanish conquerors and their Arab cooks.

INGREDIENTS | SERVES 8

3 pounds sirloin steak

2 tablespoons minced garlic

2 tablespoons ají panca paste

Salt to taste

Pepper to taste

1 teaspoon ground cumin

1 teaspoon dried oregano

2 tablespoons red wine vinegar

1 cup beer

16 bamboo sticks, soaked in water

1 recipe Twice-Cooked Potato Slices (see sidebar)

1. Cut beef in 1½-inch cubes.

2. In a bowl, add garlic, ají panca, salt, pepper, cumin, oregano, vinegar, and beer. Add beef cubes. Let marinate for 1 hour in refrigerator.

3. Drain the beef cubes, thread them onto the bamboo sticks, and grill on both sides for 5 minutes over medium-high heat, basting with the marinade. Serve immediately with Twice-Cooked Potato Slices.

Twice-Cooked Potato Slices

Boil 6 unpeeled potatoes in enough water to cover over high heat until tender, about 25 minutes. Cool. Peel them and cut in thick slices, about ¾-inch thick. Prior to serving, heat ¼ cup oil in a skillet over medium-high heat, add the potato slices, and fry until golden, turning to cook both sides, about 3 minutes per side. Season with salt and serve hot.

Lomo Saltado (Beef Stir-Fry)

This cooking method is Chinese in origin, and widely practiced in every Peruvian kitchen. To get the best results you need very high heat. If you don't have a potent stove, cooking in batches will give good results, as long as you don't let the beef steam.

INGREDIENTS | SERVES 2

1 pound sirloin steak, cut in thin slices

Salt to taste

Pepper to taste

3 tablespoons vegetable oil

2 garlic cloves, finely diced

1 red onion, cut in thick slices

2 tomatoes, cut in thick slices

1 ají amarillo, seeded and ribbed, cut in thin slices

3 tablespoons soy sauce

3 tablespoons red wine vinegar

½ cup chopped, fresh cilantro

3 cups French Fries (see Chapter 4)

1 cup Basic Peruvian Rice (see Chapter 8)

1. Season the sirloin steak with salt and pepper. Put a wok or a pan over very high heat. Add the oil and sauté the meat in batches, stirring constantly, so it doesn't steam but becomes golden instead (about 10 minutes, depending on how strong the flame is).

2. Add garlic, onion, tomatoes, and ají amarillo and stir for a couple of minutes. Add the soy sauce and vinegar on the sides of the pan and combine everything. Season with more salt and pepper as needed.

3. Turn off the heat, add chopped cilantro, and serve immediately with French Fries and rice.

Potatoes in the Old World

The first time Europeans saw Peruvian native potatoes, they couldn't believe their eyes! They thought that potatoes were mischievous spirits capable of the worst offenses, such as having aphrodisiacal benefits or causing leprosy. Nevertheless, potatoes were cultivated in Europe as an ornamental plant, because Europeans loved their purple flowers.

Beef Stew

This stew is made in every kitchen in Peru with little variations.
Sometimes it has several vegetables and sometimes only potatoes and a few carrots.

INGREDIENTS | SERVES 6

2 pounds stew meat

1 cup all-purpose flour

¼ cup vegetable oil

1 cup chopped onion

4 garlic cloves, chopped

3 large tomatoes, peeled, seeded, and diced

⅓ cup dried mushrooms

2 bay leaves

1 cup red wine

1 cup boiling water

Salt to taste

Pepper to taste

2 cups carrots, cut in ¼-inch rounds

4 potatoes, peeled and cut in chunks

1 cup green peas

4 cups Basic Peruvian Rice (see Chapter 8)

The International Potato Center

The International Potato Center in Lima, Peru, is dedicated to the research of this crop around the world. They study potatoes and some other roots and tubers—sweet potato, olluco, etc.—and develop new technologies to improve these varieties, with the goal of giving better nutrition to the millions of people that eat them on a daily basis. For more information, visit: *www.cipotato.org.*

1. Dry the meat and dredge in the flour. Heat the vegetable oil in a saucepan over medium heat; cook the meat in batches, until golden, about 3 minutes per side. Transfer to a plate.

2. In the same saucepan over medium heat, cook the onion and garlic, stirring a few times, for 5 minutes. Add the tomatoes and continue cooking 5 more minutes.

3. Put the dried mushrooms in a bowl and cover with boiling water. After 10 minutes, take out the mushrooms, chop coarsely, and add to the saucepan. Strain the water through a cheesecloth.

4. Put the meat back in the saucepan; add the bay leaves, red wine, 1 cup boiling water, salt, and pepper. Put the lid on, reduce the heat to low, and simmer for 40 minutes. Add carrots and potatoes, adding more water if needed. Simmer for 20 more minutes. Finally, add green peas and cook for 5 minutes.

5. Taste for seasoning, adding more salt and pepper if desired. Serve with Basic Peruvian Rice.

Sirloin Medallions with Huancaína Sauce

Years ago, this was a classic in many restaurants. The combination is very good, and you can serve the succulent meat with steamed vegetables or mashed potatoes.

INGREDIENTS | SERVES 2

4 sirloin medallions, about 1-inch thick

1 garlic clove, chopped

Salt to taste

Pepper to taste

2 tablespoons olive oil

1 cup Papa a La Huancaína (see Chapter 3)

2 cups mashed potatoes

1. Season the sirloin medallions with chopped garlic, salt, and pepper. Heat the oil in a skillet over medium heat. Add the medallions and cook 4 minutes per side, or until desired doneness.

2. Transfer to plates, let rest for a couple minutes. Serve with Huancaína sauce and mashed potatoes as a side.

Cooking Sirloin Medallions

This cut of beef is tender and needs little seasoning. It has a short cooking time, and it is better to use medium heat and avoid flipping the medallions continually. You can also cook them in the oven or on the grill.

Lamb Chops in Seco Sauce

If you have a special dinner and want to impress your guests, this recipe is perfect for you. Both the chops and the sauce are made separately. Faux Risotto (see Chapter 3) goes perfectly as a side dish.

INGREDIENTS | SERVES 2

½ cup beer

2 tablespoons chopped parsley

½ cup olive oil, divided

3 tablespoons chopped garlic, divided

Salt to taste

Pepper to taste

½ teaspoon ground cumin, divided

4 lamb chops

¼ cup chopped onion

1 tablespoon ají amarillo paste

½ cup cilantro leaves

1 cup beef stock

1 recipe Faux Risotto (see Chapter 3)

1. In a nonmetallic bowl, combine ½ cup beer, parsley, ¼ cup olive oil, 2 tablespoons garlic, salt, pepper, ¼ teaspoon cumin, and the lamb chops. Cover and refrigerate for 2 hours or more.

2. Heat the remaining oil in a saucepan over medium heat. Add onion, remaining garlic, ají amarillo paste, and remaining cumin. Cook until very soft, about 8 minutes. In a blender process the cilantro leaves with 2 tablespoons water to make a paste, and add to the pan with the beef stock. Bring to a boil, lower the heat, and simmer until slightly reduced, about 5 minutes. Season with salt and pepper. You may blend and strain this sauce to make it smooth or leave it as is.

3. Drain the lamb chops from the marinade and dry with paper towels. Grill them or cook in a dry skillet until golden, 3 minutes per side. Do not overcook; the center should remain pink and juicy.

4. To serve, place 2 lamb chops on a plate, drizzle with the sauce, and accompany with Faux Risotto.

Pachamanca in a Pan

Pachamanca is not an everyday dish because it involves a huge amount of time and effort. But this variation, cooked in a saucepan, is easy to make and just as flavorful as the traditional one. Chincho is the aromatic herb used for this recipe. It is of the same family as huacatay, only milder.

INGREDIENTS | SERVES 6

½ pound chincho

3 tablespoons ají amarillo paste

3 whole garlic cloves

2 cups vinegar

Salt to taste

Pepper to taste

1 teaspoon cumin

2 pounds pork leg or ribs, cut in 3" × 3" pieces

3 potatoes, unpeeled

1 pound yucca, peeled and cut in 3–4 pieces

1 pound fava beans (in the pod)

3 sweet potatoes, unpeeled

3 ripe plantains, cut in half

Ancient Cooking Methods

Ancient Peruvians cooked their food by adding hot stones to the pots, or by placing the food directly over the stones. This method cooked the food very quickly. To make Pachamanca, they dug a hole in the ground, covered the floor and walls of the hole with stones, lit a fire, and heated the stones. When very hot, layers of meats, vegetables, and herbs were placed in this "oven." The cooks then covered everything with leaves. This was buried under a layer of soil and left to cook.

1. The day before preparing the Pachamanca, place the chincho leaves, ají amarillo paste, garlic, vinegar, salt, pepper, and cumin in a blender and process until it turns into a paste.

2. Put the pieces of pork in a bowl and add the chincho mixture, stirring well to get all the pieces covered with the sauce. Cover tightly and marinate overnight.

3. The next day, put the pork in a saucepan along with the marinating liquid and cover with the lid. Bring to a boil over high heat and then turn the heat to very low to simmer the pork until it is tender, about 1 hour.

4. Transfer the pork to a roasting pan. Divide the sauce left in the saucepan into two saucepans.

5. Preheat the oven to 400°F.

6. In one saucepan with sauce, cook potatoes, yucca, and fava beans over medium heat for 30 minutes, adding water if necessary (if it looks dry).

7. In the other saucepan, cook the sweet potatoes and plantains over medium heat for 35 minutes.

8. When the vegetables are tender, cut the potatoes and sweet potatoes in half. Transfer them and the plantains to the roasting pan containing the pork.

9. Pour the remaining sauce from both pans over the pork in the roasting pan; stir well to get all the pieces covered with the sauce.

10. Roast for about 20 minutes, until the pork is golden. Serve immediately.

Apanado (Breaded Steak)

The name of this dish refers to a well-seasoned, thin steak that is pounded with a mallet and dredged in a mixture of dried bread, which is then fried to form a crusty layer. Other names for this are sábana and milanesa. Serve with rice, mashed potatoes, French Fries (see Chapter 4), beans, or a green salad.

INGREDIENTS | SERVES 6

6 thin top round steaks, about 1 pound

Salt to taste

Pepper to taste

½ teaspoon ground cumin

1 cup all-purpose flour

2 lightly beaten eggs

1 cup panko or dried bread crumbs

1 cup vegetable oil

¼ cup chopped parsley

4 cups Basic Peruvian Rice (see Chapter 8)

2 cups Salsa Criolla (see Chapter 2)

1 egg, fried (optional)

Lomo a lo Pobre

This name means "Poor Man's Steak," and it's a very popular dish for people with big appetites or cooks who are in a rush. To make it, cook the steak as instructed and serve it over Tacu Tacu, with fried ripe plantains, Salsa Criolla, and a fried egg on top.

1. Put the steaks between two sheets of plastic wrap and beat with a mallet, a stone, or a rolling pin, until very thin. Season with salt, pepper, and cumin.

2. Place the flour in one bowl, the beaten eggs in another, and panko or dried bread crumbs in a third. Dredge the steaks in the flour, shake off the excess, and dip them in the beaten eggs. Then dip in panko or dried bread crumbs to cover completely.

3. Heat the oil in a skillet over medium heat and when it is hot, fry the breaded steaks, one by one, turning, until golden on both sides, 2 minutes per side. Drain on paper towels.

4. Serve sprinkled with parsley, with Basic Peruvian Rice and Salsa Criolla on the side. Top with a fried egg, if desired.

Beef Seco

Seco is a tasty and popular green cilantro sauce, typically found in the cuisines of northern Peru. Goat, lamb, chicken, duck, or seafood can be served with this tasty sauce.

INGREDIENTS | SERVES 4

½ cup vegetable oil, divided

2 pounds stew meat

1 large onion, chopped

3 garlic cloves, chopped

1 tablespoon ají amarillo paste

½ cup cilantro leaves (tightly packed), processed with 2 tablespoons water

½ teaspoon cumin

1 cup water

Salt to taste

Pepper to taste

4 medium-sized potatoes, peeled and cut in half

½ cup green peas

4 cups Basic Peruvian Rice (see Chapter 8)

4 cups Mashed Canary Beans (see Chapter 8)

1. Heat ¼ cup vegetable oil in a saucepan over medium heat. Add the beef in batches and cook until golden, about 5 minutes. Transfer to a bowl.

2. In the same saucepan over medium heat, add remaining oil and sauté onion and garlic until soft and golden, about 10 minutes. Add ají amarillo paste, blended cilantro, cumin, water, and the seared beef. Season with salt and pepper, put the lid on, reduce the heat to low, and simmer for 45 minutes or until the meat is very tender.

3. Add potatoes and cook for 20 minutes. Add green peas and simmer for 5 more minutes. Serve immediately with Basic Peruvian Rice and Mashed Canary Beans.

Peruvian Stir-Fried Noodles

Peruvian palates love Chinese flavors. For this dish, have everything ready, chopped, and measured so that the cooking is quick and you can have dinner ready in a matter of minutes.

INGREDIENTS | SERVES 4

1 pound fresh Chinese egg noodles

⅓ cup vegetable oil

1 pound beef sirloin, cut in bite-sized pieces

Salt to taste

Pepper to taste

3 garlic cloves, grated

1 teaspoon grated ginger

1 onion, cut in ½-inch slices

1 tomato, cut in thick slices

1 ají amarillo, cut in thin slices (or any other chili pepper)

1 red bell pepper, cut in thin slices

½ cup broccoli florets, blanched

½ cup halved spring peas

2 tablespoons red wine vinegar

2 tablespoons soy sauce, or to taste

½ cup beef stock

6 scallions, chopped, including green parts

1. Cook egg noodles in boiling salted water for 3 minutes. Drain and reserve.

2. In a wok or a saucepan, heat the oil over high heat. Add the beef in batches and cook quickly until golden, 3–4 minutes. Place cooked beef in a bowl. Season with salt and pepper.

3. In the same pan, add and stir-fry in quick succession the garlic, ginger, onion, tomato, ají amarillo, red bell pepper, broccoli florets, and spring peas. Add vinegar, soy sauce, and beef stock; let boil for 1 minute. Add the noodles to the pan and sprinkle with the scallions. Taste for seasoning and add more salt and pepper if desired. Serve immediately.

Chifas Everywhere

In Peru, Chinese restaurants are called "chifas." They have great food at excellent prices, and are always packed with diners. Chifas are great places to have a delicious meal with family and friends, to celebrate birthdays or any other event, and to enjoy the wonderful flavors of the Chinese cuisine.

Canelones (Cannelloni)

Cannelloni is a classic Italian dish, but Peruvians include it as part of their family meals. The following is a mouthwatering recipe made from scratch, as is usually done at home. Preparing and enjoying this dish will remind you of how good it is to eat traditional, homemade food.

INGREDIENTS | YIELDS 30 CANNELLONI

1 recipe Tuco sauce (see Chapter 10)

3 pounds beef round eye, clean

1 pound pork leg, clean

1½ pounds stemmed chard

1 pound stemmed spinach

1¾ cups grated Parmesan cheese, divided

Salt to taste

Pepper to taste

¼ teaspoon grated nutmeg

1 egg

¼ cup vegetable oil

30 sheets lasagna noodles

2 cups coarsely grated mozzarella

1. Using beef and pork, prepare one batch of Tuco sauce (add the meat after water). Simmer for 3 hours.

2. Wash the chard and spinach. Put them in a saucepan, cover with water, and bring to a boil over medium heat for 5 minutes. Drain and reserve.

3. Take meat out of the saucepan and cut into 2-inch pieces. Reserve the Tuco sauce. Process the meat and spinach mixture in the meat grinder (or food processor) 3 times.

4. Add ¾ cup Parmesan cheese to the meat mixture, with salt, pepper, nutmeg, and egg. Combine with your hands until everything holds together.

5. Heat the oil in a large skillet over medium heat and sauté the mixture for 5 minutes or until the egg is no longer raw. Put the mixture in a bowl and stir with a wooden spoon.

6. Bring a large pot of water to a boil. Cook the lasagna sheets for 3 minutes. Drain and spread flat on a clean kitchen towel to dry.

7. Prepare a large baking sheet (17.5" × 11.5" × 1") and spread 1½ cups Tuco sauce in the base. Preheat the oven to 350°F.

8. Fill each lasagna sheet with 2 tablespoons of the meat mixture. Roll and place in the prepared baking sheet.

9. Cover the cannelloni with the remaining Tuco. Sprinkle with mozzarella and the remaining Parmesan cheese. Bake for 30 minutes until bubbly and golden. Let rest for 10 minutes before serving.

CHAPTER 12

From the Sea

Pulpo al Olivo (Octopus in Black Olive Sauce)

This famous combination is simple and easy, and after celebrity chef Rosita Yimura created it in her kitchen, it quickly became a classic at most fish and seafood eateries.

INGREDIENTS | SERVES 6

1 (2-pound) octopus, cooked and cut in thin slices

Salt to taste

2 bay leaves

1 potato, unpeeled

12 Alphonso or Kalamata olives, seeded

1 cup mayonnaise

1. Rub the octopus with coarse salt and wash under running water to get rid of the slimy substance. Then beat it with a mallet to tenderize its flesh. Rinse. Repeat as many times as needed until it is no longer slick. While doing this, have a big saucepan ready with boiling, salted water and 2 bay leaves.

2. Holding the octopus by the head, submerge the tentacles in the boiling water. On contact with the water, the tentacles will curl immediately. Drop the octopus into the water along with an unpeeled potato and cook for 35 minutes, or until the potato is tender. Turn off the heat, transfer the octopus to a chopping board, let cool, and using a sharp knife, cut it in thin slices (or leave the tentacles in one piece, as you wish).

3. In a blender, process the black olives and mayonnaise until smooth.

4. To serve, place octopus slices on six plates and cover with olive sauce.

Shrimp Cocktail

The classic combination of cooked shrimp, avocado, and "Golf sauce" is simple, yet it feels luxurious every time. Top with a teaspoon of caviar for a fancy presentation.

INGREDIENTS | SERVES 6

10 ounces medium shrimp, peeled and deveined

2 avocados, peeled and cut in cubes

1 cup mayonnaise

3 tablespoons ketchup

2 tablespoons Worcestershire sauce

Salt to taste

Pepper to taste

6 hard-boiled quail eggs, peeled

Parsley leaves for garnish

1. Cook shrimp in a saucepan, over medium-high heat, with boiling, salted water for 3 minutes, or until they turn pink. Drain and cool immediately.

2. In six martini glasses, distribute the avocado cubes and shrimp, reserving 6 large shrimp for garnishing.

3. In a small bowl, combine mayonnaise, ketchup, Worcestershire sauce, salt, and pepper. Add a couple of tablespoons to each glass. Do not mix.

4. Garnish with 1 shrimp, 1 quail egg cut in half, and parsley leaves. Serve.

Shrimp and Huancaína Mousse

Pancho Graña, in his book, Mis Recetas de Cochina Criolla, *created this fusion dish that combines two of Peru's favorite flavors: huancaína sauce and shrimp.*

INGREDIENTS | SERVES 6

1 pound medium shrimp, peeled and deveined

1 cup diced queso fresco

1 small onion, cooked

3 tablespoons ají amarillo paste

¼ cup olive oil

Salt to taste

2 tablespoons unflavored gelatin

4 tablespoons cold water

Lettuce leaves for garnish

6 large shrimp, cooked, to use as a garnish

½ cup Quick Ají Amarillo Sauce (see sidebar)

Quick Ají Amarillo Sauce

In a small saucepan, heat 1 tablespoon olive oil. Add 3 tablespoons ají amarillo paste, stirring until the mixture curdles. Turn off the heat and add ½ cup light cream, stirring continuously until smooth. Taste for seasoning and serve over the mousse.

1. Cook the shrimp in salted water over medium-high heat for 3 minutes or until they turn pink. Drain and process in a food processor until smooth.

2. In a blender, process diced queso fresco with the cooked onion, ají amarillo paste, olive oil, and salt. Add the ground shrimp, mix well, and set aside.

3. In a small pan, combine unflavored gelatin with 4 tablespoons cold water. Let rest for 5 minutes and then dissolve over low heat. Add to the queso fresco mixture.

4. Pour the mousse into oiled ramekins or into a large container. Refrigerate for at least 5 hours.

5. Unmold the mousse; garnish with a lettuce leaf on the side and a shrimp on top. Serve with ají amarillo sauce.

Fish Escabeche

Escabeche is an ancient method of marinating fish and poultry for a few hours or longer. Traditionally, bonito was the first choice of fish for this spicy dish, but you can use any type of white-fleshed fish available. Serve it cold or at room temperature.

INGREDIENTS | SERVES 6

6 white-fleshed fish fillets

Salt to taste

Pepper to taste

½ teaspoon ground cumin, divided

1 cup all-purpose flour

½ cup vegetable oil, divided

2 large red onions

2 garlic cloves, chopped

2 tablespoons ají amarillo paste

¼ cup red wine vinegar

Bibb lettuce leaves for garnish

3 hard-boiled eggs

6 black olives

Buying Fish

The freshest fish at the fish market have bright eyes with black pupils, and the flesh should feel firm when pressed with a finger. The tail should be firm, and the gills should be bright red and smell clean, like the ocean.

1. Season the fish fillets with salt, pepper, and ¼ teaspoon cumin. Dredge with flour. Heat ¼ cup oil in a skillet over medium heat and fry the fish on both sides until golden, about 3 minutes. Transfer to a serving dish.

2. Peel the onions, cut in chunks from top to root (about 1-inch thick), and separate the layers like petals. If you want, you may use only the external onion layers for an even size and reserve the remaining for other recipes. Blanch in boiling water (enough to cover) and drain after 1 minute.

3. Heat the remaining oil in a skillet over medium heat and fry the garlic and ají amarillo paste, stirring, for 3 minutes. Add vinegar, onion, salt, pepper, and ¼ teaspoon cumin. Boil for 5 minutes. The onion should become transparent, but remain crunchy.

4. Cover the fried fish with this sauce, cover tightly, and refrigerate until ready to serve. It can be refrigerated up to 24 hours (the flavors are better when allowed to marinate for this long). Do not reheat.

5. To serve, place a lettuce leaf on a plate and a piece of fish with its sauce over the lettuce. Garnish with hard-boiled eggs cut in fourths and black olives.

Grilled Octopus

Grilling gives the octopus a nice charred flavor. Use large octopus tentacles for this recipe.

INGREDIENTS | SERVES 6

1 large octopus
2 bay leaves
1 small onion
1 medium potato, unpeeled
1 tablespoon paprika
2 garlic cloves, chopped
½ cup olive oil
¼ teaspoon thyme
Salt to taste
Pepper to taste
1 cup Ají Amarillo Mayonnaise (see Chapter 2)

1. Cook the octopus in boiling, salted water with bay leaves, onion, and potato. When the potato is tender, so is the octopus (about 35 minutes). Transfer to a chopping board and let cool to room temperature.

2. In a bowl, combine paprika, garlic, olive oil, thyme, salt, and pepper. Divide the tentacles of the octopus and marinate in the spicy mixture in the refrigerator for about 30 minutes.

3. Take the octopus out of the marinade and cook on the grill until the skin has several charred spots, about 6 minutes. Serve immediately with Ají Amarillo Mayonnaise.

Scallop Tortilla

This simple yet scrumptious omelet can be made with shrimp or crab instead of scallops. It is a protein-rich dish, usually served with white fluffy rice or twice-cooked potatoes on the side.

INGREDIENTS | SERVES 4

4 tablespoons olive oil, divided
12 scallops
½ cup chopped scallions
Salt to taste
Pepper to taste
8 eggs
½ fresh or frozen rocoto, seeded, deveined, and diced
½ medium onion, finely diced
Juice of 2 limes

1. Heat 2 tablespoons olive oil in a skillet over medium heat. Add the scallops and cook for 1 minute on each side, turning when golden. Add scallions, salt, and pepper.

2. Beat the eggs in a small bowl and season with salt and pepper. Pour over the scallops and cook until set, about 4 minutes. Turn carefully to cook on the other side for 2 minutes.

3. In a small bowl, combine rocoto, onion, lime juice, and the remaining olive oil, salt, and pepper. Serve side by side with the omelet.

Seafood Chaufa

Use whatever your favorite seafood is for this dish, including snails, octopus, or any other, making sure to cook them in advance so you have everything ready to make this dish in just a few minutes.

INGREDIENTS | SERVES 2

4 tablespoons vegetable oil, divided

2 eggs

8 ounces medium shrimp, peeled, deveined, and chopped

8 ounces squid, cut into rings and blanched for 3 minutes

½ cup sliced bell pepper (any color)

2 cups cold, cooked unsalted white rice,

2 garlic cloves, chopped

2 teaspoons peeled and finely chopped ginger

½ cup soy sprouts

2–3 tablespoons soy sauce

1 teaspoon toasted sesame oil

1 tablespoon toasted sesame seeds

½ cup sliced scallions

1. Heat 1 tablespoon oil in a wok or frying pan over high heat.

2. Put the eggs in a small bowl and beat lightly to combine. Add eggs to the pan and let them spread to cook a thin omelet. When the eggs are set, about 2 minutes, turn to cook on the other side for 1 minute. Transfer to a chopping board and cut into ½-inch-wide strips. Reserve for later.

3. Add the remaining oil to the pan and stir-fry the shrimp and squid, until the shrimp turn pink (about 3 minutes). Transfer to a bowl and keep warm.

4. In the same wok, add and stir-fry the bell pepper and rice for 5 minutes. Make a well in the center and add garlic and ginger. Stir for 3–4 minutes and combine with the rice and vegetables. Incorporate the soy sprouts.

5. Season with soy sauce and sesame oil. Transfer the cooked shrimp and squid back into the wok, along with the egg strips. Turn off the heat and sprinkle with sesame seeds and scallions. Serve immediately.

Picante de Camarones (Shrimp in Spicy Sauce)

The name implies this is a heavily spiced dish, but you are in control of the amount of heat you want. The shrimp must be lightly cooked to stay juicy and tender.

Useful Shrimp

Peruvian cooks use every part of fresh shrimp to improve the flavor of their dishes. The shells and heads are the best ingredients for flavorful stocks, which are the base for sauces with an intense and rich taste. Shrimp have two sacks inside the head. You should discard the black one and keep the other one—the grayish or green roe—which is full of flavor. Just a spoonful of this is enough to transform any dish from normal to extraordinary.

1. Peel the shrimp, reserving the tails. Place heads and shells in a saucepan with 2 cups water, bring to a boil, and cook over medium-high heat for 20 minutes. Cool, transfer to a blender, and process until almost smooth. Strain through a sieve, pressing the solids with a wooden spoon to release every drop of flavorful stock. Reserve.

2. In the same saucepan, heat 2 tablespoons oil and sauté onion, garlic, ají amarillo, ají panca, and paprika over medium heat for 7 minutes.

3. Squeeze the bread, removing most of the liquid, and process in a blender. Add bread to the onion mixture along with the shrimp stock and fish stock. Bring to a boil, turn the heat to low, and simmer for 15 minutes until slightly thick. Add the reserved shrimp and simmer for 3 minutes. Season with salt and pepper.

4. Finally add cheese and evaporated milk. Turn off the heat.

5. Serve with Basic Peruvian Rice and garnish with hard-boiled egg slices and parsley leaves.

Saltado de Camarones (Shrimp Stir-Fry)

This is a seafood variation of the traditional Lomo Saltado,
the Peruvian stir-fried beef with Chinese influence.

INGREDIENTS | SERVES 6

⅓ cup vegetable oil

2 red onions, cut in thick slices

4 garlic cloves, chopped

1 fresh ají amarillo, cut in thin slices (or any other chili pepper)

2 pounds medium shrimp, peeled and deveined

2 tomatoes, cut in thick slices

2 tablespoons red wine vinegar

2 tablespoons soy sauce

1 tablespoon Worcestershire sauce

Salt to taste

Pepper to taste

2 tablespoons fresh cilantro leaves, coarsely chopped

3 cups French Fries (see Chapter 4)

3 cups Basic Peruvian Rice (see Chapter 8)

1. Heat the oil in a saucepan over high heat; then add, in quick progression, onion, garlic, and sliced ají amarillo (or any other chili pepper), stirring quickly. Add the shrimp. Stir and cook until they are pink (about 3 minutes).

2. Add tomatoes, vinegar, soy sauce, Worcestershire sauce, salt, and pepper. Stir and turn off the heat. Add the chopped cilantro.

3. Have six warm dishes ready. On each one, put a portion of French Fries, then the stir-fried shrimp, and white fluffy rice on the side.

Corvina a la Chorrillana (Chorrillos-Style Sea Bass)

Chorrillos is a fishermen's neighborhood in Lima, next to the ocean. Every day, these men come back from the sea with their nets bursting with fish and shellfish, and their wives, excellent cooks and experts in the preparation of seafood, will make the most of everything.

INGREDIENTS | SERVES 2

⅓ cup vegetable oil, divided

3 garlic cloves, chopped

1 tablespoon ají amarillo paste

½ teaspoon dried oregano

Salt to taste

Pepper to taste

1 tomato, peeled, seeded, and chopped

2 red onions, cut in thick slices

¼ cup red wine vinegar

½ cup fish or vegetable stock

2 tomatoes, cut in thick slices

2 sea bass fillets

2 tablespoons chopped cilantro leaves

1½ cups Basic Peruvian Rice (see Chapter 8)

Variations

Instead of sea bass, use any other white-fleshed fish, or use the same sauce over other seafood. To make this dish completely different, use sautéed veal liver or steaks covered with Chorrillana sauce.

1. Put ¼ cup oil in a cold saucepan, add garlic, ají amarillo paste, dried oregano, salt, and pepper, and turn on the heat to the highest setting. Bring to a boil, add chopped tomato and onion, stir, and add vinegar and fish stock. Cook for 15 seconds.

2. Add sliced tomatoes and stir. The sauce should be ready in about 45 seconds if your stove has good heat; otherwise, it will take about 4 minutes.

3. Meanwhile, season the fish with salt and pepper and fry in a skillet with the remaining oil over medium heat, turning the fillets when they are lightly golden, about 4 minutes per side. Do not overcook the fish.

4. On two plates, put half of the sauce, add a fish fillet on top, and cover with cooked onion and sliced tomato, garnished with cilantro. Serve with Basic Peruvian Rice.

Sea Bass Sudado

Light and comforting, this dish is full of flavor and color.

INGREDIENTS | SERVES 4

2 tablespoons vegetable oil

1 red onion, cut in thin slices

3 garlic cloves, finely chopped

2 tablespoons ají amarillo paste (optional)

3 tomatoes, peeled, seeded, and grated

1 tablespoon tomato paste

3 cups fish stock

¼ cup white wine

4 cilantro sprigs

Salt to taste

Pepper to taste

4 sea bass fillets

2 cups Basic Peruvian Rice (see Chapter 8)

1 boiled Yukon potato, peeled and cut in thick slices

1. Heat the oil in a saucepan over medium-high heat. Add onion and garlic, stirring occassionally, and cook for 10 minutes. Add ají amarillo, tomatoes, and tomato paste, stirring constantly.

2. Incorporate the fish stock, white wine, and cilantro sprigs and bring to a boil. Turn the heat to low, cover tightly with a lid, and simmer for 15 minutes. Season with salt and pepper.

3. Season the fish fillets with remaining salt and pepper and put in the saucepan, letting them steam in the flavorful broth until they no longer look bright, just barely opaque, about 7 minutes, depending on the thickness of the fillets.

4. On each plate, serve 1 piece of fish surrounded by the sauce, with some rice and potato slices on the side.

Gratinéed Fish Fillets

Gratinéed fish and seafood is a popular home-cooked dish and classic restaurant order as well. Use thick fillets to avoid overcooking.

INGREDIENTS | SERVES 4

2 tablespoons butter, divided

1 pound medium shrimp, cleaned, peeled, and deveined

12 scallops

1 cup fish stock

Salt to taste

Pepper to taste

4 sea bass fillets (use sole, flounder, grouper, or any other white-fleshed fish)

2 tablespoons olive oil

1 pound spinach leaves, discard the stems

2 cups Light Béchamel Sauce (see sidebar)

½ cup grated Parmesan cheese

Light Béchamel Sauce

To make the Béchamel Sauce: In a small saucepan over medium-low heat, melt 4 tablespoons butter; then add 4 table-spoons all-purpose flour, stirring constantly with a wooden spoon or a wire whisk. Add 2 cups milk (stirring to avoid lumps), 1 bay leaf, salt to taste, pepper to taste, and a pinch of grated nutmeg. Turn the heat to low and cook for 10 minutes, stirring often. The sauce should be slightly thick. Taste for seasoning.

1. Preheat the broiler. Heat 1 tablespoon butter in a skillet over medium heat. Add the shrimp and sauté until they turn pink, about 3 minutes. Transfer to a bowl using a slotted spoon and keep warm.

2. In the same skillet, add the remaining butter and sauté the scallops for 2 minutes, or until they look opaque. Put them in the bowl with the shrimp.

3. Heat the fish stock in a skillet over medium heat; season the fish with salt and pepper and simmer in the fish stock for 5–7 minutes, depending on the thickness of the fillets.

4. Heat the olive oil in a skillet; add spinach and heat until wilted. Season with salt and pepper. Divide the spinach between four plates. With a slotted spoon, transfer the fish fillets to each plate and place over the spinach.

5. Cover with ½ cup of the Béchamel sauce, sprinkle with Parmesan cheese, and place under the broiler until the cheese melts and turns golden. Garnish with shrimp and scallops and serve immediately.

Seco de Pescado (Cilantro Fish Stew)

The Pacific Ocean is bursting with fish and shellfish, and Peruvian rivers, streams, lakes, and lagoons are abundant with freshwater species. This dish is almost always made with a white-fleshed fish.

INGREDIENTS | SERVES 6

3 tablespoons vegetable oil

1 medium onion, chopped

4 garlic cloves, chopped

Ají amarillo paste, to taste (optional)

4 medium tomatoes, peeled, seeded, and chopped

¾ cup cilantro leaves, blended with ¼ cup water

Salt to taste

Pepper to taste

8 ounces shelled, fresh fava beans

2 pounds white-fleshed fish fillets

4 cups Basic Peruvian Rice (see Chapter 8)

1. Heat vegetable oil in a saucepan over medium heat. Add onion and garlic and sauté for 5 minutes. Add ají paste, tomatoes, blended cilantro, salt, and pepper and cook 5 more minutes. Add fava beans and enough water to cover; then turn the heat to low and cover tightly with a lid. Simmer for 15 minutes.

2. Add the fish fillets to the saucepan, put the lid back on, and cook for 8 more minutes, or until the fish is opaque and cooked through. Serve with rice.

Fish with Anticucho Sauce

Anticucho sauce complements the delicate flavor of fish perfectly.
Substitute Lima beans instead of yucca purée to give it some variation.

INGREDIENTS | SERVES 4

1 tablespoon ají panca paste

1 tablespoon ají mirasol paste

2 cups red wine vinegar

4 garlic cloves, mashed

1 teaspoon ground achiote (optional)

1 teaspoon ground white pepper

1 teaspoon ground cumin

1 cup fish stock

1 tablespoon butter

4 sea bass fillets, or any other white-fleshed fish

Salt to taste

Pepper to taste

2 tablespoons vegetable oil

3 cups Yucca Purée (see sidebar)

1. For the anticucho sauce: In a saucepan over medium heat, combine ají panca paste, ají mirasol paste, red wine vinegar, garlic, achiote (if using), white pepper, cumin, and fish stock. Bring to a boil and reduce by a third. Stir in the butter.

2. Season the fish with salt and pepper. Heat a skillet with oil and sear the fish fillets on both sides until cooked through, about 8 minutes.

3. Serve fish over Yucca Purée and cover with the sauce.

Yucca Purée

Peel 1 pound yucca, cut in thick slices, and cook in water with 4 garlic cloves. Bring to a boil, turn the heat to medium, and cook until tender, adding salt to taste toward the end of cooking. Drain, pass through a ricer or mash with a potato masher, and then add ½ cup evaporated milk, 2 tablespoons olive oil, salt to taste, pepper to taste, and ½ tablespoon lime juice.

Fish a lo Macho

This traditional Creole dish consists of fried fish covered with a spicy shellfish sauce. The name in Spanish is a word game, meaning either that you need to be brave enough to endure the spiciness of the dish, or that its aphrodisiacal effects will make you feel very sexy.

INGREDIENTS | SERVES 4

½ cup plus 2 tablespoons vegetable oil, divided

1 cup chopped red onion

4 garlic cloves, chopped

1 teaspoon paprika

½ teaspoon dried oregano

½ cup ají amarillo paste

2 tomatoes, peeled, seeded, and chopped

½ cup white wine

Salt to taste

Pepper to taste

2 cups fish stock

2 tablespoons potato starch (or rice flour)

3 tablespoons cold water

4 ounces cooked octopus, sliced

4 ounces scallops, cleaned

4 ounces medium shrimp, peeled and deveined

4 ounces cooked squid, cut into rings

1 tablespoon chopped cilantro

4 fish fillets, about 1-inch thick

1 pound potatoes, boiled, sliced, and fried

1. In a saucepan, heat ½ cup oil over medium heat, add onion, garlic, paprika, and oregano, and sauté for 5 minutes. Add ají amarillo paste and after 3 minutes, add tomatoes. Cook for 5 more minutes. Add wine, bring to a boil, lower the heat, and simmer for 3 minutes. Season with salt and pepper.

2. Add fish stock and simmer for 10 minutes.

3. Dissolve potato starch in 3 tablespoons cold water; add to the saucepan and stir until it is slightly thick. Finally add octopus, scallops, shrimp, and squid and stir, about 3 minutes. Sprinkle with cilantro, salt, and pepper. Turn off the heat.

4. Season the fish fillets with salt and pepper. Heat 2 tablespoons oil in a skillet over medium heat, add the fish, and sear on both sides until golden, about 8 minutes. Transfer to four plates, cover with the seafood sauce, and serve with sliced and fried potatoes.

Nutritious Potatoes

Potatoes are a great source of vitamins and minerals; rich in iron, antioxidants, fiber, potassium, magnesium, and many other nutrients. You should try to eat potatoes without peeling them because the skin contains a good amount of those vitamins.

Fish Cooked in Corn Husks

This very old recipe from Lambayeque, in the northern part of the country, shows a creative and fun way to cook fish. Grill it instead of baking it in the oven, and serve with a potato, corn, and fava bean salad.

INGREDIENTS | SERVES 2

1 pound fish fillets (flounder, turbot, etc.)

1 tablespoon ají panca paste

½ cup melted butter

Salt to taste

Pepper to taste

½ pound corn husks, cleaned

4 sprigs cilantro

1. Cut the fish into 2-inch cubes. Season with ají panca paste, melted butter, salt, and pepper.

2. Preheat the oven to 350°F. Place 2 corn husks together, wide sides overlapping, and add ½ cup fish pieces and 1 cilantro sprig. Fold to enclose the fish like a tamale. Wrap each one in aluminum foil and bake for 20 minutes. Serve immediately.

Fish and Seafood in Ancient Peru

Seafood was an important part of the pre-Columbian diet. Ancient Peruvians ate raw fish, seasoned with salt, herbs, chili peppers, and acidic fruit juices.

North-Style Grouper

The cold waters of the Humboldt Current pack the Peruvian sea with countless varieties of great-quality fish and seafood. Due to their amazing plankton diet, the fish in the Peruvian sea have a flavor that is unrivaled in the marine world.

INGREDIENTS | SERVES 4

4 fish fillets

Salt to taste

Pepper to taste

Juice of 1 lime

½ cup olive oil

4 garlic cloves, chopped

2 tablespoons ají amarillo paste

4 scallions, sliced

2 tablespoons chopped cilantro leaves

1 cup chicha de jora, beer, or white wine

1 pound cooked yucca, cut in 1-inch sticks (like matchsticks)

1. Season the fish fillets with salt, pepper, and lime juice.

2. Heat the oil in a saucepan over medium heat, stir-fry the garlic and ají amarillo for 5 minutes, add scallions and cilantro, stir, and then add chicha de jora, beer, or white wine. Bring to a boil.

3. Place the fish fillets over this mixture, put the lid on the saucepan, turn the heat to low, and cook for 5 minutes. Serve with yucca.

Jalea (Fish and Seafood Fritters with Plantains)

Jalea is one of the shining stars in cebicherías all over the country. It is served as an appetizer at the center of the table, and consists of a mixture of fish and seafood fritters with chifles (thinly sliced and fried green plantains), mayonnaise, tartar sauce, ají sauces, and salsa criolla.

INGREDIENTS | SERVES 6

10 ounces white-fleshed fish

10 ounces cooked octopus, cut in slices

10 ounces cooked squid, cut in rings

8 ounces medium shrimp, peeled and deveined

Salt to taste

Pepper to taste

2 eggs, lightly beaten

1 cup all-purpose flour

3 cups vegetable oil, divided

2 green plantains, thinly sliced

3 garlic cloves, finely chopped

1 onion, finely sliced

1 tablespoon chopped cilantro leaves

⅓ cup thin slices red or orange bell pepper

6 limes, divided

1. Cut the fish into 1½-inch squares. Season fish and seafood with salt and pepper. Dip in the lightly beaten eggs, dredge in the flour, put in a colander, and shake off the excess flour.

2. Heat 2 cups vegetable oil in a saucepan over medium heat. When oil is hot, add the seafood in batches and cook until golden, about 4 minutes. Transfer to a plate covered with paper towels to drain.

3. In another saucepan, heat 1 cup vegetable oil and fry the plantain slices until they change color to an intense yellow and take on a crispy texture, about 2 minutes.

4. In a bowl, combine garlic, onion, cilantro, bell pepper, salt, and pepper. Add the juice of 2 limes.

5. Combine the seafood with the fried plantains and serve on a plate, accompanied by the onion sauce and 4 limes cut in half.

What Is a Cebichería?

Cebicherías are gastronomic temples where cebiche is served in many forms, as well as countless other fish and shellfish dishes. They are only open for lunch, and the ambiance and décor is informal. The food is the main focus of the experience. The success of a good cebichería lies in its fresh food, and its friendly service.

Fish with Leek Cream

This recipe is simple yet elegant. The creamy texture of the leek sauce combines perfectly with the fish, giving it a mild and delicate flavor. Rice with corn kernels is a great side, as is a big green salad.

INGREDIENTS | SERVES 4

½ cup butter

2 leeks (white part only), thinly sliced

½ cup grated Parmesan cheese, divided

1 cup light cream

Salt to taste

Pepper to taste

4 flounder fillets, or any other white-fleshed fish

1. Preheat the oven to 350°F.

2. Heat the butter in a sauté pan over medium heat and add the leeks. Sauté for about 15 minutes, or until the leeks are very tender.

3. Pour in a blender with ¼ cup Parmesan cheese, cream, salt, and pepper. Process and reserve.

4. Wash the fish under running water and dry with paper towels. Place the fillets in a rectangular baking pan, add salt and pepper on both sides, and bake for 4 minutes.

5. Take the pan from the oven and remove the juice from the dish. Pour the sauce over the fillets and sprinkle with the remaining Parmesan cheese.

6. Bake covered with aluminum foil for 8 minutes. Discard the aluminum foil and broil for 2 minutes, until golden and bubbly. Serve immediately.

Fish with Ají Amarillo Béchamel

This recipe is quick to prepare, and makes an ideal dish for a dinner with guests. The sauce is creamy and has a touch of spiciness, which makes it a perfect accompaniment for the fish. Serve with garden rice.

INGREDIENTS | SERVES 4

4 flounder fillets

Salt to taste

Pepper to taste

2 limes

1 recipe Ají Amarillo Béchamel (see sidebar)

¼ cup parsley, chopped

3 cups Basic Peruvian Rice (see Chapter 8)

Ají Amarillo Béchamel

Heat 2 tablespoons oil in a skillet over medium heat and sauté 3 tablespoons ají amarillo paste. Cook until it curdles, stirring frequently. Turn off the heat and reserve. In a saucepan over medium-low heat, melt 2 tablespoons butter and add 2 tablespoons all-purpose flour, stirring constantly. When the flour is cooked (about 5 minutes), add 2 cups hot evaporated milk and stir until the sauce is slightly thick. Add the ají amarillo mixture and season with salt and pepper to taste. Stir well and reserve. The sauce should be thick enough to lightly cover the spoon.

1. Preheat the oven to 350°F.

2. Wash the fillets over running water and dry with paper towels. Place the fish fillets in a baking pan, season with salt and pepper, and squeeze the limes over them. Bake for 4 minutes.

3. Take the pan from the oven and remove the liquid, if any. Spread the Ají Amarillo Béchamel sauce over the fillets; bake for 8 minutes and broil for 2 more minutes.

4. Sprinkle with parsley and serve with Basic Peruvian Rice.

CHAPTER 13

Vegetarian, Vegan, and Gluten-Free Options

Corn with Cumin Butter

Served as a shared starter, this choclito (the word used for corn in Peru) is a very tasty way to get your appetite going. It is also ideal as a side dish for many entrées. Be careful, because it can be addictive!

INGREDIENTS | SERVES 2–4

2 cups Peruvian giant corn kernels

1 aniseed infusion bag

1 tablespoon sugar

¼ cup salted butter

1 teaspoon ground cumin

Juice of 1 lime

Salt to taste

1. Cook the corn kernels in a pan with boiling water, the aniseed bag, and sugar, until tender, about 15 minutes.

2. In a frying pan, melt the butter and add the remaining ingredients over low heat, stirring well to mix all the flavors.

3. Add the corn kernels to the frying pan, heat through, and serve.

Avocado with Corn and Vegan Huancaína Sauce

Avocados are one of the great luxuries enjoyed by vegetarians and meat eaters alike, because they are both delicious and nourishing.

INGREDIENTS | SERVES 4

4 avocados

Juice of 2 limes

Salt to taste

Pepper to taste

4 cups cooked corn kernels

2 cups Papa a la Huancaína (see Chapter 3)

8 lettuce leaves

Parsley leaves for garnish

1. Cut the avocados in half, peel them, and take out the seeds. Sprinkle with lime juice, salt, and pepper.

2. In a bowl, combine the cooked corn kernels with the Huancaína sauce and fill each avocado with about ½ cup of this mixture.

3. Put two avocado halves on each plate, over 2 lettuce leaves. Garnish with parsley leaves and serve immediately.

Solterito (Fava Bean Salad)

This is a wonderful salad from Arequipa, a city in the Andes famous for its gastronomy. The use of fresh fava beans is very typical in this region of Peru, and they add a delicious crunch and beautiful green color to this salad.

INGREDIENTS | SERVES 3

1 cup fava beans

½ cup diced red onion

1 cup diced tomato, seeds removed

1 cup giant corn kernels (or white corn), cooked

1 cup diced queso fresco

¼ rocoto, diced (or any other chili pepper)

3 tablespoons white wine vinegar

3 tablespoons olive oil

Salt to taste

Pepper to taste

2 tablespoons chopped parsley

¼ cup sliced black olives

Lettuce leaves (optional)

1. Cook fava beans in boiling salted water over high heat for 5 minutes. Drain and peel.

2. In a bowl, combine the fava beans, onion, tomato, corn, queso fresco, and rocoto. Season with vinegar, olive oil, salt, and pepper.

3. Sprinkle with parsley and garnish with black olives. Serve over lettuce (optional).

Mushroom and Asparagus Lasagna

Making this lasagna takes a lot of time, but you can make it in advance and freeze it in large baking pans or individual portions, and then bake it before serving.

INGREDIENTS | SERVES 6

3 tablespoons olive oil

2 garlic cloves, finely chopped

1 large white onion, finely chopped

5 plum tomatoes, peeled, seeded, and chopped

3 tablespoons tomato paste

1 teaspoon dried oregano

2 bay leaves

1 pound mushrooms, sliced

1 pound asparagus, cut in ½-inch pieces

Salt to taste

Pepper to taste

4 cups Light Béchamel Sauce (see Chapter 12)

2 pounds lasagna noodles

3 cups mozzarella, grated

½ cup Parmesan cheese, grated

1. Heat the oil in a saucepan over high heat; add and sauté the garlic and onion until soft, about 6 minutes. Add tomatoes, tomato paste, oregano, and bay leaves. When the tomatoes look juicy, add the mushrooms and asparagus. Season with salt and pepper, lower the heat and cook until the vegetables are tender.

2. Have the Béchamel Sauce ready. Preheat the oven to 350°F.

3. In a large baking pan, place a layer of lasagna noodles. Cover with a layer of vegetables, a layer of Béchamel, and a layer of mozzarella cheese. Sprinkle with salt and pepper. Repeat the layers and finish with mozzarella and Parmesan cheese.

4. Cover with aluminium foil, and bake for 40 minutes. Take out the foil, and continue baking for 10 minutes or until golden and bubbly.

5. Take out of the oven and let rest for 15 minutes before serving the lasagna.

Vegetarian Causa

Together with cebiche and Papa a la Huancaína, causa is probably the favorite cold appetizer for most Peruvians. The creamy potato terrine is usually filled with seafood, but there are plenty of good choices for vegetarians, too.

INGREDIENTS | SERVES 4

6 starchy potatoes (Russet or Idaho), unpeeled (yellow or white)

2 tablespoons ají amarillo paste

¼ cup vegetable oil

Juice of 3 limes

Salt to taste

1 cup cooked giant corn kernels (or regular white corn)

¾ cup mayonnaise

2 avocados, cut in thin slices

3 ounces queso fresco, in thin slices

Pepper to taste

3 hard-boiled eggs, cut in quarters

6 black olives, sliced

Make It Vegan

To turn this causa into a vegan appetizer, just replace the mayonnaise with an olive oil, mustard, lemon juice, white wine vinegar, salt, and pepper dressing. Use tofu slices instead of queso fresco and replace the hard-boiled egg with roasted pepper slices.

1. Scrub the potatoes and cook in a pan of boiling water over high heat for 20 minutes or until soft, but not mushy. Drain. Peel them while hot and mash them immediately or put them through a ricer.

2. Add the ají amarillo paste, vegetable oil, lime juice, and salt to the mashed potatoes. Mix well and keep tasting them, adding more of any of the above ingredients if needed, until you get the desired taste (you be the judge!). Reserve.

3. In a bowl, combine the corn kernels with mayonnaise.

4. Lightly oil an 8-inch round baking pan. Line the base with a layer of potato. Cover with avocado and cheese slices, and some corn and mayonnaise mix. Season with salt and pepper. Add another layer of potatoes on top and put the dish in the refrigerator until ready to serve.

5. To unmold, run a knife along the edge of the pan. Cover the pan with a large plate and turn upside down. Slowly lift the pan, giving it firm touches with your hands if it feels like the causa is stuck. Pass the knife around the edge more times if needed. Garnish with hard-boiled eggs and black olives and cut like a cake. Serve cold.

Potatoes with Amaranth Huancaína Sauce

Tiny in size, but powerful and nourishing, amaranth is the base of many dishes, mainly in the Andes region.

INGREDIENTS | SERVES 4

6 yellow potatoes, boiled, and peeled
½ cup amaranth
2 tablespoons ají amarillo paste
¼ cup vegetable oil
1 cup queso fresco
1 cup evaporated milk
Salt to taste
8 iceberg lettuce leaves
8 black olives
4 hard-boiled eggs, peeled and cut in halves

Kiwicha

Amaranth is known as *kiwicha* in Peru, where it has been used for thousands of years. It is from the same family as quinoa. It also shares many of quinoa's healthy proteins, and brings a wonderful texture to many gluten-free and vegan meals.

1. Boil potatoes over high heat for 20–25 minutes, until soft, but not mushy. Slice potatoes.

2. While potatoes are cooking, you can also cook the amaranth, boiling it in 1 cup water for 20 minutes over medium-high heat. Drain and reserve.

3. Put ají amarillo paste in a blender with ½ cup cooked amaranth, oil, cheese, milk, and salt and process until creamy.

4. Put 2 lettuce leaves on each plate. Cover with potato slices and as much sauce as you want. Garnish with 2 olives and 2 hard-boiled egg halves. Serve.

Bean Escabeche

Beans in Peru are not only eaten hot as an entrée; they are also eaten at room temperature, like in this simple salad, and as part of some desserts.

INGREDIENTS | SERVES 4

1 pound canary beans
6 garlic cloves, whole
1 onion, whole
2 thyme sprigs
Salt to taste
Pepper to taste
¼ cup olive oil
2 small red onions, cut in thick slices
3 garlic cloves, chopped
1 tablespoon ají panca paste
2 ají amarillo (fresh, frozen, or jarred)
3 bay leaves
½ cup red wine vinegar
1 teaspoon ground cumin
1 cup vegetable stock
4 iceberg lettuce leaves
4 black olives
2 hard-boiled eggs, cut in half (optional)

1. Put the beans in a bowl, cover with water, and soak overnight. The next day, drain the beans and transfer to a saucepan with enough water to cover. Bring to a boil, turn the heat to medium, add whole garlic, whole onion, and thyme sprigs, and cook partially covered with a lid for 1 hour. Season with salt and pepper to taste.

2. When the beans are soft, heat a frying pan with the olive oil over medium heat to make escabeche sauce. Add 2 of the onions, cut in thick slices, from root to top, and 3 chopped garlic cloves, together with the ají panca and ají amarillo, bay leaves, vinegar, cumin, salt, and pepper. Cook for 5 minutes; then add the vegetable stock and cook for 5 more minutes.

3. Place the beans in a serving dish, cover with escabeche sauce and serve over a lettuce leaf, garnished with black olives and, if desired, hard-boiled egg halves.

Corn Patties

Patties are easy to make and the perfect way to eat vegetables in a tasty and fun way. You need very few ingredients to cook them, which makes this the ideal meal to cook when you don't have time to go grocery shopping.

INGREDIENTS | SERVES 4

1½ cups white corn kernels
1 egg (optional)
½ cup queso fresco, diced
½ cup vegetable oil

1. Process the corn kernels with ¼ cup water in a blender. It does not need to be completely smooth. If using the egg, add it now and process a few seconds longer. Transfer to a bowl and add the diced cheese.

2. Heat the oil in a frying pan over medium heat. Add 2 tablespoons of the corn mixture and fry, about 2 minutes per side, until golden. Serve hot.

Cauliflower Fritters

Cauliflower fritters are a very creative and easy way to get kids (and yourself) to eat cauliflower, a super vegetable packed with nutrients. These are good as a side dish or even as a light dinner or snack.

INGREDIENTS | SERVES 4

1 small cauliflower
3 eggs, separated
Salt to taste
Pepper to taste
½ cup all-purpose flour
½ cup vegetable oil

1. Cut the cauliflower into medium-sized florets and steam or blanch in boiling salted water for 3–5 minutes, until tender but still firm to the bite.

2. Beat the egg whites in a mixer, until stiff. Gradually add the egg yolks, salt, and pepper. Turn off the mixer and add the flour, folding with a spatula.

3. Heat the oil in a frying pan over medium heat. Dip a piece of cauliflower in the egg batter and fry until golden, about 3 minutes per side. Repeat with all the cauliflower. Drain on a plate covered with paper towels.

4. Eat hot, or at room temperature, as an accompaniment to your favorite dishes.

Vegetable Stir-Fry (Saltado Vegetariano)

Lomo Saltado is one of the top Peruvian dishes both in popularity and taste. Portobello mushrooms give vegetarians and vegans the option to eat this dish without any changes, except for the meat. You had better be very hungry when you prepare this, because the portions are quite big.

INGREDIENTS | SERVES 2

½ cup broccoli florets

3 tablespoons vegetable oil

1 cup sliced portobello mushrooms

2 garlic cloves, finely diced

1 teaspoon grated ginger

½ cup chopped red bell pepper

1 red onion, cut in thick slices

1 cup grape tomatoes

1 seeded and ribbed ají amarillo, cut in thin slices (or any chili pepper)

3 tablespoons soy sauce

3 tablespoons red wine vinegar

Salt to taste

Pepper to taste

½ cup chopped fresh cilantro

2 cups French Fries (see Chapter 4)

1 cup Basic Peruvian Rice (see Chapter 8)

1. Blanch broccoli florets for 3 minutes in boiling, salted water. Reserve.

2. Heat a wok or a frying pan over very high heat. Add the oil and when it is hot, add and stir-fry the mushrooms until lightly golden, about 5 minutes. Add garlic and grated ginger and stir for 30 seconds.

3. Add bell pepper, broccoli, onion, grape tomatoes, and ají amarillo, stirring for 2–3 minutes. Add soy sauce and vinegar and stir. Season with salt and pepper.

4. Turn off the heat, sprinkle with chopped cilantro, and serve immediately with French Fries and rice.

Vegetarian Arroz Tapado

The beauty of arroz tapado is that it can be filled with any ingredients that you love. The greater the contrast of flavors and textures, the better!

INGREDIENTS | SERVES 4

¼ cup vegetable oil

1 red onion, chopped

2 garlic cloves, chopped

1 tablespoon tomato paste

½ cup chopped red bell pepper

½ cup chopped zucchini

½ cup baby fava beans, blanched

½ cup green beans, blanched

½ cup vegetable stock (optional)

Salt to taste

Pepper to taste

½ cup diced carrot

⅓ cup raisins

⅓ cup sliced black olives

2 hard-boiled eggs, chopped

2 tablespoons chopped parsley, plus extra for garnish

4 cups Basic Peruvian Rice (see Chapter 8)

1. Heat the oil in a pan over high heat and sauté the onion and garlic. When the onion is soft and translucent (about 5 minutes), add tomato paste, stir for 3–4 minutes, and then add bell pepper, zucchini, fava beans, and green beans. Cook for 15 minutes over medium-low heat, stirring occassionally.

2. If the mixture looks dry, add some water or vegetable stock to make it juicy (about ½ cup). Season with salt and pepper, add the diced carrot, and cook for 5 minutes more. When ready, add raisins, black olives, hard-boiled eggs, and parsley. Turn off the heat.

3. Have the rice ready and warm.

4. In the bottom of an oiled ramekin, make a layer of rice, pressing with a spoon. Over this make a layer of vegetables and cover with more rice. Put a plate over the ramekin and turn upside down. Remove the ramekin. Garnish with parsley and serve.

Locro de Zapallo (Pumpkin Stew)

Locro is the ultimate vegetarian dish in Peruvian cuisine. Not only is it delicious; it is incredibly nutritious and healthy, too. It may not look that attractive, but don't be fooled by appearances!

INGREDIENTS | SERVES 4

2 tablespoons vegetable oil

1 red onion, diced

3 garlic cloves, mashed

2 pounds pumpkin, diced

2 white potatoes, peeled and diced

1 cup giant corn kernels

2 cups vegetable stock

Salt to taste

Pepper to taste

½ cup green peas

½ cup evaporated milk

1 cup queso fresco, diced

2 tablespoons huacatay (black mint) leaves, or coriander leaves, chopped

3 cups Basic Peruvian Rice (see Chapter 8)

1. Heat a saucepan with vegetable oil over medium heat and sauté onion and garlic for 6 minutes. Add pumpkin, potatoes, corn, vegetable stock, salt, and pepper. Lower the heat to medium-low and cook partially covered, stirring a couple of times, until all the vegetables are tender, about 25 minutes. Add green peas and cook until tender, about 5 minutes.

2. Add evaporated milk and white cheese. Stir and heat through, but do not let it boil. Season with huacatay and serve immediately with rice on the side.

Zapallo Macre

In Peru, a pumpkin called *zapallo macre* is used to make locro, but you can experiment with any squash available in the market. Weighing more than 160 pounds, *zapallo macre* is the largest fruit in the whole world! It can be found in Peru, Argentina, Ecuador, Colombia, and Bolivia (all squash are native to tropical America).

Wheat Berry Risotto

*Wheat berries are delicious and nutritious. Use them in risotto,
soups, salads, or any other traditional preparations.*

INGREDIENTS | SERVES 6

1 pound wheat berries
¼ cup olive oil
1 cup diced onion
3 garlic cloves, chopped
3 tablespoons ají amarillo paste
Salt to taste
Pepper to taste
6 cups vegetable stock
½ cup fava beans
1 cup diced, raw potatoes
2 cups diced queso fresco
3 tablespoons chopped parsley

1. Put the wheat berries in a saucepan and cover with water. Soak overnight and then drain.

2. Heat the oil in a saucepan over medium heat. Add the onion and cook for 5 minutes. Add garlic, ají amarillo paste, salt, and pepper.

3. Add wheat berries and the stock; cook for 20 minutes over medium-high heat. Add the fava beans and potatoes and cook for 20 more minutes. When everything is tender, add queso fresco and parsley. Cook 3–4 more minutes and taste for seasoning. The wheat absorbs most of the liquid, but the mixture should be moist and creamy. Serve immediately.

Artisanal Queso Fresco

If you have the chance to choose, select an artisanal queso fresco instead of the industrial type. The artisanal ones have better flavor, and are salty and tender. In markets throughout Peru, cheesemongers offer an amazing variety of cheeses. Try to find a good one in your neighborhood.

Gluten-Free Yucca Cake

If you tried this yucca cake, created by celebrity chef Flavio Solórzano, the last thing on your mind would be that it has no flour or gluten whatsoever. It's hard to believe that this perfectly fluffy texture can be achieved without those ingredients, but yucca will prove you wrong.

INGREDIENTS | SERVES 4

10 ounces yucca
6 tablespoons sugar
5 tablespoons unsalted butter
2 eggs
¼ cup evaporated milk
¼ teaspoon salt
1 teaspoon baking powder
1 teaspoon grated lemon zest
1 teaspoon grated orange zest

Dry and Fluffy Yucca

To get the right texture, make sure you squeeze the yucca tightly and keep going until no more drops of liquid come out. Otherwise, instead of a cake, you will have a pudding-like dessert, which is good too, but not what this recipe wants to achieve.

1. Preheat the oven to 350°F.

2. Peel and grate the yucca with the finest side of the grater. Put yucca in a clean kitchen cloth and squeeze to get rid of all the liquid. After squeezing it well, you will be left with about 1 cup of very dry grated yucca.

3. In a mixer, beat sugar and butter until light and fluffy. Add eggs, one by one, beating well after each addition. Scrape the sides of the bowl every couple of minutes to make sure all the ingredients are mixing well.

4. Add the grated yucca, milk, salt, baking powder, lemon zest, and orange zest.

5. Pour the batter in a buttered 9-inch loaf pan. Bake for 50 minutes. The cake should be lightly golden and puffed. Turn off the oven, take the cake out, and let cool on a cooling rack.

6. To unmold, run a knife around the edges and turn the cake upside down to release it. Cool completely.

7. To serve, put a slice on a plate and, if you wish, crown with a scoop of your favorite ice cream.

Frejol Colado (Sweet Bean Confection)

In the Cañete and Chincha valleys, this toffee-like candy was created by nuns centuries ago. It is still popular and sold on the streets in little containers made of dried squash.

INGREDIENTS | YIELDS 1½ POUNDS

1 pound black beans
4 cloves
1 cinnamon stick
1 teaspoon aniseed
1½ pounds sugar
½ cup evaporated milk
2 tablespoons toasted sesame seeds

Not Only Black Beans

Use canary beans, red kidneys, garbanzos, or any other bean of your preference. Each one will give this dessert its characteristic flavor.

1. Put the beans in a bowl with enough water to cover and soak overnight. Drain well and spread the beans on a kitchen towel. Cover with another kitchen towel and rub to get rid of the peels.

2. Put the peeled beans in a saucepan with enough water to cover, cloves, cinnamon, and aniseed. Cook over medium heat until the beans are very soft, about 1 hour. Discard the cinnamon stick and the cloves and pass the beans through a strainer to make them smooth.

3. Put the beans back in the saucepan with the sugar and cook at low heat, stirring frequently until you can see the bottom of the saucepan, about 1 hour. Add the milk and stir well.

4. Turn off the heat, cool, transfer the mixture to a nice container, and sprinkle with toasted sesame seeds.

Cherimoya Alegre

If you are in the mood for the simplest, lightest, and most refreshing dessert, and if you happen to have good cherimoyas at home, this is perfect for you.

INGREDIENTS | SERVES 8

1 ripe cherimoya
1 cup freshly squeezed orange juice
2 tablespoons Cointreau (optional)
Mint leaves
Cookies

Peel the cherimoya; take out the seeds if any. Slice the fruit and put in a bowl or in glasses with orange juice and Cointreau. Serve very cold with mint leaves on top and your favorite cookies on the side.

Lima Bean Salad

The best Lima beans come from the region of Ica, south of Lima, where this salad is a delicious part of the diet.

INGREDIENTS | SERVES 3

1 pound fresh, shelled Lima beans
1 cup shredded cabbage
1 red onion, sliced
1 cup coarsely grated Danbo cheese
2 tablespoons white wine vinegar
½ cup olive oil
1 teaspoon Dijon mustard
1 teaspoon sugar
Salt to taste
Pepper to taste
½ teaspoon dried oregano
2 tomatoes, peeled, seeded, and chopped
2 tablespoons chopped parsley
1 ají amarillo, sliced (optional)

1. In a saucepan, cook the Lima beans in salted, boiling water over high heat. Reserve. Blanch the shredded cabbage and the onion and when cool combine with the cheese.

2. In a bowl, combine vinegar, oil, mustard, sugar, salt, pepper, and oregano. Add half the vinaigrette mixture over cabbage, onion, and cheese, stirring carefully. Place in a serving dish.

3. In another bowl, combine Lima beans, tomatoes, parsley, ají amarillo, and remaining vinaigrette. Pour over the cabbage mixture and serve.

CHAPTER 14

Soups and Stews

Shrimp Chupe

This soup is considered one of the highlights of Peruvian cuisine, with a balanced combination of flavors and textures. Freshwater shrimp is the best choice.

INGREDIENTS | SERVES 8

6 cups fish stock

1 pound medium-sized shrimp

¾ cup vegetable oil, divided

1 onion, chopped

4 garlic cloves, chopped

1 teaspoon dried oregano

2 tomatoes, peeled, seeded, and chopped

½ cup white rice

2 corn ears, cut in thick rounds

1 pound (about 6) medium yellow potatoes, peeled

16 large shrimp

1½ cups evaporated milk

Salt to taste

Pepper to taste

1 cup queso fresco, diced

1 cup green peas

8 slices white bread

8 fried eggs

Parsley sprigs, to garnish

Fish Stock Mini Recipe

Make your own fish stock with 2 pounds of fish and fish bones (you can get these from your fishmonger). Put the fish in a saucepan with 2 bay leaves and parsley. Cover with cold water and bring to a boil over medium heat. Turn the heat to low and simmer for 30 minutes. Strain, discarding the solids, and reserve the stock. At this point it can be frozen for future uses.

1. Heat the fish stock in a saucepan over medium heat. When boiling, cook the shrimp for 3 minutes. With a slotted spoon, take them out of the stock and transfer to a chopping board.

2. Peel the shrimp and separate the heads, reserving the tails. Inside the heads you will find two bags; discard the black one. Put peels and heads in blender, add 2 cups of the hot stock, and blend until smooth. Pass through a strainer, pressing the solids to release most of the liquid. Reserve (this is one of the secrets for a delicious chupe de camarones, because this liquid is full of flavor).

3. Heat ½ cup oil in a saucepan over medium heat. Add onion, garlic, and oregano and sauté until golden, about 5–7 minutes. Add tomatoes and continue cooking for 5 minutes; then add the fish stock that was left in the pan and bring to a boil. Turn the heat to medium-low, add rice, and simmer for 10 minutes.

4. Add corn and potatoes and after 10 minutes, add the blended and strained fish and shrimp stock and the large shrimp. Cook for 7 minutes. Add milk, salt, and pepper and turn off the heat. Add cheese and green peas.

5. Heat remaining oil in a skillet and fry the white bread until nicely golden. Drain over paper towels. Fry the eggs, sunny side up.

6. On each plate, put some medium shrimp with rice, a potato, a fried bread slice topped with a fried egg, and the hot liquid. Garnish with parsley and 2 large shrimp. Serve immediately.

Fresh Lima Bean Chupe

Chupes are traditional soups in Peru, and there are hundreds of recipes for them. Among their ingredients are potatoes, legumes, and vegetables, as in this nourishing soup. Keep in mind you can also use frozen Lima beans instead of fresh.

INGREDIENTS | SERVES 6

3 tablespoons vegetable oil
1 onion, chopped
1 whole ají panca (optional)
1 tablespoon tomato paste
2 tablespoons long-grain white rice
3 potatoes, peeled and diced
2 cups shelled, fresh Lima beans
5 cups vegetable stock
Salt to taste
Pepper to taste
¾ cup queso fresco, diced
1 cup evaporated milk
3 eggs, lightly beaten
1 teaspoon dried oregano

1. In a saucepan, heat the oil over medium heat. Add chopped onion and stir until lightly golden, about 8–10 minutes. Add ají panca, if using, and tomato paste, stirring well to incorporate. Add rice, potatoes, Lima beans, and vegetable stock. Bring to a boil, turn the heat to low, and simmer until the potatoes are tender, about 35 minutes. When ready, season with salt and pepper.

2. Add queso fresco, milk, and lightly beaten eggs. Stir and turn off the heat. Serve at once, sprinkled with oregano.

Fava Bean Chupe

A comforting and soothing soup, made with fava beans and vegetables. It can be served as a light meal, or in small soup bowls as an appetizer.

INGREDIENTS | SERVES 6

¼ cup vegetable oil
½ cup chopped onion
1 tablespoon tomato paste
1 tablespoon ají amarillo paste
2 cups fava beans, shelled
4 medium potatoes, peeled and diced
4 tablespoons long-grain white rice
5 cups vegetable stock
Salt to taste
Pepper to taste
2 eggs, lightly beaten
½ cup diced queso fresco
½ cup evaporated milk
2 tablespoons chopped parsley

1. Heat the oil in a saucepan over medium heat. Sauté the onion until tender, about 3–5 minutes. Add tomato paste and ají amarillo paste, stir, and cook for 5 minutes. Add fava beans, potatoes, rice, and stock, bring to a boil, turn the heat to low, and simmer until the vegetables are cooked, about 30 minutes. Season with salt and pepper.

2. Add beaten eggs, queso fresco, and evaporated milk. Turn off the heat. Sprinkle with parsley and serve.

Green Chupe

This soup is very popular in the Andes of Peru and a great treat for cool days. It has an amazing mix of flavors, and in the Andes it is considered an aphrodisiac.

INGREDIENTS | SERVES 4

4 Russet potatoes
¼ cup vegetable oil
1 garlic clove, minced
½ white onion, chopped
7 cups water, divided
Salt to taste
Pepper to taste
¼ cup parsley leaves
¼ cup cilantro leaves
1 sprig muña (the leaves)
1 sprig paico (epazote or hierba santa)
1 sprig ruda (the leaves)
1 sprig hierbabuena (the leaves)
¼ cup chopped scallion (the green part)
2 eggs, lightly beaten
½ cup milk
1 cup diced queso fresco

1. Peel the potatoes and coarsely grate them. Place the grated potatoes in a bowl and wash them two or three times under running water to get rid of the starch. Leave them in the bowl covered with water until ready to use.

2. Heat the oil in a saucepan over high heat and sauté the garlic and onion. When the onion is soft and translucent (about 5 minutes), add 6 cups cold water and bring to a boil.

3. Drain the potatoes and transfer to the saucepan with the boiling water. Add salt and pepper. Do not stir.

4. Put the leaves of parsley, cilantro, muña, paico, ruda, hierbabuena, and the scallions in a blender with 1 cup water and process until smooth.

5. When the potatoes are tender, about 5 minutes, pour the lightly beaten eggs in a thin stream, stirring with a wooden spoon. Wait until the eggs are cooked, about 2 minutes.

6. Turn off the heat and incorporate the milk, queso fresco, and herb mixture. Serve immediately.

7. Reheat the soup over medium heat, but do not let it boil. If the soup boils, the protein in the milk will curdle and the herbs will turn a dark and unappetizing color.

Fish Chupín

Peru is a coastal country, with fish and seafood present in many dishes in the daily diet for the last 10,000 years. This soup is one of countless ways to enjoy fish in all its glory.

INGREDIENTS | SERVES 6

½ cup vegetable oil, divided

1 onion, chopped

2 garlic cloves, chopped

1 teaspoon dried oregano

6 cups fish stock

½ cup long-grain white rice

6 medium-sized potatoes, peeled

1 cup corn kernels

1 cup green peas

Salt to taste

Pepper to taste

2 tablespoons Chinese dried shrimp

6 fish fillets

½ cup all-purpose flour

2 ounces diced queso fresco

3 eggs, lightly beaten

1 cup evaporated milk

2 tablespoons chopped cilantro

1. Heat ¼ cup oil in a saucepan over medium heat. Sauté onion, garlic, and oregano, until translucent, about 5 minutes, stirring from time to time. Add fish stock and bring to a boil.

2. Add rice, potatoes, corn, green peas, salt, pepper, and Chinese dried shrimp. Turn the heat to low, cover partially, and simmer until the vegetables are tender, about 30 minutes.

3. Meanwhile, season the fish fillets with salt and pepper. Dredge with flour and fry in a skillet with ¼ cup hot oil for 3 minutes per side. Transfer to a plate and reserve.

4. Add cheese to the soup along with the lightly beaten eggs and the milk, stirring well. Turn off the heat. Serve in soup bowls, top with a fried fish fillet, and sprinkle with cilantro. Serve immediately.

Chinese Dried Shrimp

Many cooks swear by the delicious flavor these tiny shrimp bring to dishes. They are regular shrimp, sun-dried and salted, and can be eaten as a snack. They are easy to find in Chinese grocery stores and large supermarkets.

Chicken Aguadito

This hearty and succulent soup received the name levantamuertos *(which means to get the dead up), because of its energizing powers.*

INGREDIENTS | SERVES 4

4 chicken legs with thighs

Salt to taste

Pepper to taste

¼ cup vegetable oil

½ cup red chopped onion

2 garlic cloves, chopped

2 tablespoons ají amarillo paste

2 cups cilantro leaves (stems discarded)

¼ cup water

4 cups chicken stock

1 cup beer

½ red bell pepper, cut in slices

1 cup diced carrot

½ cup long-grain white rice

2 medium yellow potatoes, peeled and cut in half

½ cup green peas

Variations

With duck: Substitute duck for the chicken and add duck stock. With scallops: Use scallops instead of chicken and fish stock, adding them toward the end of cooking, to just steam in the hot soup. With fish: Toward the end of cooking, add white-fleshed fish fillets cut into 2-inch pieces. Use fish stock.

1. Season the chicken with salt and pepper. Heat vegetable oil in a saucepan over medium heat, add the chicken pieces, and sear them, about 4 minutes per side. Transfer to a plate. In the same saucepan, sauté onion, garlic, and ají amarillo, until golden (about 8–10 minutes).

2. Process cilantro leaves with ¼ cup water in a blender. When smooth, add to the onion mixture, along with the chicken stock, beer, chicken, bell pepper, and carrot. Bring to a boil, turn the heat to low, cover with a lid, and simmer for 15 minutes. Add rice and after 10 minutes, add potatoes and green peas.

3. Put the lid on and simmer until the potatoes are tender and the rice is cooked, about 20 minutes. If the soup is too thick for your taste, add more stock. Taste for seasoning and serve immediately.

Mussel Aguadito

Aguadito is a brothy soup that has potatoes, rice, and some protein in it, in addition to lots of vegetables and the distinct flavor and green color of cilantro. In Peru it is very common to have this dish in the early morning, after partying all night long.

INGREDIENTS | SERVES 6

3 dozen fresh mussels

6 cups fish stock, divided

2 tablespoons vegetable oil

1 onion, chopped

5 garlic cloves, chopped

2 tablespoons ají amarillo paste

1 red bell pepper, diced

Salt to taste

Pepper to taste

2 cups cilantro leaves

¼ cup water

1 cup green peas

1 cup diced carrots

1½ cups Basic Peruvian Rice (see Chapter 8)

4 yellow potatoes, peeled

1. Put mussels in a heavy saucepan, add 2 cups fish stock, cover tightly with a lid, and steam over high heat until the shells open, about 5 minutes. Take them out of the stock and discard any shells that remain closed. Reserve the mussels.

2. In a saucepan, heat the vegetable oil over medium heat and fry onion, garlic, and ají amarillo. When the onion looks translucent (about 10 minutes), add the bell pepper and stir for 5 minutes. Add salt and pepper.

3. Add the remaining fish stock and bring to a boil.

4. In a blender, process the cilantro leaves with ¼ cup water until smooth. Add to the stock with green peas, carrots, and rice. Turn the heat to low and simmer until all the vegetables are tender, about 15 minutes.

5. Add potatoes and 15 minutes later, put the mussels back in the saucepan. Taste for seasoning and cook, covered, for 3 minutes over low heat. Serve immediately.

Sopa a la Minuta (Quick Beef and Noodle Soup)

This cheap and quick soup can be prepared in a matter of minutes. Some believe that many years ago, home cooks made it with no meat, using only onion, garlic, ají panca, stock, and pasta.

INGREDIENTS | SERVES 4

3 tablespoons vegetable oil

½ onion, chopped

2 garlic cloves, chopped

2 teaspoons ají panca paste

1 teaspoon dried oregano

2 tablespoons tomato paste

1 pound ground beef

4 cups beef stock, or water

4 ounces angel hair pasta

2 eggs, lightly beaten (optional)

Salt to taste

Pepper to taste

½ cup evaporated milk

1. Heat the oil in a saucepan over medium heat. Add and sauté onion, garlic, and ají panca, stirring for 5 minutes. Add oregano and tomato paste, stir. Add ground beef, cook until brown, about 10 minutes, and then add 4 cups boiling stock or water. Put the lid on, lower the heat, and simmer for 10 minutes.

2. Add pasta and cook for 3 minutes; then add lightly beaten eggs (if using) and stir quickly. Season with salt and pepper. Turn off the heat and incorporate the milk.

3. Serve immediately.

Sopa Seca (Dry Soup)

This is not a regular soup, but a thick pasta dish popular in Chincha, south of Lima. It is usually served with Carapulcra, a tasty potato dish (see recipe in this chapter).

INGREDIENTS | SERVES 4

¼ cup vegetable oil

2 tablespoons ají panca paste

½ teaspoon ground cumin

2 garlic cloves, chopped

½ teaspoon ground black pepper

2 tomatoes, peeled, seeded, and grated

1 grated carrot, about ½ cup

2 tablespoons chopped parsley

4 chicken thighs

Salt to taste

Pepper to taste

1½ cups chicken stock

12 ounces cooked spaghetti

1. Heat the oil in a saucepan over medium heat. Fry the ají panca, cumin, garlic, and black pepper about 4 minutes. Add tomatoes, carrot, and parsley, stirring, and cook for 10 minutes.

2. Add chicken pieces, salt, and pepper, cover with the vegetable mixture, and then add chicken stock. Bring to a boil, turn the heat to low, put the lid on, and simmer until the chicken is tender, about 40 minutes. Add the cooked spaghetti and heat through. Serve immediately.

Sancochado

This dish is a banquet in itself, with an abundance of meat and vegetables, and is accompanied by several sauces.

INGREDIENTS | SERVES 6

2 pounds brisket, or flank steak

2 pounds bones for stock

1 cup garbanzo beans, cooked

1 pound yucca, peeled and cut in pieces

½ leek, cut in half lengthwise

2 celery ribs

Salt to taste

Pepper to taste

6 potatoes, peeled

3 sweet potatoes, cooked

2 white corn ears, cut in thick rounds

1 medium head green cabbage, cut in 6 pieces lengthwise

2 tablespoons finely chopped parsley leaves

6 limes, cut in halves

A Colonial Feast

In pre-Columbian times, ancient Peruvians made a hearty soup with alpaca or llama meat, called T'impu. The Spanish brought with them the traditional Puchero, or Cocido, and the two soups combined into what is now known as Sancochado. In colonial times, it was customary to prepare Sancochado with fifteen different meats: beef's sirloin, brisket, round, tail, and flank; rooster; pork's feet, skin, neck, jowl, belly, and bacon; and Creole sausage, chorizo, and blood sausage; all of this in addition to a cornucopia of vegetables, with the addition of vegetables, garbanzo beans, and rice. Nowadays the list of ingredients is shorter, but the dish is still powerful. It is not only a complete meal in itself; it is a banquet.

1. In a saucepan, place meat and bones, cover with cold water, and bring to a boil over high heat. Turn the heat to medium-low, partially cover the pan, and simmer for 2 hours, skimming the fat from the surface. When the meat is tender, transfer to a bowl, discard the bones, and strain the stock.

2. Add cooked garbanzo beans, yucca, leek, and celery to the stock. Season with salt and pepper. Simmer for 15 minutes or until the vegetables are tender. Add potatoes and corn and continue cooking until tender, about 20 minutes.

3. In another saucepan, boil the cabbage in salted water for 15 minutes. Drain.

4. To serve, place meat and vegetables on a serving dish. In individual soup bowls, serve the stock, sprinkled with finely chopped parsley. Pass lime slices with the soup. Place small ramekins with Salsa Criolla, salsa huancaína, salsa de perejil, Huacatay Salsa, scallions and egg salsa, to accompany the dish. See recipes for Salsa Criolla and Huacatay Salsa in Chapter 2.

Cazuela

This is another Peruvian classic soup. It is healthy and delicious, and the broth has an amazing flavor because of the wide variety of vegetables included. You can add any vegetable you want!

INGREDIENTS | SERVES 8

2 tablespoons vegetable oil

2 onions, chopped

3 garlic cloves, minced

12 cups water

2 pounds beef ribs, cut in pieces

2 teaspoons dried oregano

Salt to taste

Pepper to taste

½ pound yucca, peeled and cut in thick slices

3 Russet potatoes, peeled and cut in 6 parts

1 cup sliced celery

1 cup peeled and diced acorn squash

1 cup sliced green beans

1 cup peeled and diced carrots

1 cup green peas

1 cup fava beans

1 small head green cabbage, thinly sliced

1 cup corn kernels

1 cup broccoli florets

¼ cup chopped parsley

1. Heat the oil in a saucepan over medium heat. Add onions and garlic and sauté until the onions are soft and translucent (about 10 minutes).

2. Pour 12 cups water in the saucepan, incorporate the ribs, bring to a boil over high heat, and turn the heat to medium-low. Add oregano, salt, and pepper and simmer with the lid on for 2 hours or until the meat is fork tender. Add more water if needed (in case the soup looks dry).

3. When the meat is done, take it out and cut into 2-inch pieces. Put the meat back in the broth.

4. Add yucca and potatoes and simmer for 10 minutes. Add the celery, squash, green beans, carrots, green peas, fava beans, cabbage, corn, and broccoli and simmer for 10 minutes more, or until all the vegetables are tender. If using frozen or canned vegetables, the cooking time will be shorter (half the time).

5. Taste and add more salt and pepper if desired. Serve in soup bowls, sprinkled with parsley.

Variation

There are many ways to make a variation of this recipe. You can add quinoa or wheat berries; legumes like beans, chickpeas, or lentils; or pasta like orzo or angel hair. It always tastes great topped with Parmesan cheese!

Menestrón (Peruvian Minestrone)

For this Peruvian version of the Italian Minestrone, you can substitute the fresh ingredients with frozen ones, in the same quantities.

INGREDIENTS | SERVES 4

1 cup chopped celery

1 cup chopped onion or leek

4 garlic cloves, chopped

1 cup chopped carrot

1 cup sliced green beans

1 cup baby Lima beans

1 cup peeled and chopped potato

1 cup peeled and chopped yucca

1 cup chopped cabbage (optional)

1 cup corn kernels

8 cups beef, chicken, or vegetable broth, or water

Salt to taste

Pepper to taste

1 cup penne or rigatoni

1 recipe Quick Pesto (see sidebar)

½ cup diced fresh queso fresco

1. In a saucepan over medium heat, cook the vegetables with the broth or water until everything is very tender, about 45 minutes. Season with salt and pepper. If you want to add some herbs while cooking, feel free to do so. Parsley, bay leaf, and cilantro are some flavorful additions.

2. Add penne or rigatoni and cook a few minutes longer, about 12 minutes (or according to package instructions).

3. Pour the pesto into the soup. Simmer for 5 minutes longer, add queso fresco, and serve immediately.

Quick Pesto Mini Recipe

Heat 2 tablespoons oil in a small skillet over medium heat, add ½ chopped onion and 2 chopped garlic cloves, and sauté for 5 minutes. Add 1 cup basil leaves and 1 cup spinach and season with salt and pepper, to taste. Transfer to a blender and blend until finely chopped.

Bean Soup

This soup is popular because it's hearty and gives you a lot of energy. Serve warm crusty bread with it.

INGREDIENTS | SERVES 8

2 cups canary beans

25 cups water, divided

¼ cup vegetable oil

2 pounds pork leg, cut in 2-inch pieces

2 garlic cloves, minced

1 large red onion, chopped

2 tomatoes, peeled and chopped

2 teaspoons dried oregano

2 Russet potatoes, peeled and diced

½ pound penne

Salt to taste

Pepper to taste

¼ cup chopped cilantro

1 cup grated Parmesan cheese

1. Put the beans in a bowl, add 5 cups water, and soak overnight. Drain before using.

2. Put a saucepan over medium heat with 4 cups water, add the beans, and bring to a boil. Cook for 5 minutes, drain, and put the beans back in the saucepan. Add 4 cups water and bring to a boil one more time for 5 minutes. Drain and reserve.

3. Heat the oil in a big saucepan over medium heat and fry the pork, stirring occasionally until golden, about 7 minutes. Add garlic and onion and sauté until the onion is tender and translucent (about 10 minutes). Incorporate tomatoes and oregano and stir for 3 minutes.

4. Add 12 cups water, turn the heat to high, and bring to a boil. Add the beans, turn the heat to low, and simmer partially covered for 40 minutes or until the pork and beans are tender.

5. Add potatoes and pasta; simmer for 10 more minutes and season with salt and pepper.

6. Turn off the heat and add cilantro. Taste for seasoning. Serve hot with a sprinkling of Parmesan cheese.

Carapulcra

The Quechua word qarapullka *refers to a dried potato and dried meat dish. On the other hand, the Aymara word* calapurca *describes a cooking technique in which hot stones are added to the clay pot with the purpose of cooking the ingredients.*

INGREDIENTS | SERVES 8

1 pound papa seca (dried potatoes)
½ cup vegetable oil
1 pound pork leg, cut in 2-inch cubes
1 pound pork ribs, cut in 2-inch pieces
1 onion, chopped
4 garlic cloves, chopped
1 teaspoon dried oregano
1 teaspoon ground cumin
Salt to taste
Pepper to taste
¼ cup ají panca paste
2 cups chicken stock
⅓ cup sweet wine (like Port)
½ cup ground peanut butter cookies
1 (1-ounce) square 70–72% chocolate, grated
¼ cup ground and toasted peanuts

Papa Seca

This is an ancient method of preserving potatoes after the harvest, still used to this day. First, they are cooked in boiling water, drained, peeled, and cut in medium dices or thin sticks. Then, these pieces are sun-dried until they lose all their moisture and look like small crystals. Now they are ready to be stored for a very long time. When buying papa seca, choose the ones with yellowish color, because they are of better quality.

1. Place the papa seca in a dry saucepan and toast it over medium heat for 3–4 minutes, stirring constantly. Be careful, because it burns quickly. Transfer to a bowl, add boiling water or chicken stock to cover, and soak overnight. Drain and reserve.

2. In a saucepan, heat the oil over medium heat and fry the pork until nicely brown, about 7 minutes. Transfer to a plate.

3. In the same oil, sauté onion and garlic until golden, about 5 minutes, and then add oregano, cumin, salt, and pepper. Add ají panca.

4. Add chicken stock, sweet wine, ground peanut butter cookies, the reserved meats, and finally, the drained papa seca. Turn the heat to low, cover with a lid, and cook for 50–60 minutes, adding more boiling stock or water if the mixture looks dry.

5. When the papa seca is tender (you know it when you gently press a piece of potato with the spoon and it feels soft), add salt to taste, grated chocolate, and ground peanuts. Stir until incorporated. Turn off the heat and let rest for at least 30 minutes before serving to let the flavors meld. This is a flavorful stew that gets better when reheated.

Adobo

This is a classic dish whose name comes from the spicy sauce in which the pork is marinated and cooked. There are celebrated versions in Arequipa, Cusco, Tacna, Ayacucho, and other regions of Peru.

INGREDIENTS | SERVES 10

1 cup red wine vinegar

½ cup water

3 tablespoons ají panca paste

5 garlic cloves, chopped

1 teaspoon ground cumin

1 teaspoon ground turmeric

Salt to taste

Pepper to taste

1 teaspoon dried oregano

2 pounds pork shoulder, cut in medium-sized pieces

½ cup vegetable oil

3 sweet potatoes, cooked, peeled, and sliced

8 cups Basic Peruvian Rice (see Chapter 8)

1. In a nonmetallic bowl, combine vinegar, ½ cup water, ají panca, chopped garlic, cumin, turmeric, salt, pepper, and oregano. Add pork meat, turning to cover each piece. Cover and refrigerate for at least 12 hours.

2. Drain the pork, reserving the marinade. Heat the oil in a saucepan over medium heat; add and sear the pork, about 3 minutes per side. Incorporate the reserved marinade, put the lid on, turn the heat to low, and simmer until the pork is tender, about 45 minutes. Add more water if the mixture looks dry; this dish should be saucy.

3. Serve with cooked sweet potatoes and Basic Peruvian Rice.

Cau Cau

The original recipe for this dish uses tripe, but there are versions with chicken and with seafood.

INGREDIENTS | SERVES 4

1 pound tripe

2 sprigs hierbabuena (or spearmint)

2 tablespoons milk

½ cup vegetable oil

1 onion, chopped

2 garlic cloves, chopped

2 tablespoons ají amarillo paste

½ teaspoon ground cumin

1 teaspoon ground turmeric

Salt to taste

Pepper to taste

4 tablespoons chopped hierbabuena, divided

1 pound potatoes, peeled, diced, and cooked

1 cup green peas (optional)

4 cups Basic Peruvian Rice (see Chapter 8)

1. Wash the tripe well and simmer in a saucepan over medium heat with enough water to cover (more than 4 cups), hierbabuena, and milk. When very tender, about 45 minutes, drain, reserving the cooking water, and cut into 1-inch dice.

2. Heat the oil in a saucepan over medium heat and sauté the onion and garlic until lightly golden (about 10 minutes). Add ají amarillo, cumin, turmeric, salt, and pepper. Cook for 5 minutes; then add the tripe and 4 cups of the cooking liquid and simmer for 15 minutes. Incorporate half the chopped hierbabuena.

3. Add potatoes and green peas (if using) and continue cooking until tender, about 10 minutes. Taste for seasoning, sprinkle with remaining hierbabuena, and serve with rice.

Hierbabuena

The flavor of Cau Cau is complemented by the minty hint of hierbabuena, an aromatic herb used in savory dishes, including soups. If you can't find it anywhere, substitute for it with spearmint. In natural medicine, it is used as a relaxing tea, and it soothes and alleviates cramps and nausea.

Goat Seco

Piura, with its hot weather and good food, has this dish as one of its favorites.
They serve it with green tamales, as if they were bread.

INGREDIENTS | SERVES 8

6 pounds baby goat

Salt to taste

Pepper to taste

1 teaspoon ground cumin

4 garlic cloves, chopped

½ cup red wine vinegar

4 tablespoons vegetable oil

1 cup onion, chopped

1 red bell pepper, diced

4 fresh ají amarillo, seeded and sliced

½ cup peeled, seeded, and chopped tomato

2 cups goat stock, or chicken stock

4 scallions (green part), sliced

1 cilantro sprig, chopped

8 cups Basic Peruvian Rice (see Chapter 8)

1 recipe Tamalitos Verdes (see Chapter 6)

1. Cut the goat into 6 pieces. Add salt, pepper, and cumin. Put in nonmetallic bowl with garlic and vinegar. Marinate for 1 hour in the refrigerator.

2. Heat the oil in a saucepan over medium heat. Sauté onion, bell pepper, and ají amarillo for 5 minutes. Add tomato.

3. Drain the goat, reserving the marinade. Add goat to the saucepan and stir to cover every piece with the onion mixture. Add the reserved marinade and the stock, turn down the heat to low, put the lid on, and simmer for 45 minutes, or until the goat meat is very tender. Taste for seasoning.

4. Finally, add scallions and cilantro. Serve with rice and green tamalitos.

Ají Amarillo

Ají amarillo (yellow chili) is extensively used in Peruvian cooking. It has different names besides ají amarillo, like ají verde (green chili) and ají escabeche. The funny part is that it is not yellow or green, but orange. It gives a subtle fragrance to the dishes, a lovely color, and a nice kick.

CHAPTER 15

Desserts

Suspiro Limeño

*The poet José Galvez gave this dessert its name (which means "Lima girl's sigh")
because of its sweetness and softness. For delicious variations, you can flavor it with
manjarblanco or by adding 1 cup fresh cherimoya or lúcuma pulp.*

INGREDIENTS | SERVES 6

2 (12-ounce) cans evaporated milk

1 (14-ounce) can sweetened condensed milk

5 egg yolks

1 cup sugar

¼ cup Port wine

2 tablespoons water

3 egg whites

2 teaspoons ground cinnamon

A Little Goes a Long Way

This is a very sweet dessert and it is wise to serve small portions. If you want to enjoy Suspiro Limeño with a dessert wine, it is better to choose something stronger like Pisco to cut the sweetness and richness of this dessert.

1. In a heavy saucepan, cook the evaporated milk and the sweetened condensed milk over low heat, stirring constantly with a wooden spoon until the mixture thickens and turns a pretty caramel color, or until you can see the bottom of the saucepan, about 45 minutes. Turn off the heat.

2. Put the egg yolks in a bowl and beat with a wire whisk. Add 4 tablespoons of the hot milk mixture and keep beating for a few seconds. Pour everything back in the saucepan, mix carefully, and cool.

3. To make the Italian meringue: In another saucepan, mix the sugar, the Port wine, and 2 tablespoons water, stirring to dissolve the sugar. Bring to a boil over high heat for 6 minutes without stirring. The syrup is ready when it forms a caramel thread when dropped from a spoon, or reaches 123°F on a candy thermometer.

4. Meanwhile, beat the egg whites with an electric mixer at high speed until soft peaks form (when you lift one of the beaters and it has a soft cloud of meringue foam around it). Add the hot syrup in a thin stream while beating the meringue. Continue beating until cool.

5. To serve: Pour about ¼ cup of the caramel mixture, cooled to room temperature, into martini or any other nice glasses. Put the meringue in a pastry bag and crown the glasses with a nice, tall dollop of meringue. Sprinkle with cinnamon and refrigerate until serving time.

Simple Syrup

If you love to bake, you'll end up using this syrup time and time again. Make extra to keep on hand!

INGREDIENTS | YIELDS 1½ CUPS

1 cup sugar
1 cup water

Combine sugar and water in a saucepan. Bring to a boil over high heat, stirring until dissolved. Lower heat to low and simmer for 5 minutes. Cool and store in a jar in the refrigerator for up to a month.

Arroz Zambito

This is a dark and fragrant rice pudding studded with dried fruits and spices. The earthy sweetness of the chancaca is very unusual.

INGREDIENTS | SERVES 6–8

4 cups milk
2 cups water
4 cloves
2 cinnamon sticks
½ teaspoon aniseed
¼ teaspoon salt
1 cup long-grain rice
2 pieces chancaca, chopped
½ cup grated dried coconut
½ cup raisins
½ cup chopped walnuts
1 tablespoon unsalted butter
1 teaspoon vanilla essence

1. In a heavy saucepan, put milk, 2 cups water, cloves, cinnamon sticks, aniseed, salt, and rice. Bring to a boil over high heat, turn the heat to medium-low, and continue cooking until the rice is al dente, about 20 minutes. Turn the heat to low.

2. Add the chancaca, coconut, and raisins. Continue cooking, stirring every few minutes until the chancaca melts, the rice is very soft, and the texture of the dessert is creamy, about 40 minutes.

3. Turn off the heat; add walnuts, butter, and vanilla. Discard the cinnamon sticks and the cloves. Serve in nice glasses or in ramekins at room temperature.

About Chancaca

This is a kind of raw sugar with a flavor between brown sugar and molasses. Because it is artisanal, the same batch has lighter and darker colors. You can replace it with molasses or dark brown sugar.

Arroz con Leche (Rice Pudding)

This is basic comfort food loved by many people around the world. Regular long-grain rice is good for this dessert, but Arborio rice gives it a wonderful creaminess.

INGREDIENTS | SERVES 8

4 cups whole milk
2 cinnamon sticks
1 cup Arborio rice
¼ teaspoon salt
2 cups evaporated milk
1 cup water
¾ cup sugar
Peel of 1 lemon
1 teaspoon vanilla essence
2 tablespoons unsalted butter
2 teaspoons ground cinnamon

1. In a heavy saucepan, combine the milk with cinnamon sticks, rice, and salt. Bring to a boil over high heat; then lower the heat to medium-low and cook uncovered, stirring every few minutes and taking care that the milk does not boil over.

2. When the rice is tender (about 25 minutes), add the evaporated milk, water, sugar, and lemon peel. Continue cooking over low heat, stirring every now and then with a wooden spoon until it is creamy, about 30 minutes. Do not let it dry too much, because the pudding will become thicker as it cools and the rice absorbs the liquid.

3. Remove from the heat and discard the lemon peel and the cinnamon sticks. Add vanilla essence and butter. Cool to room temperature.

4. Pour the pudding into ramekins, glasses, or nice containers. Dust with ground cinnamon and serve. Can be refrigerated and served cold, but most people like it at room temperature or lukewarm, especially in the winter.

Pionono (Manjarblanco Jelly Roll)

*Brazo Gitano, Jelly Roll, Arrollado: These are some other names for Pionono,
a basic sponge cake filled with manjarblanco, marmalade, or pastry cream.*

INGREDIENTS | SERVES 8

5 eggs
6 tablespoons granulated sugar, divided
5 tablespoons self-rising flour
1 teaspoon vanilla essence
¼ teaspoon salt
1 teaspoon grated lemon zest
2 cups Manjarblanco (see Chapter 16)
¼ cup confectioners' sugar
Whipped cream (optional)
1 cup berries (optional)

Changing Proportions

This is a little baking secret for you: To change the size of this cake, change the quantities of the basic ingredients—eggs, sugar, and flour—in the same proportion. Do you want it smaller? 4-4-4. Larger? 7-7-7.

1. Preheat the oven to 350°F. Grease a 10" × 13" × 1" baking sheet, cover with parchment paper, and grease again.

2. In a mixer (make sure the bowl is completely clean and dry), beat the eggs at high speed until they are thick and foamy, about 8 minutes. Gradually add 5 tablespoons sugar, beating well after each addition. Continue beating 8 more minutes. The egg mixture should triple in volume, and will be very thick. Using a spatula, fold in the flour. Add vanilla, salt, and lemon zest. Turn off the mixer.

3. Pour the batter and spread evenly on the baking sheet and bake for 12 minutes. To check for doneness, touch the cake with your fingertips; if the dough is a little sticky, continue baking 2 more minutes. Take out of the oven.

4. Have a clean kitchen cloth ready on the counter, sprinkled with the extra tablespoon of granulated sugar. Turn the cake upside down over the cloth, remove the tray and the parchment, and with the help of the cloth, roll the cake in one direction. Let rest on a cooling rack, undisturbed until cool.

5. After a couple of hours, unroll the cake carefully, cut the edges with a sharp knife so that they look smooth, spread with Manjarblanco, and roll again, this time without the cloth. Transfer to a plate and sprinkle confectioners' sugar on top.

6. To serve, cut in thick slices. If desired, you can garnish the cake with whipped cream and berries.

Tres Leches Cake

This delicious dessert is common in many countries. Some say that it is from Nicaragua, but every Latin American country claims it as its own. Peru is no exception, and this cake has become a lovely staple in every household and in many restaurants and bakeries.

INGREDIENTS | SERVES 12

2 cups all-purpose flour

3 teaspoons baking powder

6 eggs

1½ cups sugar

½ cup milk

2 (14-ounce) cans sweetened condensed milk

2 (12-ounce) cans evaporated milk

2 cups heavy cream, divided

1 teaspoon vanilla essence

Whipped cream

Variations on This Dessert

With this basic recipe, you can make several variations of Tres Leches Cake. Substitute heavy cream with coconut cream in the milk mixture; flavor the milks with coffee or chocolate; or blend mango, pineapple, or lúcuma into them and skip the heavy cream. The possibilities are endless. Be creative and have fun!

1. Preheat the oven to 350°F. Sift the flour together with the baking powder.

2. Beat eggs at high speed for about 8 minutes. They have to grow at least 3 times in volume. Gradually add the sugar and continue beating for 3 minutes until the sugar is incorporated and the mixture looks glossy.

3. Turn off the mixer. Using a spatula, fold one-third of the flour into the egg mixture, then one-third of the milk (it should be at room temperature, not cold), and then fold in the next third of flour, followed by another third of the milk. The folding should be very gentle in order to keep the air in the beaten eggs. Repeat until milk and flour are combined.

4. Transfer the cake batter to a rectangular 15" × 10" × 2" baking pan and bake for 30 minutes.

5. While the cake is in the oven, use a large bowl or pitcher to combine the condensed milk, evaporated milk, and cream with the vanilla. Mix well and refrigerate.

6. Turn off the oven and take out the cake. Prick it everywhere with a knife or a toothpick. Do this as soon as it comes out of the oven so it is still hot. Pour the refrigerated milk mixture over the cake immediately, making sure you do this evenly and cover every part of the cake.

7. Let cool and then refrigerate to serve it cold. It keeps well in the refrigerator for several days, even better if covered with a lid or plastic film.

8. Serve each portion of Tres Leches Cake with a dollop of whipped cream. You can serve with meringue or grated chocolate instead, or just eat it as is. Some colorful fruits are a nice garnish.

Sweet Corn Cake

Corn goes well in both savory and sweet dishes. This simple cake brings out the best of its sweet side.

INGREDIENTS | SERVES 8

½ cup unsalted butter, at room temperature

1 cup plus 2 tablespoons sugar

8 egg yolks, divided

2 cups cream cheese

3 cups white corn kernels

3 egg whites

2 tablespoons all-purpose flour

2 teaspoons baking powder

1 cup cream

½ cup milk

1 teaspoon vanilla

Ice cream

1. Preheat the oven to 350°F. In the mixer, beat the butter and gradually add 1 cup sugar at high speed, until light and fluffy. Add 5 egg yolks, one by one. Add the cream cheese and continue beating for 5 minutes.

2. Process the corn in a food processor until very smooth. Add to the butter mixture and beat for 1 more minute.

3. In another bowl, beat the egg whites until stiff, but not dry, and fold into the corn mixture. Add the flour with the baking powder. Pour into 2 (8-inch) round baking pans lined with parchment paper. Place the pans over a larger pan with an inch of water and bake in this water bath for 40 minutes. Take out of the oven and cool.

4. To make the custard: In a small saucepan, heat cream and milk over medium heat. In a small bowl, beat 3 egg yolks and 2 tablespoons sugar with a wire whisk, until pale and light, about 4 minutes. Add the hot cream mixture to the beaten egg yolks.

5. Strain and transfer the mixture to the saucepan and cook over very low heat, stirring constantly with a spatula or a wooden spoon, until the cream is slightly thick, about 5 minutes. Do not let it boil because it curdles. Add the vanilla, turn off the heat, strain into another bowl inside a larger bowl filled with water and ice to stop the cooking, and cool.

6. Serve slices of the corn pudding with custard or ice cream, or both.

Chocolate Turrón

This dessert is rich, crunchy, and intensely flavored: exactly how Peruvians love their sweets!

INGREDIENTS | SERVES 6

½ cup unsalted butter

1½ cups sugar

3 eggs, separated into yolks and whites

1 cup self-rising flour

½ cup unsweetened cocoa powder

1 teaspoon vanilla essence

2½ cups chopped pecans, divided

2 cups Chocolate Fudge (see recipe in this chapter)

1. Preheat the oven to 350°F. In the mixer, beat butter and sugar at high speed until light and fluffy; add egg yolks, one at a time. Turn off the mixer, sift the flour and cocoa, and add to the butter, mixing carefully with a rubber spatula.

2. In another bowl, beat egg whites until stiff. Fold into the batter, along with the vanilla essence and 1½ cups pecans.

3. Pour into 2 greased and floured 8½" × 4½" loaf pans and bake for 30 minutes. Take out of the oven and put on a cooling rack to cool. Cover with fudge and garnish with 1 cup chopped pecans. Serve.

Large Alfajor

Every Peruvian cook has the best recipe for alfajores, or so they think.
Some of them are crispy and some are tender and crumbly, like this one.
Truth is, this delightful cookie is a pleasure to have, whatever form it takes.

INGREDIENTS | SERVES 6

1 pound all-purpose flour
1½ cups margarine, at room temperature
4 tablespoons milk
2 cups Manjarblanco (see Chapter 16)
1 cup pineapple marmalade
Confectioners' sugar, for decoration

1. Sift the flour on a kitchen counter and make a well in the center. Add margarine and milk, working with a fork to incorporate all the ingredients. Knead lightly with your hands. When dough is formed, wrap in plastic film or in a plastic bag and refrigerate overnight.

2. Preheat the oven to 350°F. Drop a little water on a kitchen counter or table; place a sheet of waxed paper on it and over this, put one-third of the dough. Roll with a rolling pin to form a big circle. Cut a big, round cookie using a plate as a guide. With the help of the waxed paper, transfer the cookie to a greased baking tray. Prick it several times with a fork and bake for 15 minutes or until lightly golden. Repeat with the rest of the dough, until you have 3 or more large cookies. Cool on cooling racks.

3. Place one cookie on a plate, spread with Manjarblanco, cover with another cookie, and spread pineapple marmalade. Keep going like this. Finish with a cookie and sprinkle heavily with confectioners' sugar. Serve.

Champuz

*Traditionally from Lima, this is a comforting dessert, thick and full of fruits and hominy.
Serve it hot, especially during the winter.*

INGREDIENTS | SERVES 6

1 cup dried mote (hominy)

8 cups water

2 cinnamon sticks

4 cloves

2 cups chopped pineapple

2 quinces, peeled and chopped

1½ cups sugar

1 cup yellow cornmeal

1 guanábana (soursop)

Ground cinnamon, to decorate

Mote

This is the Peruvian name for hominy, used in many dishes in the Andes. It is corn that has been boiled with lime powder, peeled, and then dried.

1. Soak the hominy in plenty of water for 24 hours or more, changing the water 3 times.

2. In a heavy saucepan, put 8 cups water, cinnamon sticks, cloves, pineapple, quinces, and sugar. Bring to a boil over high heat, turn the heat to medium, and cook for 25 minutes. Drain the hominy and add it to the mixture. Cook for 20 minutes more and then turn the heat to low.

3. Add the yellow cornmeal, dissolved in ¾ cup cold water, and cook, stirring with a wooden spoon, until thick and creamy, about 15 minutes. Add the soursop, peeled and cut in medium-sized pieces, bring to a boil over high heat, and turn off the heat.

4. Serve hot in tall glasses, sprinkled with ground cinnamon.

Huevo Chimbo

This popular dessert, originally from Ancash where it is known as Tajadón, needs a long beating of the egg yolks, but the hard work is worth it.

INGREDIENTS | SERVES 8

2 cups sugar

1 cup water

1 cinnamon stick

Peel of 1 orange

¼ cup Pisco

10 egg yolks

1 egg

2 tablespoons all-purpose flour

1 teaspoon baking powder

½ cup raisins

½ cup almonds

About Pisco

Pisco is a grape distillate produced in the south of Lima. It is prepared with grapes, but not the ones that are used for wine-making (this is what makes this brandy so special). Seventeen pounds of grapes are necessary to create one bottle of Pisco.

1. To make the syrup, put sugar, water, cinnamon stick, and orange peel in a saucepan over high heat. Bring to a boil, turn the heat to medium, and cook for 10 minutes. Turn off the heat. Discard the orange peel and add Pisco. Cool.

2. Preheat the oven to 350°F. In a standing mixer, beat egg yolks and whole egg at high speed until tripled in volume. Turn off the mixer and fold in the flour and baking powder. Pour into a greased 8" × 8" baking pan and bake for 20 minutes.

3. Take out of the oven and while hot, cut into squares. Drench with the cool syrup and garnish with raisins and almonds. Serve very cold.

Prune Bavarois

What better way to finish a meal than with this light and airy dessert? It has the right amount of sweetness, and the prunes add a wonderfully distinct flavor.

INGREDIENTS | SERVES 6

6 eggs, separated into whites and yolks

1 cup sugar

1 cup chopped soft prunes

2½ tablespoons unflavored gelatin

⅓ cup cold water

½ (14-ounce) can sweetened condensed milk

1 (12-ounce) can evaporated milk

1 teaspoon vanilla essence

Whole prunes for garnish

Baked Bavarois

To bake this dessert, omit the unflavored gelatin, line a tube pan with caramel (the way you do with Crema Volteada, also in this chapter), and bake the bavarois for 50 minutes at 350°F. Let cool in the refrigerator up to 1 day. Serve with custard.

1. In the bowl of a mixer, beat the egg whites at high speed until soft peaks form. Gradually add the sugar, beating continuously. When the sugar is fully incorporated, turn off the mixer and using a spatula, fold the chopped prunes into the meringue.

2. In a small saucepan, combine gelatin and ⅓ cup cold water. Let stand 5 minutes and then put over low heat, stirring to dissolve the gelatin. Turn off the heat. Cool. Fold into the meringue and pour into an oiled 10-inch tube pan. Refrigerate until set.

3. To make the custard, in a saucepan, cook condensed milk and evaporated milk over medium-high heat until slightly thick, about 20 minutes. Turn the heat down to low. Whisk the egg yolks, add 4 spoonfuls of the hot milk mixture, combine, and strain over the hot milk. Continue cooking for 2 minutes and then turn off the heat. Add vanilla essence and cool in the refrigerator for several hours.

4. Unmold the bavarois by running a knife around the edges of the pan. Turn upside down on a plate.

5. To serve, slice the bavarois, garnish each slice with a prune, and serve on plates with some custard.

Crema Volteada (Flan)

This is the Peruvian name for Flan, which is one of the most loved desserts in the country. There is no café or family restaurant where Crema Volteada is not on the menu, and no house where it is not prepared on a regular basis.

INGREDIENTS | SERVES 8

1½ cups sugar

2 (14-ounce) cans sweetened condensed milk

2 (12-ounce) cans evaporated milk

1 cup water

6 eggs

2 teaspoons vanilla essence

1. Preheat the oven to 350°F.

2. For the caramel: In a saucepan, heat the sugar over medium-high heat, stirring until it melts and forms a liquid caramel, about 15 minutes. It should have a beautiful golden color, but not too dark because the caramel will become bitter. Pour into a 10-inch round baking pan, covering the bottom and sides of the pan with the caramel. You have to move quickly to complete this, but be very careful when working with hot caramel because you can burn yourself easily. Let cool.

3. In a blender, process condensed and evaporated milks, 1 cup water, eggs, and vanilla essence. Pour into the baking pan and place the baking pan over a larger pan filled with an inch of hot water. Bake for 1 hour. Take out of the oven, put the pan with the flan on a cooling rack, and let cool. Refrigerate for several hours, as it is easier to unmold when very cold.

4. To unmold, run a knife around the edge of the pan and turn upside down over a bigger plate. The caramel will form a pool of sauce on the plate. Serve this sauce over the dessert. Keep refrigerated.

Carob Crème Brûlée

This is a French dessert that has been Peruvian-ized by the addition of algarrobina, or carob. The resulting crème is an absolute delight.

INGREDIENTS | SERVES 4

2 cups heavy cream

3 tablespoons algarrobina (carob syrup)

1 cup sugar, divided

5 egg yolks

1 teaspoon vanilla

Algarrobina or Carob

In the northern part of Peru, there are thousands of algarrobo trees that produce a delicious syrup called algarrobina. It is widely known as carob in other countries, and is used in desserts, drinks, some savory dishes, and as a diet supplement to give you energy.

1. Preheat the oven to 300°F. In a saucepan, heat the cream with the carob syrup over medium heat for 7 minutes. Do not let it boil.

2. Meanwhile, beat ¼ cup sugar, egg yolks, and vanilla until pale and thick, about 5 minutes. Add the hot cream and carob mixture in a thin stream, stirring all the time.

3. Put into small ramekins and place them in a larger pan filled with an inch of hot water. Bake for 35–40 minutes. They are ready when they are set, but quiver slightly in the center when shaken. The water bath should not boil at any time; if this happens, add more tepid water to the baking pan.

4. Take out of the oven and cool to room temperature. Transfer to the refrigerator. Prior to serving, sprinkle each ramekin with a generous amount of sugar and, using a blowtorch or under the broiler, melt the sugar until golden. Serve cold.

Leche Asada

Every bakery that sells traditional desserts has this dessert. Leche Asada is lighter that flan, less sweet, and has a thin crust on top. Even though it is easy to make, it is rarely baked at home.

INGREDIENTS | SERVES 6

3 cups whole milk

4 egg yolks

4 eggs

1 cup sugar

1 teaspoon vanilla essence

1. Preheat the oven to 300°F. Process all the ingredients in a blender, strain, and pour into 6 ramekins. Place the ramekins in a large pan filled with an inch of hot water. Bake for 1 hour. Take out of the oven, cool, and refrigerate.

2. Do not unmold. Serve this dessert in the ramekins.

Churros

Peru has a deep love for these fritters, which are originally from Spain. Buy them plain or filled with Manjarblanco, pastry cream, or fudge, but they are even more enjoyable when accompanied by a thick and steamy cup of hot chocolate, or with chocolate sauce to dunk them in.

INGREDIENTS | SERVES 6

1 cup water

1 cup unsalted butter

¼ teaspoon salt

½ cup sugar, divided

1½ cups all-purpose flour

4 eggs

3 cups vegetable oil

3 cups Chocolate Sauce (see recipe in this chapter)

1. In saucepan, put water, butter, salt, and ¼ cup sugar. Bring to a boil over high heat. Turn off the heat and add the flour, stirring until all of it is incorporated. Continue to cook over low heat, stirring constantly with a wooden spoon, for 5 minutes. Turn off the heat.

2. Add the eggs, one by one, stirring continuously. When the batter is ready, put it in a pastry bag with a rosette tip.

3. In another saucepan, heat the oil over medium-high heat. With the help of the pastry bag, form the churros and fry in the hot oil until golden, about 3 minutes. While hot, roll over remaining sugar and serve with a cup of Chocolate Sauce to dip them in.

Cherimoya Meringue

Crispy layers of meringue combine perfectly with the fluffy whipped cream and fresh cherimoya pieces. This local fruit is so sweet, and the texture of this combination so appealing, that this dessert has been a favorite for many years.

INGREDIENTS | SERVES 6–8

1 cup egg whites

2 cups sugar, divided

3 cups cold heavy cream

2 ripe cherimoyas

1 cup Chocolate Sauce (see recipe in this chapter)

Working with Cherimoyas

The pulp of cherimoyas is almost white in color, but oxidizes quickly and turns an unappealing brown color, especially if you use a metal knife to cut it. You have two choices: drizzle the fruit with a few drops of lemon juice, or use a plastic knife to peel and cut the cherimoya. The seeds are not edible, so take them out with your clean hands and discard.

1. Preheat the oven to its lowest temperature (200°F). In a very clean mixer bowl, beat the egg whites until stiff, adding 1½ cups sugar, spoonful by spoonful until well incorporated. Put in a pastry bag with a round piping tip. Pipe three 9-inch-wide circles on a baking sheet covered with parchment paper. Bake for 2 hours. Turn off the oven and leave the meringue in the oven several hours or overnight with the door ajar.

2. When ready to assemble the merengado, whip the cold heavy cream with ½ cup sugar, until thick, about 4 minutes. Do not overbeat or you will have butter instead of whipped cream.

3. Peel the cherimoyas, take out the seeds, and cut into small pieces, about ½-inch thick. Combine with ⅔ the whipped cream.

4. To assemble the dessert, put one meringue on a large plate. Spread half of the cream mixture on top. Cover with the other meringue, and repeat the layers. Finish with meringue. You can freeze the merengado for a few hours, or keep it refrigerated to serve very cold.

5. To serve, cover with more whipped cream and drizzle with Chocolate Sauce.

Lúcuma Ice Cream

Serve this ice cream with chocolate sauce or as a side to many cakes and desserts. Substitute 2 pounds cherimoya for a completely different, but equally tasty, flavor.

INGREDIENTS | SERVES 4

1½ pounds lúcuma pulp

1 (14–ounce) can sweetened condensed milk

1 cup heavy cream

½ cup sugar

1 cup Chocolate Sauce (see recipe in this chapter)

Buying Lúcumas

Choose lúcumas that are soft to the touch, and if their peels are tearing apart and show some of the orange pulp, buy them immediately and use them within the same day. These fruits are not easy to find in the United States; sometimes you can spot them in the freezer section of Latin American grocery stores. If you find lúcuma flour, substitute as follows: Combine 4 tablespoons lúcuma flour with 8 tablespoons water and let rest for 2 hours. Use as indicated in the recipe.

1. Peel the lúcumas; take out the bright seeds and discard them. Process the pulp in the food processor with the sweetened condensed milk.

2. In the mixer, whip the heavy cream and the sugar at high speed until thickened. Add to the lúcuma mixture, stir well, and pour in a bowl or a glass baking dish. Freeze for at least 7 hours or overnight. Transfer to the refrigerator 15 minutes prior to serving time to soften it a little bit. Serve cold with Chocolate Sauce.

Mazamorra Morada

This is a simple and homey dessert, but it has a very unusual color, and the complexity of flavors will surprise you.

INGREDIENTS | SERVES 8

3 pounds maíz morado (purple corn)

3 cloves

3 cinnamon sticks

½ pineapple, peeled and chopped (save the peel)

1 Granny Smith apple, peeled, cored, and chopped

1 quince, chopped

8 cups water

½ cup prunes

½ cup dried apricots

1 cup sugar

6 tablespoons sweet potato starch

Juice of 1 lime

Ground cinnamon, for decoration

The Real Thickener

This dessert owes its silky texture to a unique thickener: sweet potato starch. Potato starch is a fine substitute; just be aware that potato flour is not the same thing, and though it is still a thickener, it has a very strong potato flavor and aroma that you do not want in your dessert. Cornstarch is not the best option, but works just fine if you do not have the real thing.

1. Break the corn in several pieces. Put in a heavy saucepan along with the cloves, cinnamon sticks, pineapple peels, apple cores and peels, quince, and 8 cups water. Bring to a boil over high heat and cook for 15 minutes. Turn the heat to medium and cook partially covered for 1 hour, or until reduced to 6 cups of purple water. Strain, reserving the liquid and discarding the solids. (If you add sugar and lime juice to this water, it is called chicha morada.)

2. In the same saucepan, put the purple water, 1 cup chopped pineapple, the chopped apple, prunes, dried apricots, and sugar. Cook for 20 minutes over medium heat to soften the fruits.

3. In a bowl, dissolve the sweet potato starch in ½ cup purple corn liquid and add to the saucepan, stirring constantly. Cook for 5 more minutes or until thick. Turn off the heat and add the lime juice. Cool to room temperature.

4. Serve in ramekins or glasses, sprinkled with ground cinnamon.

Ranfañote

This is a dessert from colonial times that has, somehow, almost been forgotten. Luckily, new pastry chefs are bringing back Peruvian traditional recipes and trying to revive this rustic sweet.

INGREDIENTS | SERVES 6

8 ounces chancaca
3 cloves
1 teaspoon aniseed
1 cinnamon stick
4 allspice
1 piece orange peel
2½ cups sugar
2½ cups water
1 cup pecans
1 cup Brazil nuts
1 cup dark raisins
1½ cups finely diced coconut meat
1 cup stale bread
1 tablespoon unsalted butter
1 cup cubed queso fresco

Do You Have Stale Bread?

If the answer is no, making bread stale is really easy. Just leave the bread on the kitchen counter at room temperature for a couple of days. It will be dry and . . . stale. Ready for this dessert!

1. To make the syrup: Chop or grate the chancaca and put in a saucepan with cloves, aniseed, cinnamon stick, allspice, orange peel, sugar, and 2½ cups water. Boil over medium-high heat for 30 minutes to thicken the syrup. Strain and discard the spices and orange peel. (If you drop a teaspoonful of syrup in a glass of cold water, it should form a soft ball.) Reserve. You can replace chancaca with molasses syrup or dark brown sugar.

2. Chop the pecans and the Brazil nuts into small squares. Toast in a frying pan until fragrant, about 4 minutes over medium-low heat. Cut the raisins in half. Peel the coconut and cut into small squares.

3. Cut the bread into small cubes and fry in the butter over medium heat until the bread is golden, about 3 minutes.

4. Add the pecans, Brazil nuts, raisins, and coconut to a saucepan with the syrup. Cook over medium-low heat for 5 minutes. Finally, add the fried bread and the cubed cheese. Stir and turn off the heat. Serve in glasses or dessert bowls at room temperature.

Picarones

Have you ever eaten buñuelos or beignets? Picarones are similar to these, but quite different at the same time. They are eaten hot from the frying pan, with bare hands and plenty of napkins on the side.

INGREDIENTS | SERVES 12

1 pound sweet potatoes
1 pound pumpkin
2 teaspoons aniseed
1 tablespoon sugar
1¾ tablespoons active dry yeast
1 pound all-purpose flour
4 cups vegetable oil
4 cups Chancaca Syrup (see sidebar)

Chancaca Syrup Mini Recipe

The chancaca syrup is made in advance because it takes a long time to prepare, and it needs to be at room temperature to drizzle over the picarones. Chop 2 chancaca pieces and put in a heavy saucepan with 2 cinnamon sticks, 6 cloves, 1 fig leaf, and 2 star anise. Add pineapple peels or a whole orange, peel and all, for extra flavor. Cover with water and cook over medium heat until the chancaca is dissolved and forms a thick syrup. Drain, discarding the solids, cool, and put in a jar to have it ready to pour over picarones. You can substitute the chancaca with molasses syrup or dark brown sugar.

1. Peel the sweet potatoes and cut into medium-sized squares. Peel and chop the pumpkin. Put sweet potatoes and pumpkin in a heavy saucepan with the aniseed, add water to cover, and cook over medium-high heat until soft, about 25 minutes. Drain, reserving the water, and process in the food processor, or mash the sweet potatoes and pumpkin to form a soft purée.

2. Cool the water to lukewarm in a bowl. In another bowl, put 1 cup cooking water and the sugar; add the active dry yeast, stirring until dissolved. Cover and let rest for 10 minutes in a warm place, until it forms a sponge.

3. Put the potato and pumpkin purée in a large bowl. Add the activated yeast mixture. Add the flour and, mixing with your hands, add ½ cup of the cooking water, until the dough is no longer sticky and feels soft and silky. Cover with a kitchen towel and let rest in a warm place, until double or triple in volume, at least 2 hours.

4. When the dough is ready, heat oil in a big saucepan over high heat to deep-fry the picarones.

5. This is a fundamental step and requires skill and training. With practice, you will get there. Have a bowl with cold water nearby. With one wet hand, take a portion of dough and quickly try to make a ring shape with your thumb while you put it in the hot oil. Fry for 2 minutes before flipping. With a long wooden stick, turn the picarones around (you can use a kitchen fork to do this, too). Remove from oil, drain on paper towels, and serve drenched with syrup.

Chocolate Cake

This is the essential chocolate cake. It's dark, rich, dense, moist, and incredibly sweet.
Serve thin slices with large glasses of cold milk.

INGREDIENTS | SERVES 10–12

3 cups self-rising flour

8 tablespoons unsweetened cocoa powder

1 teaspoon instant coffee

1 teaspoon salt

2½ teaspoons baking soda

1 cup vegetable oil

2 cups milk

1 tablespoon vinegar

2 teaspoons vanilla essence, divided

3 eggs

2½ cups sugar, divided

1 cup water

1 recipe Chocolate Fudge (see recipe in this chapter)

½ cup toasted almonds (optional)

1. Grease a 10-inch tube baking pan and cover the bottom with parchment paper. Preheat oven to 350°F.

2. In a big bowl, sift flour, cocoa, coffee, salt, and baking soda. Make a well in the center and add oil, milk, vinegar, 1 teaspoon vanilla, eggs, and 2 cups sugar. Mix with a spatula or wooden spoon. Pour in the prepared baking pan and bake for 1 hour. Let cool.

3. To make the syrup, put remaining sugar and 1 cup water in a small saucepan. Bring to a boil over high heat until sugar dissolves. Add remaining vanilla essence, remove from heat, and cool.

4. To assemble the cake, cut the cake into three layers. Drizzle every layer with 3 tablespoons syrup. Spread the fudge on the first layer and cover with another cake layer. Repeat. Cover the cake with more fudge and sprinkle with toasted almonds.

Chocolate Fudge

Have all the ingredients of this recipe ready before you start the dessert.
Don't refrigerate when you are done or the fudge will be too thick to spread.

INGREDIENTS | YIELDS 2½ CUPS

½ cup unsweetened cocoa powder
3 tablespoons hot water
1 (12-ounce) can evaporated milk
1 (14-ounce) can sweetened condensed milk
2 tablespoons unsalted butter

1. Stir cocoa in 3 tablespoons hot water until dissolved.

2. In a saucepan, cook evaporated milk, condensed milk, and cocoa over medium-low heat, stirring frequently, until the mixture thickens and you can barely see the bottom of the pan, about 40 minutes. Turn off the heat and add the butter. If the fudge is too thick, add a little whole milk to thin it. To serve, place the fudge in a saucer and use it to fill and frost cakes or cupcakes, or serve over ice cream.

Chocolate Sauce

Many desserts taste better with a chocolate sauce, like ice creams, churros, cakes, bavarois, and more!

INGREDIENTS | YIELDS 2 CUPS

1 cup sugar
¼ cup water
1½ (12-ounce) cans evaporated milk
⅓ cup unsweetened cocoa powder
3 tablespoons hot water
⅓ cup unsalted butter

1. In a saucepan, cook the sugar with ¼ cup water over high heat, stir to dissolve the sugar, and boil uninterrupted until the syrup turns lightly golden, about 15 minutes. Turn the heat to low.

2. Add evaporated milk and cocoa powder dissolved in 3 tablespoons hot water. Stir constantly until thick. You don't need to see the bottom of the pan, unless you want to make fudge (this sauce should be thinner than fudge). Turn off the heat and add the butter. Cool to room temperature and serve.

CHAPTER 16

Sweet Bites

Manjarblanco (Peruvian Dulce de Leche)

Many Peruvian sweets and desserts have manjarblanco as one of their ingredients. There are several recipes for this creamy caramel, but modern cooks adore the quick method using canned milks.

INGREDIENTS | YIELDS 2 CUPS

1 (14-ounce) can sweetened condensed milk

1 (12-ounce) can evaporated milk

Dulce de Leche or Manjarblanco

Dulce de leche, as it is known in Argentina, is very similar to manjarblanco. The texture is lighter in dulce de leche, but they can be used interchangeably. Similar sweets go by the names arequipe in Colombia and cajeta in Mexico.

In a saucepan, pour sweetened condensed milk and evaporated milk. Bring to a boil over medium-high heat, lower the heat, and cook, stirring continuously until the mixture is thick and you can see the bottom of the saucepan, about 40 minutes. Remove from heat and cool.

Manjarblanco Express

If you want to have several cans of homemade manjarblanco in your cupboard, this recipe is perfect for you. No stirring, no babysitting the cans; just cook and relax.

INGREDIENTS | YIELDS AS MANY CANS AS YOU WANT

(14-ounce) cans sweetened condensed milk

Cooling and Handling

This method is convenient and easy, but do not open the cans for at least a day or two, until completely cool. You may want to make things go faster, but if you open one of these cans and it is still hot inside, it will explode in your face. Be extremely careful!

1. In a heavy saucepan, big enough to make as many cans as you want, put the cans in one layer, cover with plenty of water, and bring water to a boil over high heat. Turn the heat to low, put the lid on, and cook for 3 hours, checking on the water. If the level is lowering, add more boiling water (not cold water). If you have a pressure cooker, use it to cook the cans for 30 minutes instead of using a regular pan.

2. When completely cool (1 or 2 days at least), store the manjarblanco in the pantry. It will last many months, and you will always have some on hand.

Lima Bean Manjarblanco

Creamy, smooth, and delicious, this is the kind of sweet you can eat with a spoon when you are feeling indulgent. Some cooks like to sprinkle it with 1 teaspoon toasted and ground sesame seeds. Use it to fill alfajores, macaroons, or jelly rolls.

INGREDIENTS | YIELDS 1 POUND

2 cups dried Lima beans
1 cinnamon stick
2 cups sugar
1 (12-ounce) can evaporated milk
¼ teaspoon salt
1 teaspoon ground cinnamon

Peeling Lima Beans

If you are running short on time, put the Lima beans in a pan with hot water. Bring to a boil, turn down the heat to low, and cook until the beans are plump, about 20 minutes. At this point, the peels should come off easily.

1. Cover Lima beans with water and soak for 8 hours or overnight. Drain and then peel each one, slightly squeezing with your fingertips to release the beans. Discard the peels.

2. Put the beans in a heavy saucepan, add enough water to barely cover them, and cook at medium heat until very soft, 30–40 minutes. Drain, pass them through a ricer or just process in the blender to make them smooth, and put them back in the saucepan. They should have the consistency of soft mashed potatoes.

3. Add cinnamon, sugar, evaporated milk, and salt and cook over low heat, stirring frequently with a wooden spoon until you can see the bottom of the pan, about an hour. Remove the cinnamon stick.

4. Pour into a bowl or small ramekins and sprinkle with cinnamon. Serve at room temperature.

Yemecillas Acarameladas (Candied Egg Yolk Confections)

With their shiny and polished look, these little gems are a great addition to any party spread. These do not keep well, though. Eat them the same day because the caramel topping melts within a few hours, especially in humid weather.

INGREDIENTS | YIELDS 25 SWEETS

15 egg yolks

3 cups confectioners' sugar, sifted

3 tablespoons whole milk

2 cups granulated sugar

1 cup plus 1 teaspoon water, divided

½ teaspoon cream of tartar

Working with Caramel

Be very careful when dealing with the caramel and work as quickly as possible, as it is extremely hot and can cause burns if you touch it. Children should not be in the kitchen when you are preparing these sweets.

1. In a saucepan, combine egg yolks, confectioners' sugar, and milk. Bring to a boil over high heat, lower the heat to medium-low and cook, stirring often with a wooden spoon until you can see the bottom of the pan, about 30 minutes. You know it is ready when you drop a teaspoon of the mixture in a glass of cold water and it forms a soft ball.

2. Take the pan off the heat. Beat the mixture with the wooden spoon until no more liquid is visible in the pan and it is cool enough to handle. With your hands, form little balls the size of a marble. Insert a toothpick in each ball and keep on doing this until all the dough is used. They will look like lollipops.

3. To make the caramel, in a saucepan, cook granulated sugar and 1 cup of water over high heat, stirring with a wooden spoon or spatula until the sugar dissolves, about 5 minutes. Bring to a boil and add the cream of tartar mixed with a teaspoon of water. Combine quickly. Continue boiling without stirring until it has a beautiful golden color, about 15 minutes. (If you keep on cooking past this point and stir the caramel, it will harden.) Turn off the heat.

4. Holding the toothpick, take the reserved balls and submerge the candy in the caramel, one by one, turning to cover completely. Let the excess caramel drip and then stick the toothpick in Styrofoam or in an orange (cut a slice from the bottom so it can stand without rolling), until the caramel is cool and has hardened. Then remove the toothpick by turning it and pulling slowly.

5. Serve each sweet in a paper candy cup.

Maná

Maná is a sweet and popular confection invented by nuns in colonial Lima. It takes a lot of time and effort to make, but the milky flavor and delicate texture that results is exquisite. Eat within a few days to enjoy its freshness.

INGREDIENTS | YIELDS 50 SWEETS

4 cups whole milk
2 cups granulated sugar
7 egg yolks
1 egg
1–1½ cups confectioners' sugar, sifted
Food coloring (optional)

Kneading by Hand

Instead of using the mixer, you can beat the mixture with a wooden spoon until it is cool to the touch. Then knead on a clean kitchen counter, previously dusted with confectioners' sugar, adding sugar until it is soft and pliable. This is a relaxing job.

1. Put milk, granulated sugar, egg yolks, and egg in a bowl and beat with a wire whisk. Strain and pour into a heavy saucepan. Bring to a boil over high heat, stirring occasionally with a wooden spoon. Lower the heat to medium-low. When the mixture curdles, takes a golden color, and the liquid is absorbed, about 45 minutes, start stirring constantly.

2. When the liquid evaporates and the mixture looks almost dry, after 20 minutes, transfer to the mixer and beat with the paddle attachment on low speed, until it is cool and dry, about 10 minutes.

3. While beating, add confectioners' sugar until the dough is no longer sticky.

4. Using your hands, form little balls the size of walnuts. You can create fruit shapes, like bananas, strawberries, peaches, lemons, pears, etc. Have fun and form braids, half-moons, flowers, etc. Maná looks pretty if the fruits and flowers are painted with food coloring. Use a brush and a light hand to get the best results.

Nuez Nada

Nuez Nada or No Es Nada: both are names given to these delicious sweets.

INGREDIENTS | YIELDS 20 SWEETS

4 egg yolks

2 eggs

4 cups whole milk

2 cups granulated sugar

1 cup confectioners' sugar

1. In a bowl, combine egg yolks, eggs, milk, and granulated sugar. Strain and pour in a heavy saucepan. Cook over low heat, stirring every few minutes until the mixture curdles (you know it has curdled when the mixture has a combination of lumps and clear liquid).

2. Continue cooking, stirring often, and when the liquid evaporates and you can see the bottom of the pan, about 45 minutes, turn off the heat and beat with a wooden spoon until smooth. When cool enough, knead with your hands, using confectioners' sugar to keep the dough from sticking to your hands. Form balls the size of cherries and serve in paper candy cups.

Manjarblanco Mini Potatoes

These candies, covered in ground cinnamon and confectioners' sugar, look like tiny potatoes. Press to form small indentations before adding the cinnamon, and they will look perfect!

INGREDIENTS | YIELDS 20 SWEETS

1 (12-ounce) can evaporated milk

1 (14-ounce) can sweetened condensed milk

2 tablespooons confectioners' sugar

2 tablespoons ground cinnamon

1. Put the evaporated milk and sweetened condensed milk in a saucepan. Cook over medium heat, stirring with a wooden spoon until you can see the bottom of the pan, about 40 minutes. Turn off the heat and cool the mixture.

2. Roll the mixture into a ball, flatten it, wrap in plastic film, and refrigerate.

3. When the mixture is completely cool, make little balls the size of cherries.

4. On a plate, combine confectioners' sugar and ground cinnamon. Roll the candy over these and serve.

Tocinitos del Cielo (Thick Mini Flans)

Like many Peruvian sweets, these are from Spain, where they are called Tocinillos. Some believe that after using egg whites for the process known as wine clarification, instead of discarding the egg yolks, creative cooks invented this flan variation.

INGREDIENTS | YIELDS 50 SWEETS

2 cups sugar
10 egg yolks
1 (14-ounce) can sweetened condensed milk
1 (12-ounce) can evaporated milk

Water Bath

The temperature for the water bath, or *bain-marie*, should be hot but not boiling. It is a good idea to put a folded kitchen towel or a paper bag between the baking pans while baking the flan. This will prevent bubbles from forming on the tocinitos while baking, and the texture will be smoother and creamier.

1. To make the caramel, in a heavy saucepan, cook the sugar without water, stirring constantly over medium-high heat. When the sugar melts, stop stirring and cook until golden, about 15 minutes. Do not let it get too much color, because it will burn and take on a bitter flavor. Carefully pour into a square 8" × 8" baking pan and let cool.

2. Preheat the oven to 350°F. In a blender, process the egg yolks with the milks until smooth. Strain the mixture and pour over the cooled caramel. Put the baking pan inside a larger baking pan filled with hot water, up to 1 inch.

3. Bake for 1 hour, turn off the oven, take out the pan with the tocinito, let cool, and put in the refrigerator. When cold, run a knife around the inner edge of the pan, turn upside down over a plate, and cut into 1-inch squares.

4. Serve very cold.

Queso de Flandes

Despite their name, these sweets do not have cheese, and since their origin is unknown, no one is sure if they were named because they were first made in the Flanders region, in Belgium, or if the name is a deformation of the word flanes *(plural of* flan, *in Spanish).*

INGREDIENTS | YIELDS 50 SWEETS

1 (12-ounce) can unsweetened evaporated milk

1 cup granulated sugar

1 cup Brazil nuts, peeled and ground

⅔ cup pecans, ground

8 egg yolks

1 teaspoon ground cloves

1 teaspoon ground cinnamon

¾ cup confectioners' sugar, sifted

1. In a heavy saucepan, combine milk and sugar. Cook over high heat and when the milk is hot, add Brazil nuts and pecans.

2. Cook, stirring constantly, until you can see the bottom of the saucepan, about 45 minutes. Turn off the heat and let cool.

3. Beat the egg yolks in a mixer until light and fluffy. Add them to the milk mixture, stirring. Add cloves and cinnamon and cook over low heat until the mixture is almost dry, about 35 minutes. Let it cool.

4. Form balls the size of a walnut and roll each one in confectioners' sugar. Serve.

Melcochas de Chocolate (Fudgy Chocolate Balls)

With a soft but chewy, toffee-like texture, these chocolate balls, which resemble truffles, look their best when rolled over different coarsely grated chocolates. Use milk, dark, and white chocolate for a fantastic result.

INGREDIENTS | YIELDS 50 SWEETS

1 (12-ounce) can evaporated milk

1 (14-ounce) can sweetened condensed milk

1 cup sugar

5 tablespoons unsweetened cocoa, sifted

1 tablespoon unsalted butter

1 tablespoon vegetable oil, divided

1 cup coarsely grated chocolate

1. In a heavy saucepan over medium-high heat, cook evaporated and condensed milks and sugar, stirring to dissolve. When the mixture is hot, add the cocoa.

2. Cook, stirring often, until you can see the bottom of the saucepan, about 40 minutes. Incorporate the butter. Pour on a lightly oiled 8-inch plate or baking tray and cool.

3. Put a few drops of oil on your hands and form little balls the size of marbles.

4. Roll each ball over grated chocolate and serve in paper candy cups.

Hot Pepper Truffles

With the intensity of dark chocolate and the unexpected heat of panca peppers, these truffles are a delight for the palates of those looking for new and exciting flavors.

INGREDIENTS | YIELDS 20 TRUFFLES

2 ají panca
⅔ cup heavy cream
1½ cups coarsely chopped dark chocolate
⅛ teaspoon salt
1 cup finely chopped dark chocolate

Ají Panca (Panca Chili Pepper)

Ají panca is one of the most flavorful ingredients in Peruvian savory dishes, and its presence in a sweet dish is unusual. It is a sun-dried chili pepper, with smoky and earthy flavors, but you can replace it with any other hot peppers of your liking.

1. Slice the ají panca lengthwise; take out the seeds and veins and dry fry in a skillet for 5 minutes over medium heat. Turn off the heat and let the peppers cool. When cold, put in a saucepan and cover with cold water. Boil them twice for 3 minutes, changing the water each time. Drain and cool.

2. In a heavy saucepan, bring the heavy cream and the reserved ají panca to a boil over high heat. Turn off the heat, cover, and infuse for 20 minutes.

3. Put the coarsely chopped chocolate and salt in a bowl. Discard the ají panca and heat the cream again over low heat until hot. Pour over the bowl of chocolate. After a couple of minutes, start stirring very gently from the center outwards with a spatula, until smooth and no chocolate pieces remain. This is a ganache. Refrigerate at least 2 hours or until firm.

4. When the ganache is firm, take out of the refrigerator and start forming 1-inch balls. If the balls are too soft, put ganache back in the refrigerator for approximately 30 minutes. You can even leave the ganache balls overnight in the refrigerator.

5. To make the outer layer, melt the finely chopped dark chocolate in a bowl placed over a pan of boiling water. Cool to room temperature and dip each truffle in the melted chocolate to cover completely. Transfer to a lightly oiled dish and let harden. Serve.

Alfajores with Manjarblanco

These delicate cookie sandwiches melt in the mouth, and are beloved by kids and adults alike. Nobody can resist the sweet temptation of an alfajor, and even with Manjarblanco and drenched in powdered sugar, they are not overly sweet.

INGREDIENTS | YIELDS 50 SWEETS

1 cup cornstarch

2 cups all-purpose flour

1 teaspoon baking powder

6 tablespoons plus ½ cup confectioners' sugar, divided

1 cup unsalted butter, at room temperature

2 cups Manjarblanco (see recipe in this chapter)

Baking in Advance

Bake the cookies up to three days in advance. Let them cool and store in an airtight container to keep them fresh. Fill them with Manjarblanco before serving.

1. On a kitchen table, sift cornstarch, flour, baking powder, and 6 tablespoons confectioners' sugar. Form a well in the center.

2. Cut the butter into small cubes, put in the center of the flour, and work with your fingertips, incorporating butter and dry ingredients quickly. When it forms a soft dough that doesn't stick to your hands anymore, roll into a ball, flatten it, wrap in plastic film or put in a plastic bag, and refrigerate for 20 minutes.

3. Preheat the oven to 350°F. Take the dough out of the refrigerator and roll on a floured surface with a rolling pin until ¼-inch thick.

4. Using a round cookie cutter (1½ or 2 inches in diameter), cut little cookies and place them on baking trays covered with parchment paper. Bake for 10 minutes. Take out of the oven and transfer to cooling racks to cool.

5. To form the alfajores, fill two cookies with a teaspoon of Manjarblanco. Sift remaining confectioners' sugar over them and serve.

Cornstarch Alfajores

These almost white alfajores are incredibly delicate and a nice treat with a cup of coffee or tea.

INGREDIENTS | YIELDS 50 SWEETS

½ cup margarine

1¾ cups confectioners' sugar, divided

4 egg yolks

Zest of ½ lemon

2 cups cornstarch, sifted

½ cup all-purpose flour

1 teaspoon baking powder

¼ teaspoon salt

2 cups Manjarblanco (see recipe in this chapter)

1. In a mixer, beat margarine with ¾ cup confectioners' sugar until creamy. Add egg yolks, one by one, and then the lemon zest. Add the sifted cornstarch, flour, baking powder, and salt. Wrap in plastic film or put in a plastic bag and let rest for 15 minutes at room temperature.

2. Preheat the oven to 325°F. On a floured kitchen table, roll the dough with a rolling pin until it is ¼-inch thick. Cut with 1½-inch cookie cutters. Put on clean baking sheets and bake for 10 minutes. Watch them closely and do not let them take color.

3. Take out of the oven. Cool on cooling racks, fill with Manjarblanco, and sift remaining confectioners' sugar over them. Serve.

Chocolate Alfajores

These are an addictive treat for chocolate lovers. You can choose to make the cookies chocolate-flavored, as in this recipe, and fill them with Manjarblanco, or use regular alfajor cookies and fill them with fudge. Or make both!

INGREDIENTS | YIELDS 40 SWEETS

4 tablespoons unsweetened cocoa powder

4 tablespoons milk

½ cup plus 1 tablespoon unsalted butter, at room temperature

¾ cup sugar

1 egg yolk

1 egg

½ teaspoon vanilla essence

2½ cups all-purpose flour, sifted, divided

1 teaspoon baking powder

2 cups Manjarblanco (see recipe in this chapter)

1. Preheat the oven to 350°F. In a small bowl, combine cocoa powder and milk, until the cocoa dissolves and forms a paste. Reserve.

2. In the bowl of a mixer, beat ½ cup butter with sugar until creamy. Add the egg yolk and whole egg, beating well after each addition. Incorporate vanilla essence and the cocoa paste. Turn the speed to low and add 1¼ cups flour and baking powder, until incorporated.

3. Scrape the dough onto a floured kitchen table (using remaining flour) and knead lightly. With a floured rolling pin, roll dough to a thickness of ¼-inch and cut 2-inch rounds with cookie cutters. Bake on greased (using remaining butter) baking sheets for 12 minutes. Transfer to cooling racks.

4. When cool, fill two cookies with a teaspoon of Manjarblanco. Serve.

Voladores

These triple-layered cookies filled with Manjarblanco and marmalade (usually pineapple or apricot) are the stylish version of alfajores. The cookie layers are incredibly thin and fragile and always look very pretty when arranged on silver trays.

INGREDIENTS | YIELDS 50 SWEETS

1 cup all-purpose flour

5 egg yolks

2 tablespoons melted, unsalted butter

2 tablespoons Pisco

2 tablespoons white vinegar

2 cups Manjarblanco (see recipe in this chapter)

1 cup pineapple marmalade

½ cup confectioners' sugar, sifted

Using a Pasta Maker for Sweet Doughs

Whether you believe it or not, the best way to achieve the perfectly thin layers of dough for these sweets is by rolling the dough through a pasta machine. It works like magic and is so much quicker! Keep in mind that you can do the same job with a rolling pin, patience, and a fierce determination.

1. Sift the flour on a kitchen table. Make a well in the center and add egg yolks, melted butter, Pisco, and vinegar. Work with your fingertips until the dough no longer sticks to your hands. Cover with a kitchen towel and let rest for 10 minutes at room temperature.

2. Preheat the oven to 350°F. On a lightly floured surface, use a rolling pin to spread the dough until very thin, almost translucent. Cut 1½-inch circles with a cookie cutter. Place them on baking trays covered with parchment paper. Bake until the edges are lightly golden, about 7 minutes. Take them out of the oven and cool on cooling racks.

3. To form the voladores, put a teaspoon of Manjarblanco on a cookie, put another cookie on top, and spread with marmalade. Cover with a third cookie.

4. Sift confectioners' sugar over the cookies and serve immediately.

Guargüeros (Little Fried Napkins)

These are another example of the light and gifted hands of Peruvian nuns. They were the queens of colonial patisserie, and many convents in Lima still make the best traditional sweets.

INGREDIENTS | YIELDS 50 SWEETS

1 cup all-purpose flour

1 egg

6 egg yolks

2 tablespoons Pisco

2 tablespoons unsalted butter, melted

3 cups vegetable oil

2 cups Manjarblanco (see recipe in this chapter)

1 cup confectioners' sugar, sifted

1. On a kitchen table, sift the flour; make a well in the center and add egg, egg yolks, Pisco, and melted butter. Working quickly with your fingertips, incorporate all the ingredients until they form a soft dough that does not stick to your hands. Cover the dough with a clean kitchen towel or plastic film and let rest for 10 minutes at room temperature.

2. With the help of a rolling pin, roll the dough until very thin, almost transparent. Using a knife, cut 3-inch squares. Lift two opposite corners and stick them together with a drop of water, to form a napkin-like shape.

3. In a heavy saucepan, heat the oil over high heat and fry the guargüeros for about 3 minutes, taking care that they keep a tube-like form. Take them out when they look lightly golden and drain them on a cooling rack covered with paper towels.

4. When cool, fill with Manjarblanco and sprinkle with confectioners' sugar. Serve.

Fried Alfajores

Fried alfajores are easy to make, with a crispy texture and wonderful flavor.
This is a good recipe if you are not in the mood for baking.

INGREDIENTS | YIELDS 12 SWEETS

3 tablespoons plus 1 cup vegetable oil, divided

3 egg yolks

3 tablespoons granulated sugar

3 cups all-purpose flour, divided

2 cups Manjarblanco (see recipe in this chapter)

½ cup confectioners' sugar

1. In a bowl, combine 3 tablespoons vegetable oil, egg yolks, and granulated sugar. Gradually add 2 cups flour and form a dough with your hands. Cover with plastic wrap or a kitchen towel and let rest for 10 minutes.

2. On a lightly floured (using remaining flour) kitchen table, roll the dough with a rolling pin until it is ¼-inch thick. Cut 2-inch rounds with a cookie cutter.

3. Fry in remaining oil, for 3 minutes, or until lightly golden, and drain on a plate covered with paper towels. Fill two cookies with a teaspoon of Manjarblanco and sift confectioners' sugar over them. Serve.

Cocadas (Peruvian-Style Macaroons)

Many years ago, cocadas were a popular confection sold in the streets of every city. The ideal texture is almost crunchy on the outside and chewy on the inside.

INGREDIENTS | YIELDS 30 SWEETS

5 cups grated, unsweetened, dried coconut

1¼ cups sugar

10 egg whites

Grated Coconut

The coconut usually sold in Peru is unsweetened and finely grated. Do not substitute with the sweetened flaked variety, because the results will be completely different.

1. In a metal bowl, combine the ingredients. Heat bowl over (not inside) a saucepan of boiling water, stirring the mixture for 7 minutes.

2. Preheat the oven to 350°F. With lightly wet hands, form small balls (about 1 tablespoon each) and place on a greased 15" × 10" baking sheet. Bake for 15–20 minutes or until lightly golden. Take out of the oven and cool on cooling racks. Serve.

Encanelados (Cinnamon Bites)

When it comes to encanelados, just one square is enough to satisfy a sweet craving.
It is so rich that it needs to be enjoyed in small portions.

INGREDIENTS | YIELDS 35 SWEETS

6 eggs

2 cups granulated sugar, divided

½ cup self-rising flour

½ cup water

2 cloves

1 cinnamon stick

4 tablespoons Pisco

2 cups Manjarblanco (see recipe in this chapter)

½ cup confectioners' sugar

3 tablespoons ground cinnamon

Tip for Beating the Eggs

Make sure the mixer and the beater are completely clean and dry before using. Otherwise, the eggs will not increase in volume as desired.

1. Preheat the oven to 350°F. Grease a 13" × 9" baking pan.

2. In the mixer, blend eggs and 1 cup granulated sugar at high speed until it has tripled in volume. Turn off the mixer and fold the flour in with a spatula. Scrape the dough into the baking pan and bake for 25 minutes. Transfer to a rack to cool.

3. In the meantime, make the syrup in a saucepan by boiling water, cloves, cinnamon stick, and 1 cup granulated sugar for 7 minutes over high heat, without stirring. Turn off the heat and add Pisco.

4. Unmold the cake by running a knife along the edge and turning the pan upside down on a tray. Then cut the cake in half (making two layers) and place each half side by side. Drench one layer with half the syrup. Spread with Manjarblanco and cover with the other cake layer. Drizzle with remaining syrup. Sprinkle with a mixture of confectioners' sugar and cinnamon.

5. Cut into small squares, about 1½ inches in size, and serve.

Baked Mini Meringues with Manjarblanco

White, light, and ethereal, but at the same time crunchy and fudgy, these merenguitos are a real delight. Use leftover egg whites to make a batch whenever you have the time.

INGREDIENTS | YIELDS 50 SWEETS

1 cup egg whites
1 cup granulated sugar
1 cup confectioners' sugar, sifted
1 cup Manjarblanco (see recipe in this chapter)

1. Preheat the oven to 200°F. In the bowl of a mixer, beat the egg whites at high speed. Gradually add the granulated sugar and continue beating until very stiff.

2. Turn off the mixer and with the help of a spatula, fold the confectioners' sugar into the meringue. Transfer the meringue into a piping bag with a piping tip and squeeze little meringues on a baking sheet lined with parchment paper.

3. Bake for 2 hours or until the meringue is dry, but still white. Turn off the oven and let rest with the door ajar for several hours.

4. When cool, fill two meringues with a teaspoon of Manjarblanco.

Marquesas de Pecanas (Pecan Balls)

Toasting the pecans before grinding them gives them an extra layer of flavor and brings out their perfume.

2 (14-ounce) cans sweetened condensed milk

3 egg yolks

2½ cups ground pecans, divided

1 tablespoon softened butter

Perfect Size Every Time

An ice cream scoop is the best tool to make candies and sweets exactly the same size. This works when making cookies or cupcakes, too.

1. In a saucepan over medium heat, cook sweetened condensed milk, egg yolks, and 2 cups pecans. Stir constantly with a wooden spoon until the mixture thickens and does not stick to the pan, about 30 minutes. Turn off the heat and cool completely.

2. Put butter on your hands and form balls the size of a cherry. Roll over remaining ground pecans. Serve.

Chocotejas

These are the chocolate version of a traditional sweet from the southern coast of Peru, called Tejas. Chocotejas are not only popular; they are also easy to make.

40 pecan halves

2 cups Manjarblanco (see recipe in this chapter)

3 cups chopped dark chocolate

Variations

To make the filling, use your imagination. You can use pecans, walnuts, raisins macerated in Pisco, candied orange or lemon peels, prunes, figs, guava paste, lúcuma ganache, passion fruit . . . you name it. The Manjarblanco for the filling should be thick and firm.

1. Fill 2 pecan halves with 1 tablespoon Manjarblanco. Repeat with all the pecans.

2. Put the chocolate in a bowl over a saucepan with hot water and melt, stirring every few minutes. Cool to room temperature.

3. Dip each pecan sandwich to cover completely with dark chocolate. Put on an oiled baking sheet to harden.

4. To serve, wrap in silk or silver paper.

Prestiños

Prestiños come from the central part of Peru. They have the shape of doughnuts, but their texture is crispy and spongy at the same time. They are perfect for teatime or as a snack in the morning.

INGREDIENTS | YIELDS 25 PRESTIÑOS

3 cups all-purpose flour
1 teaspoon baking powder
2 egg whites
5 egg yolks
⅓ teaspoon salt
1 tablespoon shortening
2 cups vegetable oil
2 cups sugar
¾ cup water
Juice of ½ lime

1. Sift the flour together with the baking powder.

2. In a mixer, beat egg whites at the highest speed for about 5 minutes, until they triple their volume (or more). Add the egg yolks, lower the speed, and add the flour with the baking powder, salt, and shortening. Turn off the mixer and with a spatula, incorporate the ingredients. Knead lightly with your hands, about 30 minutes.

3. Divide the dough into 25 portions and with your hands, make a small doughnut with each portion, about 2 inches wide. With a very thin knife, make a cut on the outer edge of the prestiño. That cut will let the cookie expand when fried.

4. Put several paper towels on a plate, stacked on top of one another to quickly absorb the oil after frying the prestiños. Heat the oil in a frying pan over high heat and fry the prestiños until they are lightly golden, about 40 seconds on each side.

5. In a saucepan, mix the sugar with ¾ cup water and lime juice and bring to a simmer, stirring constantly over medium heat. Stop stirring when the color of the mixture changes to a pale yellow, about 10 minutes.

6. Turn off the heat and beat with a wooden spoon until it turns a white color.

7. Drop the prestiños, one by one, into this glaze. Submerge completely and remove with a slotted spoon.

8. Let them sit on a cooling rack until the glaze is dry. Serve.

Rosquitas de Manteca

These rosquitas are a favorite Peruvian snack, especially when you are traveling, because they are sold in most gas stations. The flavor is delicate, and they have a crispy texture. This recipe is easy and fun to make.

INGREDIENTS | YIELDS 30 ROSQUITAS

3 cups enriched flour

1 cup confectioners' sugar

½ teaspoon salt

¾ cup shortening, melted

1 teaspoon aniseed

¼ cup water

1. Sift the flour, sugar, and salt into a bowl and make a well in the center. Add the shortening, aniseed, and ¼ cup water. Knead with your hands until mixture forms a soft dough. Cover with a cloth and let it rest for 15 minutes.

2. Preheat the oven to 325°F. To make the rosquitas, roll two small parts of the dough (the size of a walnut) with your hands, making two ropes, about ½-inch wide. Join the ends of both ropes and intertwine, making a braid. Finally, seal the ends to make a ring shape. The size of the rosquitas should be between 2–3 inches wide.

3. Place the rosquitas on a greased and floured baking sheet. Bake for 15–20 minutes, or until they are lightly golden. Cool on cooling racks.

4. Store in a container with a tight-fitting lid.

CHAPTER 17

Delicious Drinks

Chicha Morada

With an intense purple color and a citrusy flavor, this drink is enjoyed in every Peruvian home, come rain or shine. The purple corn does not have much flavor on its own, so it allows the spices and fruit flavors to sparkle.

INGREDIENTS | SERVES 6

2 pounds purple corn

Peels of ½ pineapple

1 Granny Smith apple, chopped

1 quince, chopped

3 cinnamon sticks

6 allspice

6 cloves

8 cups water

Sugar to taste

Juice of 4 limes

1. Take the kernels off the corn ears and put in a large saucepan along with pineapple peels, chopped apple, chopped quince, cinnamon sticks, allspice, cloves, and 8 cups water.

2. Bring to a boil and simmer without a lid for about one hour over low heat, so the water takes on a vibrant purple color.

3. Turn off the heat, cool, and drain, discarding the solids. Add sugar and the juice of 4 limes. Serve.

Other Uses for Purple Liquid

If you make the purple water and do not add lime juice, you can make Mazamorra Morada, a traditional dessert from Lima (see Chapter 15). You can also use this water to cook Purple Rice (see Chapter 8). The purple liquid gives a wonderful color, and some say it is a diuretic and helps regulate blood pressure.

Agua de Manzana (Apple Water)

Agua de locos, or "crazy man's water," as it is known in Peru, is not only delicious and refreshing, but a good way to avoid artificial sugary beverages. The apples are relaxing, hence the funny nickname.

INGREDIENTS | SERVES 6

2 pounds Granny Smith apples, chopped
3 cinnamon sticks
6 allspice
3 cloves
8 cups water
Sugar to taste

1. Put apples, cinnamon, allspice, cloves, and 8 cups water in a saucepan. Bring to a boil over high heat, turn the heat down to low, and simmer, partially covered, for 35 minutes or until the apples are very tender. Turn off the heat and cool.

2. Discard the spices, process in a blender or pass through a strainer, and add sugar. Serve cold. Keep refrigerated.

Tart Apples

The best apples for this beverage are tart ones, because of their concentrated flavor. Sweet and delicate ones do not work well in this preparation. The beverage should have the texture of nectar, bursting with an intense apple flavor.

Emoliente

This warm beverage is made with a mix of herbs and spices. Each emolientero (a person who sells emoliente in the streets) has a secret recipe, but in general, it always has barley, flaxseed, and lime. In winter, it is a welcome mid-morning treat.

INGREDIENTS | SERVES 4

1 cup toasted barley
½ cup dried horsetail
½ cup dried lemongrass
½ cup flaxseed
4 leaves fresh llantén (plantain leaf)
½ quince, chopped
6 cups water
Juice of 2 limes
Sugar or honey to taste

1. Place barley, horsetail, lemongrass, flaxseed, plantain leaf, and quince in a saucepan with 6 cups water. Bring to a boil and simmer over low heat, uncovered, for 35 minutes.

2. Turn off the heat, cool, strain, add lime juice, and sweeten with sugar or honey. Serve warm or at room temperature.

Chicha de Jora

Chicha was the sacred drink of the Incas, used for ceremonies and commemorative events. It is an ancient beverage with a long tradition all over America, and is still regularly consumed in the Andes, where it is known as a strong Andean beer.

INGREDIENTS | YIELDS 12 CUPS

24 cups water
½ pound jora corn kernels
½ pound quinoa
½ pound barley
¾ cup molasses
2 cinnamon sticks
10 cloves
1 cup sugar (optional)

1. Heat 24 cups water in a big saucepan over medium heat and add the jora corn, quinoa, barley, molasses, cinnamon sticks, and cloves. Bring to a boil and simmer for 3 hours over low heat, partly covered.

2. Cool and strain through a cheesecloth. To accelerate the fermentation process, add the sugar, stir, pour in an earthenware jar, and cover with a cloth.

3. Let it rest up to 4 days at room temperature, stirring once a day. If you want it stronger and with higher alcohol concentration, let it ferment up to 30 days.

4. To serve, add sugar if needed.

Hot Chocolate

For this recipe, if you like a thicker chocolate, add 1 teaspoon cornstarch diluted in 1 tablespoon water before turning off the heat. If something lighter is preferred, add more hot water or regular milk.

INGREDIENTS | SERVES 4

3 cups water
2 cinnamon sticks
4 cloves
4 ounces semisweet chocolate, chopped
1 (12-ounce) can evaporated milk
Sugar to taste
½ teaspoon grated nutmeg
2 teaspoons vanilla essence
1 cup whipped cream (optional)
Ground cinnamon for decoration (optional)
Ground grated chocolate for decoration (optional)

1. In a heavy saucepan, bring 3 cups water, cinnamon, and cloves to a boil over high heat for 10 minutes. Add the chopped chocolate, stirring until melted. Add evaporated milk, sugar, nutmeg, and vanilla essence.

2. Serve immediately with a dollop of whipped cream and a sprinkling of ground cinnamon or grated chocolate, if desired.

Hot Chocolate Tradition

Drinking hot chocolate is an old tradition in Peru, especially in the colder weather of the Andes, where it's extremely cold at night for most of the year. Some cooks love to add egg yolk and a teaspoon of butter to this decadent beverage, while the adventurous add a shot of Pisco to make it stronger.

Peanut Chicha

This is one more version of the many Peruvian chichas. Similar to many others, this one comes from the fermentation of peanuts. It is consumed in the Andes and is typically shared with friends and family.

INGREDIENTS | YIELDS 10 CUPS

20 cups water, divided

½ pound dry white corn kernels

2 pounds peanuts, toasted and ground

½ pound sesame seeds, toasted and ground

½ pound walnuts or pecans, ground

10 cloves

2 cinnamon sticks

1 teaspoon aniseed

1 cup sugar

1. In a saucepan over high heat, pour 10 cups water and add the white corn kernels. Bring to a boil and simmer over low heat for 3 hours with the lid on.

2. In another saucepan pour 10 cups water, peanuts, sesame seeds, walnuts or pecans, cloves, cinnamon sticks, and aniseed. Bring to a boil over high heat, turn the heat to low, and simmer, partially covered, for 3 hours.

3. Combine both mixtures while still hot. Let cool and strain through a cheesecloth or a fine colander.

4. To accelerate the fermentation process, add sugar, stir, and pour the mixture into an earthenware jar. Cover with a cloth.

5. Let it rest for up to 4 days at room temperature. Add more sugar if desired.

The Many Faces of Chicha

Peru has a variety of chichas in every part of the country, with different names and styles: Frutillada in Cusco; Kañiwa and Gui-ñapo in Arequipa; Masato in the Amazon jungle; Aloha in Ancash; among many others. Fruits, cereals, and legumes are the base of most of these drinks, which once fermented have alcoholic properties, even though they are not as strong as beer or liqueur.

Hot Corn Beverage

This drink shows you just how versatile corn can be. You can drink it!
This drink is warm and comforting for those cold winter nights.

INGREDIENTS | YIELDS 4½ CUPS

2 cups corn kernels
3 cups whole milk
2 cinnamon sticks
Sugar to taste
¼ teaspoon salt
1 teaspoon vanilla essence

1. Process corn kernels with milk in a food processor or blender.

2. Heat in a saucepan over medium heat with cinnamon sticks, stirring all the time, until slightly thick, about 20 minutes. If you find it is too thick, add more milk.

3. Add sugar, salt, and vanilla. Strain and serve immediately.

Te Piteado

Arequipa is the birthplace of this beverage. It is simple to make and oh, so delicious!

INGREDIENTS | SERVES 1

1 teaspoon black tea, or 1 tea bag
1 ounce anise liqueur
Sugar to taste

Put tea leaves or tea bag in a cup, pour ¾ cup hot water over it, and let infuse for up to 4 minutes. Drain and discard the solids. Add the anise liqueur to the tea and sweeten with sugar. Serve immediately.

Orange and Papaya Juice

A refreshing and healthy juice for any time of the year.
Serve it at breakfast or as a mid-morning pick-me-up. You will feel wonderful!

INGREDIENTS | SERVES 1

Juice of 3 oranges
1 cup papaya

Process in a blender until smooth and serve immediately.

Fresh Oranges

There is nothing better than a glass of freshly squeezed orange juice, except maybe when it is combined with other good-for-you fruits or vegetables. Instead of papaya, you can also use carrot or beet juice. One more tip: Combine orange juice with Greek yogurt and some raisins for a great snack.

Strawberries and Milk Smoothie

What could be more delicious than a shake—or smoothie—made with strawberries and milk?
Use a mixture of fruits for even more goodness.

INGREDIENTS | SERVES 1

1 cup strawberries, cut in half
1 cup milk
1 tablespoon sugar

Process in a blender until smooth and serve immediately.

Strawberries and Cream

Not in the mood for a shake? Combine sliced strawberries with whipped cream. Not as healthy, but really delicious.

Passion Fruit Nectar

*Boiling passion fruits, peel and all, makes a delicate nectar.
It is slightly thick and has only a touch of acidity.*

INGREDIENTS | SERVES 4

5 cups water
5 passion fruits
1 cup sugar

1. Wash and cut the passion fruits in half, scoop out the pulp, and place, along with the peels, in a saucepan with 5 cups water. Simmer, partially covered, over medium heat until tender, about 30 minutes. Cool.

2. Process in a blender, strain, and add sugar. Keep refrigerated.

Prickly Pear Juice

Tunas, in Spanish, are the fruit of the prickly pear cactus, and they are so sweet and colorful that everyone loves them. You can find them in many colors . . . red, green, orange, and yellow. Serve them as part of fruit salads or eat them alone with a few drops of lime juice. Some say they are good for hangovers.

INGREDIENTS | SERVES 4

6 red prickly pears
4 cups water
Sugar to taste
Juice of 2 limes

Peel the fruits, but do not hold them with your hands because they have tiny thorns. Cut into pieces and process with 4 cups water, sugar, and lime juice. Strain and pour in a jar, or serve immediately.

Camu Camu Juice

Did you know that camu camu is the fruit that contains the highest amount of vitamin C in the world? They are not easy to find, but if you happen to have some, make juice with them!

INGREDIENTS | SERVES 2

1 pound fresh camu camu

Sugar to taste

2 cups water

Cover whole camu camu with hot water. After 4–5 minutes, squeeze the fruit with your hands, strain it discarding the solids, and add sugar and 1 cup water to the juice. Keep refrigerated and serve cold.

Banana, Milk, Carob, and Maca Shake

Banana shakes are a breakfast staple in many Peruvian homes. Bananas are good for you because of their high potassium levels, and carob and maca give you tons of energy. Have this smoothie at breakfast and if you want, add a couple of tablespoons of cooked quinoa.

INGREDIENTS | SERVES 1

1 banana

1 cup milk

1 tablespoon carob syrup, or to taste

1 teaspoon maca flour

Process banana, milk, carob, and maca in a blender until smooth. Serve immediately.

Super Vegan Banana Ice Cream

Freeze bananas and process in a food processor with carob and maca. You will have a delicious ice cream without the sugar, dairy, or fat. If you don't like carob flavor, replace with 1 teaspoon vanilla extract.

Lúcuma Milk Shake

*This is another delicious shake that many Peruvians like to enjoy,
especially if it's very cold or, even better, made with lúcuma ice cream!*

INGREDIENTS | SERVES 1

1 medium-sized lúcuma, peeled and chopped

1 cup whole milk

1 teaspoon vanilla

2 tablespoons sugar or condensed milk

Process lúcuma, milk, vanilla, and sugar or condensed milk in a blender until smooth. Serve immediately.

Strawberry Frappé

*This frozen treat is refreshing and can be made in seconds if you have the fruit in the freezer.
Great for days with steamy, hot weather.*

INGREDIENTS | SERVES 1

1½ cups frozen strawberries

Juice of ½ lime

1 tablespoon sugar

⅔ cup water

Process strawberries, lime juice, sugar, and ⅔ cup water in a blender until smooth. Serve immediately with straws.

Variations

Substitute strawberries with any other frozen fruit. Peel the fruits of your preference (even better if they are in season), cut in pieces, and store in freezer bags. Use one kind at a time, or use a mixture of different fruits. Try melon, watermelon, papaya, soursop, mango, raspberries, grapes, plums, pineapple, etc.

Tangerine and Lemon Balm Juice

Lemon balm is relaxing and soothing, the perfect addition to a fruit juice. It goes well with orange, tangerine, granadilla, tumbo, etc.

INGREDIENTS | SERVES 2

1 cup water
2 bags lemon balm tea
3 cups freshly squeezed tangerine juice
2 tablespoons sugar

1. Bring water to a boil in a medium saucepan over high heat, and infuse the lemon balm tea bags for 15 minutes. Discard the bags.

2. When the water is cool, combine with tangerine juice and sugar. Serve at room temperature or with ice.

Caspiroleta

For those nights when you are feeling under the weather, there is nothing more comforting than a mug of steaming caspiroleta. The best moment to have it is before going to sleep. In the morning, you will feel refreshed.

INGREDIENTS | SERVES 1

1 cup milk
1 cinnamon stick
1 egg
1 tablespoon honey
2 tablespoons Pisco
⅛ teaspoon ground cinnamon

1. In a small saucepan, bring the milk and cinnamon stick to a boil over high heat. In the meantime, whisk the egg until foamy. Add the boiling milk, honey, and Pisco to the egg.

2. Pour in a mug, sprinkle with cinnamon, and serve immediately.

Pisco, Rum, or Whiskey

Substitute Pisco with the same amount of rum or whiskey, if you have any. Follow the instructions and serve. The flavor will be somewhat different, but equally enjoyable. A virgin version is also perfect for kids.

Pisco Sour

Are you concerned about the safety of raw eggs? If you are, do not include egg white in your Pisco Sour. It does not affect the flavor, only the look, because the drink will not have the foamy topping.

INGREDIENTS | SERVES 1

3 ounces Pisco

1 ounce lime juice

1½ ounces Simple Syrup (see Chapter 15)

5 ice cubes

⅓ egg white, lightly mixed

1 drop Angostura bitters

1. Process Pisco, lime juice, syrup, ice cubes, and egg white in the blender until frothy, about 15 seconds.

2. Serve in a short glass with a drop of Angostura bitters on top.

Passion Fruit Sour

Peruvian maracuyá, or passion fruit, has a far more intense flavor than its American counterpart. It is larger, with a yellowish skin, and it is full of acid. If only the purple variety is available, feel free to add ½ or 1 tablespoon of lime juice to balance the flavors of this sexy cocktail.

INGREDIENTS | SERVES 1

4 passion fruits (about 2 ounces juice)

1 ounce Pisco

1 ounce Simple Syrup (see Chapter 15)

5 ice cubes

1. Cut passion fruits in half and scoop the pulp into a strainer over a bowl. Press with a spoon to separate the juice from the seeds. Measure the juice—you should have 2 ounces—and discard the seeds.

2. Process Pisco, passion fruit juice, simple syrup, and ice cubes in a blender for 30 seconds. Serve immediately in a glass.

Algarrobina

For many years, this was considered a ladies' drink, maybe because there is something feminine in its creamy sweetness. But beware of Pisco drinks! They look mild and innocent, but they are not.

INGREDIENTS | SERVES 1

3 ounces Pisco

1½ ounces carob syrup

2 ounces evaporated milk

1 egg yolk (optional)

4 ice cubes

⅛ teaspoon ground cinnamon

Mix all ingredients, except cinnamon, in a blender for 30 seconds. Serve immediately, sprinkled with ground cinnamon.

Pisco Punch

With a romantic story that dates back to the Gold Rush in San Francisco, this fresh and fruity punch is worth the effort it takes to prepare it.

INGREDIENTS | SERVES 4

1½ cups Pisco

1½ cups soda water

¾ cup lime juice

1 cup Pineapple Syrup (see sidebar)

8 cooked pineapple pieces

4 maraschino cherries

In a jar, combine Pisco, soda water, lime juice, and Pineapple Syrup. Stir. Serve in wine glasses and garnish each glass with 2 pieces of cooked pineapple and a maraschino cherry.

Pineapple Syrup

Boil the diced pulp of one pineapple with 4 cups water and 2 pounds sugar, over high heat, for 30 minutes. Cool and use as directed.

Chilcano

Normally ginger ale is used for this drink, but you can use any other lemon-lime soda.

INGREDIENTS | SERVES 1

2 ounces Pisco
¼ ounce lime juice
1 iced ginger ale
1 lime slice

Put Pisco and lime juice in a tall glass filled with ice. Top with ginger ale, stir, and enjoy. Garnish with a lime slice.

Glossary

Achiote

(*Bixa orellana*) Its seeds, whole or ground, are used to give color and flavor to many Latin American dishes, including savory and sweet dishes, and even hot chocolate. Some tribes use achiote paste to color the skin and hair of their people.

Aderezo

Every savory dish starts with aderezo, a sautéed mixture of onion, garlic, and ají (amarillo, mirasol, or panca), cooked in oil until very soft.

Aguaymanto (Golden Berries)

(*Physalis peruviana*) Fresh aguaymantos, or golden berries, have a sweet and acidic flavor. They are good in salads, or cooked in compotes, sauces, jams, marmalades, juices, and desserts. They look like yellow cherry tomatoes, and can be found fresh or dehydrated in many health food stores or supermarkets around the world.

Ají Amarillo

(*Capsicum baccatum*) Ají escabeche and ají verde are other names for this popular chili pepper. It is mostly used for its flavor and color, not for its spiciness, so it is usually deseeded, deveined, and blanched to get rid of the potency.

Ají Charapita

Tiny but powerful, maybe the smallest of Peruvian chili peppers, they are the size of blueberries, but fire-hot.

Mostly used in Amazonian food, they only recently made their debut in some restaurants in Lima.

Ají Limo

(*Capsicum sinense*) These have bright and varied colors, and are smaller than ají amarillo, but at the same time are very spicy. Use for cebiches and tiraditos.

Ají Mirasol

This sun-dried ají amarillo can be toasted and rehydrated in hot water. It can then be blanched and processed with a little water or vegetable oil in a blender to make a paste. Store this paste in the refrigerator, or freeze in small amounts.

Ají Panca

(*Capsicum baccatum*) This sun-dried red ají, used for stews and other slow-cooked preparations, has a long shelf life, and its heat does not diminish with time. It needs to be toasted and blanched before using.

Algarrobina

The syrup of the algarrobo, or carob tree, is used to sweeten milk and desserts, or as the main ingredient in Algarrobina, a drink made with Pisco, egg yolks, and milk.

Anticuchera

A street vendor who sells anticuchos.

Batán

It is a heavy stone—similar to a mortar—used to grind cereals and chili peppers. Years ago, every kitchen in the country had one, but in recent years they have been replaced by blenders and food processors. In the Andes, they are still an important part of food preparation.

Camu Camu

(*Myrciaria dubia*) This fruit grows wild in the Peruvian and Brazilian rainforests, and even though it is small, it is extremely acidic. Use it in juices, sauces, or desserts.

Carambola (Star Fruit)

Carambolas are not only decorative fruits; they can also be used as part of salads, in juices and nectars, or for sweet and savory sauces.

Castaña (Brazil Nut)

(*Bertholletia excelsa*) Peruvians use it for many desserts, and simply call it castaña. It is rich in selenium, and eating one per day is recommended for good health. In colonial times, the Spanish used to call them "almonds from the Andes."

Cherimoya

(*Anona cherimolia*) In Quechua, its name means "cold seeds." Peruvian cherimoyas weigh up to 3 pounds, with a flavor that is reminiscent of apples, bananas, and strawberries. They are perfect when eaten on their own, discarding the black seeds, but are also used in desserts and fruit salads. Cherimoya Cumbe is the most famous variety. Serve them very cold and eat them with a spoon.

Chincho

(*Tageteselliptica smith*) This fragrant herb is used to flavor pachamanca and other Andean dishes, mostly soups and stews.

Chonta

(*Astrocaryum chonta*) The edible and tender heart of this palm tree is known worldwide as heart of palm, but chonta is the fresh and unprocessed heart. It is eaten mostly raw in the Amazon jungle. Its white color, and its crisp and fragile texture, make it perfect in salads.

Chuño (Potato Starch)

It is used as a thickener in several sauces and cakes. In the Andes, chuño is a freeze-dried potato that has a long shelf life, and can be used for stews and soups.

Coca

(*Erythroxylon coca*) The bad image of the coca leaf has shadowed its many nutritional benefits. Andeans use coca not only as food, but as a medicine, because it is soothing to the nervous and digestive systems. When visiting the Andes, it is customary to receive a cup of mate de coca, or coca tea, to overcome the effects of mountain sickness.

Corn

(*Zea mays*) Corn, or choclo, as it is called in Peru, has been a main staple of the daily Peruvian diet for thousands of years. There are more than thirty varieties, in every color and size imaginable, but the giant kernel corn from Cusco is one of the most popular. Interestingly enough, and despite the amount of corn consumed, Tortillas or Arepas are not a part of the Peruvian diet, as they are in many other corn-producing countries. Peruvian Giant Corn can be found frozen in many Latin American grocery stores in the United States and elsewhere.

Culantro

(*Eryngium foetidum*) European in origin, its leaves are widely used in Peruvian cooking. In the Amazon, there is another kind called sacha culantro, with long leaves and a similar but milder taste.

Cushuro

This is a kind of seaweed that grows in the highest Andean lakes, lagoons, rivers, and streams. It has a round shape—like oversized green caviar—and a neutral flavor, and is rich in protein and calcium, among other nutrients.

Guitarra

(*Rhinobatos planiceps*) Find this fish salted and sun dried along the Peruvian coast. It is cheap, and mostly used to make chiringuito (a dried fish cebiche) and in place of salted cod.

Hierbabuena

(*Micromeria douglasii*) Along with other aromatic herbs, hierbabuena is an ingredient in many dishes, like cau cau and sancochado. It is soothing, and gives a wonderful aroma to food.

Huacatay

(*Tagetes minuta*) A fragrant Andean herb used in many dishes, along with several kinds of chili peppers. It is also known as black mint, and its pungent aroma and flavor is better when used in small quantities.

Kion (Ginger)

(*Zingiber officinale*) The Chinese that came to Peru called it *kion*, and this became the only name for it in Peru. It is grown in the Amazon jungle and mostly used for Chinese recipes, and some infusions, but it has found its way into many cebiche recipes and other Peruvian dishes.

Kiwicha (Amaranth)

(*Amaranthus caudatus*) *Kiwicha* is the Quechua name for this grain, which is very similar to quinoa, but smaller, and used for stews, soups, breads, and as part of breakfast.

Lime

(*Citrus aurantifolia*) This small and intensely flavored lime of Peru is an important ingredient for cebiche. It has been given the name of Limón Sutil. A delicious confection made with this fruit and sugar, and sometimes filled with manjarblanco, has been a well-kept secret recipe in Lima's convents for centuries (its name is Limón Relleno).

Lonche

This is the name for the Peruvian teatime. It is a century-old custom to have tea, coffee, or hot chocolate in the afternoon, accompanying one or more kinds of mini sandwiches, cookies, cakes, or tarts.

Lúcuma

(*Pouteria lucuma*) With its floury and orange pulp, this is the darling of Peruvian desserts, especially for mousses, ice creams, and milk shakes. This fruit has a peculiar aroma, and a completely unique and earthy flavor, similar to Zapote but without the juicy texture. Use the flour only if you live abroad and this is your only option.

Maca

(*Lepidium meyenii*) It is known as the Peruvian gingseng, but its beneficial powers exceed this reputation. Use it sparingly in cooking because of its strong flavor.

Manjarblanco

The first manjarblanco, which is the Peruvian version of dulce de leche, was prepared during colonial times with chicken and almonds. The recipe evolved and turned into a sweet milk-cream, used as part of countless desserts and drinks.

Maracuyá (Passion Fruit)

(*Passiflora edulis*) Its fruity juice has an intense acidic and sweet flavor, with a delicious floral aroma. Buy it fresh, when the skin is bright and spotless and the fruit feels heavy for its size. Use it for juices, ice creams, desserts, cebiches, and sweet and savory sauces.

Molle

(*Schinus molle*) This pink peppercorn has a sweet and delicate flavor, like allspice. Use it in savory dishes and desserts.

Muña

(*Minthostachys mollis*) The Spanish called it poleo or oregano, because they thought this herb tasted similar. It flavors Andean soups and stews.

Novoandean Cuisine

A new style of making Andean dishes, using ancient ingredients and modern cooking techniques.

Olluco

(*Ullucus tuberosus*) Also known as *papalisa* or lisas (smooth potato/smooth), the word *ullucu* means tuber in Aymara and Quechua. It looks like a small potato with beautiful and bright colors. It is used in soups, stews, and salads.

Paico

(*Chenopodium ambrosioides*) The aromatic leaves and flowers of this plant, a member of the quinoa and cañihua variety, are used in chupes, soups, and beans, among many others.

Pallar (Lima Bean)

(*Phaseolus lunatus*) Native Lima beans are used fresh or dried in salads, soups, purées, desserts, etc.

Panetón

From the Italian panettone, panetón is a yeast bread usually consumed during Christmas. With the Italian immigration to Peru, this bread became a tradition in Peru as well.

Panko

A Japanese grated bread, especially used for breading fish, seafood, meats, or chicken. It gives a crispy and golden texture.

Pepino

(*Solanum muricatum*) It is a very sweet and juicy fruit with a mild and flowery flavor. It has been around for more than 6,000 years. You can eat it by itself, or in fruit salads, juices, or even grilled.

Potato

(*Solanum tuberosum*) The name comes from a Quechua word meaning something like "roots as bread." Native to Peru, there are thousands of varieties, in different colors, sizes, and textures, but all of them are nutritious. Potato is one of the main crops of the world.

Quinoa

(*Chenopodium quinoa*) Quinoa still grows in what was once the Inca Empire, from Argentina to Colombia. There are hundreds of ways to cook quinoa in both savory and sweet dishes.

Rocoto

(*Capsicum pubescens*) Its appearance is very innocent (resembling a bell pepper), but this is one of Peru's hottest chili peppers. This is why rocotos are mainly used as a condiment; just a little bit to give a kick to some dishes. They have beautiful colors ranging from green and yellow to red.

Sachatomate

(*Solanum betaceum*) This is a tomato produced by small trees. Native to Peru, it has a dark red skin and sweet aroma that goes particularly well in sauces, savory and sweet dishes, and in juices.

Sauco (Elderberry)

(*Sambucus peruviana*) The fruit of a medium-sized tree, it grows in clusters, and is very popular in the form of marmalades, compotes, and wines.

Seco

The name of a flavorful stew made with a variety of meats, like goat, beef, chicken, or lamb. Cilantro gives the sauce its green color. Potatoes and rice are the side dish, as well as canary beans.

Soy Sauce

Peruvians call it *sillao* and consume huge amounts of this sauce. It is used to flavor Chinese and Peruvian dishes, as well as soups and sauces.

Suspiro Limeño

The most famous Peruvian dessert; incredibly sweet, it has many variations with fruits and spices.

Tarwi

(*Lupinus mutabilis*) Tarwi is eaten like peanuts, but first you need to get rid of the bitterness and toxins contained in its beans by cooking it before eating.

Tuna (Prickly Pear)

(*Opuntia ficus-indica*) A refreshing fruit of the cactus. It is juicy, full of edible seeds, and it comes in red, orange, yellow, and green. Use in juices, in salads, or in syrups.

Wonton Dough

Sold in the refrigerated section of grocery stores, it is not only used for fried wontons but also to wrap tequeños, and to make quick ravioli, amongst other things.

Yucca

(*Manihoc esculenta*) Golden or white, yucca is used in many dishes as a side dish or the main ingredient. The golden one is tender and silky. It is widely harvested in the Amazon jungle.

Yuyo

These are seaweeds widely used on top of cebiche. They have a jelly-like texture and look like ribbons. They are known as yuyo and cochayuyo, and are high in protein.

Zapallo Loche

(*Cucurbita moschata*) From Lambayeque, in the northern part of Peru, this squash is very aromatic and gives a delicious and distinctive flavor to the cuisine of this region.

Online Resources

Websites

www.deanandeluca.com
www.labodegaperuana.com
www.vallartasupermarket.com
www.latinfood.com
www.tubodeguita.com
www.mamatinas.com
www.spiceworlds.com
www.westernbeef.com
www.comparesupermarkets.com
www.kalustyans.com
www.aofwc.com
www.leeleesupermarket.com
www.shoppersfood.com
www.tienda.com
www.sabortropicalsupermarkets.com
www.facebook.com/Catalinasmarket
www.sedanos.com
www.costsavermarket.com
www.liborio.com
www.oceanicmarketlatino.com
www.amazon.com
http://www.facebook.com/pages/Casa-Lucas-Market/141731415866534
www.bouminggourmet.com
www.blog.rumbadesserts.com
www.amigosfoods.com
www.yelp.com/biz/el-chico-produce-san-francisco
www.theperuvianmarket.com

Grocery Stores

- PUBLIX
- Xtra Supermarket
- Food Star Supermarket
- HMart
- Azteca Produce

INDEX